THE EPISTLE OF S. JAMES

THE
EPISTLE OF S. JAMES

LECTURES

BY

H. MAYNARD SMITH
VICAR OF HOLY TRINITY, MALVERN
RURAL DEAN OF POWYKE, EXAMINING CHAPLAIN TO THE BISHOP OF ZANZIBAR
AUTHOR OF
"CHURCH TEACHING AT HOME," "IN PLAYTIME," "PLAYMATES," ETC

WIPF & STOCK · Eugene, Oregon

Wipf and Stock Publishers
199 W 8th Ave, Suite 3
Eugene, OR 97401

The Epistles of S. James
Lectures
By Smith, H. Maynard
Copyright © 1914 by Smith, H. Maynard All rights reserved.
Softcover ISBN-13: 979-8-3852-3819-4
Hardcover ISBN-13: 979-8-3852-3820-0
eBook ISBN-13: 979-8-3852-3821-7
Publication date 11/5/2024
Previously published by Oxford, 1914

This edition is a scanned facsimile of the original edition published in 1914.

To
MY BROTHER

PREFACE

THESE Lectures were not delivered to theological students, but to a mixed congregation; and for that congregation, in the first place, they have been rewritten and amplified. The author is a busy parish priest, with no pretensions to special learning; but it is his business to expound the Scriptures; and, in publishing this book, he not only hopes to help others, but to receive criticism which may be helpful in his work. He has had access to no library but his own, and his authorities are such as may be found on most clerical book-shelves. In acknowledging his indebtedness to others, he would also express his gratitude; and he hopes that the distinguished scholars mentioned below will forgive his temerity where he has ventured to disagree with them.

ACKNOWLEDGMENTS

The author is very much indebted to the great Commentary on the Epistle of S James by Professor J. B. Mayor. He has also found much help from the Commentaries of Professor Knowling, Dean Plumtre, Canon Carr, Dr. Hort, and Dr. Oesterley. He has consulted the older works of Cornelius à Lapide, Bengel,

Alford, Wordsworth, and Scott. For information on other books of the New Testament he has received help from Lightfoot, Westcott, Salmon, Swete, Plummer, Bigg, Sanday, Headlam, Rackham, and Gore Dr Thayer's edition of Grimm's Lexicon of New Testament Greek has been constantly consulted. For information on special points he is indebted to Fr. Puller's Tract upon Unction, to George Adam Smith's *Historical Geography of Palestine*, and to articles in Hastings' *Dictionary of the Bible*, Smith's *Dictionary of the Bible*, and to Smith and Cheetham's *Dictionary of Christian Antiquities*. For the history of the period, besides Josephus and Eusebius and Lightfoot's *Apostolic Fathers*, he has used Schurer's great book on *The Jewish People in the Time of Jesus Christ*, Hort's *Judaistic Christianity*, Harnack's *Expansion of Christianity*, and the works of Sir William Ramsay. Lastly, he has adhered to the Greek text of the Revisers, except in two places, where he has preferred that of Westcott and Hort.

H. M. S.

MALVERN,
SS. Simon and Jude, 1914

CONTENTS

LECTURE	PAGE
I. INTRODUCTION. S. JAMES I. I	1
II. TRIALS S. JAMES I. 2-12	44
III. TEMPTATION S. JAMES I. 13-18	57
IV. HEARING AND SPEAKING S. JAMES I 19-21	69
V HEARING AND DOING S. JAMES I 22-27	81
VI RESPECT FOR PERSONS S JAMES II 1-9	98
VII. THE ROYAL LAW S. JAMES II. 10-13	116
VIII FAITH AND WORKS S JAMES II. 14-26	133
IX. TEACHERS S. JAMES III. 1, 2	159
X. PERILS OF SPEECH S JAMES III. 2-12	172
XI WISDOM S. JAMES III 13-18	190
XII. THE WORLD S. JAMES IV. 1-6	210
XIII HUMILITY: S. JAMES IV. 7-10	234
XIV CRITICISM: S. JAMES IV. 11, 12	248
XV. PRESUMPTION AND PLANS S JAMES IV 13-17	262
XVI THE SINS OF THE RICH S JAMES V 1-6	274
XVII. THE PAROUSIA S JAMES V. 7-11	290
XVIII OATHS AND TRUTHFULNESS. S. JAMES V. 12	314
XIX. IN SICKNESS AND HEALTH S. JAMES V 13-15	333
XX. A MEDIATORIAL CHURCH: S. JAMES V. 16-20	362

NOTES

THE LORD'S BRETHREN	38
THE ELDERS OF THE CHURCH	343
UNCTION FOR THE SICK	347
ABSOLUTION	352

THE EPISTLE OF S. JAMES

LECTURE I

INTRODUCTION

"*James, a servant of God and of the Lord Jesus Christ, to the twelve tribes that are of the Dispersion, greeting*"—JAS. 1. 1.

I.—DIRECT EVIDENCE.

THE direct evidence for the authenticity of the Epistle is slight. It is not mentioned in the Muratorian fragment, and although it is contained in the Peshitto Syriac, "the Queen of Versions," it is doubtful if the Church of Edessa accepted it as canonical before the fourth century. Origen is the first extant writer who cites the Epistle as by S. James. Eusebius, who once quotes it as Scripture, looked upon its authorship as doubtful, although he confesses that many received it. S. Jerome believed it was by S. James, but immediately adds: "It is asserted that it was published by some other person under his name." S. Cyril of Jerusalem in 348, and S. Athanasius in 367, include it in their lists of New Testament writings. The Council of Laodicea in 363 accepted it as authentic, and since the Council of Carthage, in 397, its place in the sacred Canon has been assured.

The fact that the Epistle won its way to Catholic acceptance very slowly need not disquiet us. It was not directly useful for theological instruction, and was therefore little quoted and little regarded by writers who were primarily concerned with the maintenance and definition of the faith. Secondly, the Epistle seemed to controvert S. Paul, and this would render it obnoxious to many whose views were only over-emphasized by the heretic Marcion. Thirdly, to S. James had been attributed more than one apocryphal book written in the interests of Ebionism, and in Ebionite legend S. James had been exalted far above all the Apostles. In consequence any writing bearing his name would be suspect in orthodox circles.

These reasons render it also very unlikely that the Epistle was written at Rome in the middle of the second century. An orthodox forger would have attributed his work to anyone rather than S. James; while an Ebionite would have had no reason for concocting an Epistle which does not favour his peculiar opinions. An Ebionite of the second century wishing to glorify S. James would not have written *James the bondslave of God and the Lord Jesus Christ*, but have emulated the forger who makes S. Clement write to "James, the Lord and Bishop of Bishops, ruling the Holy Church of the Hebrews in Jerusalem."

II.—INDIRECT EVIDENCE.

Eusebius, when classing the book among the Antilegomena, tells us it was disputed, but does not tell us why. He only adds: "At least, not many of the ancients have mentioned it." Direct quotations, prior to Origen, are indeed rare, but a good case can be made out for believing that the Epistle was known to S. Clement of Rome, who may have written much earlier than the year 98, and certainly not later. Parallel passages in *the Testaments of the Twelve Patriarchs*—a work which in its Christian form probably emanated from the Nazarenes at Pella—are too striking to be altogether accidental. It is also impossible to maintain that there is no connexion between *the Shepherd of Hermas* (*circa* 130) and the Epistle of S. James. Dr. Hort is convinced that Irenæus used the Epistle, and Professor Mayor piles up quotations, not all of them very convincing, to prove that it was known to many other early Fathers. Such quotations, it is true, prove nothing as to authorship, and it is always precarious to argue from possible allusions and verbal coincidences, but this evidence is not to be despised by those who think that they have other weighty reasons for believing in the authenticity of the Epistle.

III.—Internal Evidence.

Let us now turn to the internal evidence. The Epistle is Hebraic throughout. It is not only inspired by the Old Testament Scriptures, but it is almost impossible to resist the conviction that it was written by a Jew. The author has references to Genesis, Exodus, Leviticus, Deuteronomy, Joshua, Job, the Book of Proverbs, and Isaiah. He calls Abraham "our Father," and appeals to the examples of Isaac, Rahab, Job, and Elijah.[1] *The Twelve Tribes* still ideally

[1] Jas ii. 21, 25, v. 11, 17

remain for him. He takes for granted that his readers observe the Law. He never uses the word Gospel, because the Gospel for him is the perfected Law—*the Law of Liberty*, prophesied of by Jeremiah.[1] He does not pause to explain a reference to *the Shema*.[2] He finds a metaphor in the *first fruits*.[3] It is the *Lord of Sabaoth*, who hears the cry of the oppressed, and disloyalty to God is spiritual adultery.[4] Throughout the Epistle we are constantly reminded of the Wisdom Literature, and Wisdom for him is the Hebrew *Chochma*. Illustrative passages may be found in the Rabbinical writings, and the whole mental atmosphere is that of a devout Jew, who has not ceased to be a Jew by becoming a Christian. He is not an enthusiastic man of letters aping the style of Jeremiah, Micah, and Amos. He does not quote them, but he shares their spirit. So with an equal moral exaltation and a like conviction of God's holiness, he faces the facts of his own day and prophesies to the men of his own time.

But if it be clear that the Epistle was written by a Jew, there is also very good reason for believing that it was written in Palestine. It is a land where agricultural illustrations are natural. It is a land of the fig, the olive, and the vine,[5] it is the land that needs "the former and the latter rains."[6] It is a land of salt springs and where fountains gush from the limestone rocks.[7] There is a reference to the scorching wind which withers the wild flowers of Galilee.[8] The sea is

[1] Jer xxxi 33
[2] Jas ii 19
[3] Jas. i 18
[4] Jas. iv. 4.
[5] Jas. iii 12
[6] Jas. v 7
[7] Jas iii 11
[8] Jas i 11.

Introduction 5

also near, and the surge of the wave upon the shore furnishes the author with a metaphor.[1] He may well have held a rudder in a sudden squall on the dangerous lake of Galilee. Such being the case, there are critics who believe that the Epistle, far from being the pseudonymous work of a second-century Roman, is in reality by a pre-Christian writer, and they reject as interpolated the words, *and the Lord Jesus Christ*, in i. 1, and *Our . . . Jesus Christ*, in ii. 1. For this contention there is no manuscript authority, while such a view overlooks much that is implicit in this Epistle In the course of these lectures it will often be seen how the author by some slight change, or because of his context, shows that he has passed beyond the teaching of the Wisdom Books, which furnish verbal parallels, and is in full agreement with the loftier teaching which we associate with Our Lord. Secondly, those who would interpret the Epistle from a purely Jewish standpoint have to explain away the continual correspondences with the Gospels.

These correspondences will be repeatedly noted in the following Lectures. Here I would only call the reader's attention to the fact that though the Epistle is so full of the Gospel spirit, there is no sign of literary dependence on any of the four Evangelists. The verse on swearing[2] most nearly approaches to a quotation, but a careful comparison of the Greek will show that S. James is independent of S. Matthew. Now it is almost impossible to believe that anyone who had received his knowledge of Christianity through hearing and reading the Gospels could have written this particular Epistle without betraying by his lan-

[1] Jas 1 6 [2] Jas. v. 12.

guage the source of his inspiration. We must conclude therefore that this Epistle was written prior to the Gospels by someone with first-hand knowledge of Our Lord's teaching.

The social conditions revealed in the Epistle seem quite compatible with a date before the fall of Jerusalem. The author addresses *the Brethren*, which we gather from the Acts was the designation of Christians in the earliest days. They are represented as suffering from manifold trials, but there is nothing to suggest persecution by the State. Their troubles apparently are caused by their own countrymen. It is especially the rich who *oppress them and drag them before the judgment seats*.[1] Now it was the wealthy Sadducean sect which was most bitterly opposed to Christianity, and among them were the chief of the Priests. At any rate, in the Synagogues of the Dispersion, *the gold ringed men*[2] were pre-eminent, and before the great insurrection the Jews were allowed to administer their own law and exercise extensive judicial powers within their own community. Migratory Jewish merchants, intent on gain, might, of course, be found at any time in history,[3] but large Jewish landowners who stored their crops and withheld wages were not to be found after the war.[4] A tendency to hoard and a tendency to squander on their pleasures was characteristic of the Jewish aristocrats described by Josephus, and the hatred of the masses for them found vent in the siege of Jerusalem. Both in the Acts[5] and in Josephus we read of the great drought and resulting famine in the

[1] Jas ii 6.   [2] Jas. ii. 2.   [3] Jas iv. 13-17
[4] Jas. v 1-6.   [5] Acts xi. 27-30

reign of Claudius, and this adds significance to several passages in the Epistle. S. James alludes to the scorching heat, to the naked and hungry asking alms, to the hoarded crops which were corrupting while starving labourers were not paid, to the patient husbandman dependent on the early and latter rains; and when he urges men to prayer and intercession, the prayers of Elijah for rain are insisted on. The time of the insurrection of Theudas and the war between Philadelphia and Pella might well be described as a time of *wars and fighting*.

It is also worth noting that the Epistle presupposes public worship.[1] A rich or poor man might be expected to enter the Christian synagogue as an unknown visitor. This would hardly have been the case in the second century. Again, the immediate expectation of the Parousia is evidence of an early date;[2] and the teaching of this letter is in close agreement with S. Paul's earliest Epistles—those to the Thessalonians. It seems that the time of complete separation of Jew from Christian had not come. There is not a single reference to Gentiles. The Old Testament Scriptures are alone referred to, and this suggests the inference that they were the only Scriptures then existing.

IV.—OBJECTIONS TO AN EARLY DATE.

But Professors of great name assert that the worldliness condemned in this Epistle is inconsistent with the purity and fervour of the early Church. "The moral tone," they say, "is low; the day of corruption

[1] Jas. ii. 2   [2] Jas v. 7, 8

had come; and our scheme of development does not admit of corruption manifesting itself so early."

There was, however, more corruption and a lower moral tone in the Church of Corinth shortly after S. Paul's visit than in the Churches of the Dispersion addressed in this Epistle. Primitive Christians were not free from sin; from the first there have been tares among the wheat. Ananias and Sapphira were converts of the first days,[1] the murmuring of the Grecians against the Hebrews occurred in the early years.[2] Simon Magus even wished to make money out of the Sacraments.[3] All the early converts did not join the Church on the same spiritual level, all were not inspired by the same purity of motive, all were not equally well instructed, all were affected by ingrained habits, and none could be wholly free from the traditions of their past. The author of our Epistle looked on men as they were, and not as they ought to have been had they conformed to pattern, and there never has been a time in the history of the Church when his moral exhortations would have been inappropriate or inapplicable.

The same authorities sometimes argue that the tone of the Epistle is far too authoritative for it to have been written at an early date. It is said to presuppose an ecclesiastical development for which there had been no time.

This objection is raised in the interests of a theory with which we are not immediately concerned. It is here sufficient to answer that such documents as we possess dealing with the Church in Jerusalem agree with the evidence to be found in the Epistle.

[1] Acts v. 1-11. [2] Acts vi. 1. [3] Acts viii. 18.

Introduction

In the Gospels we find that Our Lord came as a King to establish a Kingdom, and that after His Resurrection He vested His power in the Apostles. From the Day of Pentecost there was a Church, and the members "abode steadfastly in the Apostles' doctrine and fellowship, in the breaking of bread and the prayers."[1] We read of the institution of the Diaconate, and very soon of a presiding officer at Jerusalem surrounded by his Presbyters.[2] Order and discipline were conspicuous in the community. The organization was simple but enduring. It exists to-day and is divine. For those who disbelieve in the supernatural origin of the Church this rapid development is inconceivable, although in bodies like the so-called Church of Christian Science they might see an equally rapid development to-day. The fact which many critics leave out of consideration is that the Jewish converts were accustomed to act together:—the formation of a new sect was no new thing. As Jews they had been trained and schooled in the synagogue system, and a synagogue often represented quite a small society or clique. Ten men formed a legal congregation, and synagogues were more numerous than Welsh chapels. There were 380 in Jerusalem alone. Secondly, the synagogue was not merely a place of worship, but a school and place of business. Its rulers exercised discipline, settled disputes, interpreted the law, and administered funds. The synagogues were all in touch with the hierarchy at Jerusalem, just as unity was maintained in the Christian communities by the authority of the Apostolate. Men trained and disciplined in the

[1] Acts ii. 42.   [2] Acts xv. 4.

synagogue system found no difficulty in organizing themselves. Difficulties only began when the Church spread into Europe, for the Gentile converts had not the same traditions, lacked the training, and were unfamiliar with Jewish customs. But at first the Church, which started in Jerusalem, provided the standard of ecclesiastical organization. It was the great war, ending in the siege and destruction of the Holy City, which deprived the Church of a centre just at the time when the expansion among the Gentiles made the maintenance of unity a problem of the greatest difficulty. We need not in consequence be surprised that the evidence as to ecclesiastical organization is for a time confusing and confused. But the last of the Apostles, S. John, stereotyped in Asia the true tradition of what was from the beginning; and it is to Asia, taught by S. John, and to Antioch, which had been in closest touch with the Church in Jerusalem, that we owe the orderly evolution of the Catholic system and the establishment throughout the world of the monarchical episcopate.

But the Church in Jerusalem was not only the model for other Churches elsewhere, it was also the source from which authority flowed forth. When the Church was founded at Samaria, S. Peter and S. John went down from Jerusalem to confirm the members.[1] When Cornelius was converted it was before the Church at Jerusalem that S. Peter justified his action.[2] When Christians at Antioch began to preach to the Gentiles, the Church at Jerusalem sent S. Barnabas to inquire and report.[3] S. Paul was formally received

[1] Acts viii. 14.   [2] Acts xi 4   [3] Acts xi 22.

by the Apostles,[1] and when he went up to Jerusalem, fourteen years afterwards, he gave an account of his teaching, "lest haply he had run in vain."[2] It was at Jerusalem that the first Council was summoned to decide as to the necessity of circumcision, and from Jerusalem went forth the first ecclesiastical decree.[3] Those who came from James persuaded S. Peter and even S. Barnabas to alter their conduct;[4] and lastly, at the close of his third missionary journey, S. Paul at Jerusalem made his official report.[5]

V.—OBJECTIONS TO S. JAMES'S AUTHORSHIP.

We have now reached a point at which we may reasonably assume that the Epistle is by the James who presided over the Church in Jerusalem. We have no means of proving it, for the external evidence is of little value; but from internal evidence the Epistle seems to have been written by a Palestinian Jew who had become a Christian, and wrote before the fall of Jerusalem. The tone of the Epistle is authoritative, and it is addressed to the Hebrew Dispersion. It claims to be by James, and until evidence is forthcoming that he could not have written it, we seem to be justified in accepting that claim.

The reason alleged against his authorship may be stated as follows: (1) He was a peasant. (2) He came from a little out-of-the-way village in a backward province of the Roman Empire. (3) He must in consequence have been utterly illiterate, and could not

[1] Acts ix. 27   [2] Gal ii. 1, 2.   [3] Acts xv 1-35
[4] Gal. ii. 12   [5] Acts xxi 18, 19.

have written such Greek as we find in this Epistle. Let us take these objections one by one and consider their validity.

First, the term "peasant" is altogether misleading. In a society like our own, which has emerged from feudalism, a peasant originally belonged to a conquered race, while manners, education, and standpoint still sever the upper and lower classes. In Galilee, on the other hand, there were Jews and Gentiles, rich and poor, free men and some slaves, but among the Jews there was no inequality based on birth and breeding— the peasant, as we imagine him, did not exist. Neither are we justified in supposing that the family of Joseph belonged to the lowest class. Joseph himself pursued what was looked on as an honourable calling. He was fully conscious of his royal descent and alive to the Messianic hopes of his race.[1] The Blessed Virgin was the cousin of Elizabeth, the wife of a well-known priest.[2] S. John, possibly her nephew, was acquainted with the Chief Priest.[3] Zebedee and his partners, S. Peter and S. Andrew, had hired servants,[4] and the house of S. Peter had a courtyard large enough to accommodate a crowd.[5] The story of the feast at Cana of Galilee describes a social circle of limited means, but far removed from destitution.[6] Our Lord was no doubt poor when He gave up His work as a carpenter to save the world. The Apostles became poor when they forsook all to follow Him, but their poverty was willingly embraced.

Secondly, many have pictured the Holy Family at

[1] Luke ii. 4 [2] Luke i. 36 [3] John xviii. 16
[4] Mark i. 20. [5] Mark ii. 4. [6] John ii. 1-12

Nazareth as dwelling in rustic surroundings. Unconsciously perhaps they provide them with a background, like that of cottagers in a Devonshire village. Nothing could be more misleading. The area of Galilee was about 1,600 square miles. It was about the size of an English county. The land was exceedingly fertile, well cultivated, and densely peopled. Josephus estimated that it had a population of three millions, but this was doubtless an exaggeration. There were many towns, some of them altogether Greek in character, with temples, fora, baths, schools, and race-courses. More than one distinguished man of letters and several Stoic philosophers were born and brought up in the neighbourhood. The Lake of Galilee hummed with life, and several towns melted into one another about its shores. The country was crossed in every direction by great roads, which were veritable highways of the nations. Nazareth, indeed, was probably not a place of great importance, but the road from Damascus went winding round the hill on which the town was built to join the great highway up the plain of Esdraelon. The land was full of historic associations, and from a neighbouring hill-top the famous Way of the Sea could be traced for miles. Any day the boys of Nazareth may have watched the tramp of Roman legionaries on their way to the frontier, caravans of pilgrims on their way to Jerusalem, invalids and pleasure-seekers journeying to the lake, and merchants bringing the treasures of the East to the great markets of the world.

Such sights were among the earliest impressions of S. James, and colour his style. His education was not primarily the result of books and schools, but was picked up on the road. There is a sense of life and a remembrance of things heard and seen throughout his Epistle. He says *behold* this or that, and uses the Attic ἰδού with a frequency that is not Attic. But was he illiterate? This brings us to our third point. Like other Jewish boys, S. James was probably taught to read by the Hassan in the local synagogue. We may be sure that in his home the Scriptures were household words. The Jews, like the Scotch until recently, were chiefly educated by means of an open Bible and a polemical pulpit. They searched the Scriptures, and listened to the disputations of the Rabbis. As in many a humble home Scotch students have learned to read the Greek Testament, it is not improbable that in the devout home in Nazareth a student should have read the Septuagint and sapiential books of his race. The Jews were indeed proud of their own language, and jealous for its preservation; but Galilee contained a very mixed population, and its inhabitants were almost necessarily bi-lingual. Dwellers in Capernaum who knew no Greek were probably as rare as dwellers in Llandudno who know no English. S. James, indeed, spent the last thirty years of his life in Jerusalem where Greek was officially discouraged from political motives, but even there it was generally understood, or the crowd would not have expected S. Paul to address them in that language.[1] S. James, as head of the Church in the city, constantly in touch with pilgrims, and with connexions at Antioch and other places, could scarcely have fulfilled his duties had he been ignorant of Greek.

[1] Acts xxii. 2

All this, however, may be granted, and yet many critics find it difficult to believe that S. James could have written such Greek as we find in this Epistle. He has many words of some rarity, many of them also are archaic. He shows a careful felicity in choosing the right word, and in placing it in such a way as to secure the right emphasis. His sentences are carefully written, his grammar, on the whole, is accurate. His Greek is everything that S. Paul's is not, but that is because S. Paul thought in Greek: the language of the Levant was his native tongue. S. Paul wrote, as he spoke, with impetuous eloquence, he had at command a tumultuous flood of words, while his parentheses and subordinate clauses can only be compared to whirlpools and eddies. S. James, on the other hand, thought in Aramaic. He translated his sentences carefully one at a time, and this partly accounts for his dislocated style. With a large vocabulary of nouns and adjectives, almost all of them to be traced in the Septuagint or apocryphal books, he has but a limited number of verbs, so that $\pi o \iota \epsilon \hat{\iota} \nu$, $\H{\epsilon} \chi \epsilon \iota \nu$, and $\lambda \alpha \mu \beta \acute{\alpha} \nu \epsilon \iota \nu$ are engaged for very varied service. His grammar, we have said, is accurate, but he only ventures on simple constructions, and in this short Epistle there are no less than 140 sentences without a subordinate clause, and only seven sentences with more than one. But when all deductions are made, he still must be credited with exceptional literary power, and this is an endowment which can never be accounted for. Some people speak of Shakespeare as "the boor of Stratford," and yet most men are agreed that he wrote *Hamlet*. We can call Burns, if we please, the drunken ploughman of Ayr, but none the less he wrote with an unequalled purity of diction. A Caroline divine would have dismissed John Bunyan as "an unlearned and ignorant man," but the Tinker of Bedford wrote *Pilgrim's Progress*, which is a "well of English undefiled." It is only professors who imagine that no one can know anything or write anything unless they have had an academic training, and, as facts disprove their assumption, we may dismiss the dogmatic assertion, that one who was born in Galilee could not possibly have written the Epistle of S. James.

VI.—LIFE OF S. JAMES.

The authorship of a particular treatise may be a matter of no consequence, but it is always important if we would understand a letter to know who wrote it, to whom it was written, and when. So we will go on to collect the scattered notices about S. James, and try with their aid to reconstruct his life.

Assuming[1] that S. Joseph was a widower when he espoused the Blessed Virgin, we can think of S. James as the eldest of a family of six children by a former wife. He was probably born in Nazareth, and certainly lived there. Hegesippus, who collected the traditions concerning him in Palestine, tells us that "he was holy from his mother's womb; drank no wine or strong drink, nor ate animal food; no razor came upon his head, nor did he anoint himself with oil or use the bath."[2] S. James was, as we should judge from the Epistle, an ascetic; and there is nothing surprising in

---

[1] See *Note on the Lord's Brethren*, p. 38.
[2] The Roman bath is of course intended.

Introduction

the fact that the first-born son of Joseph was dedicated to be a perpetual Nazarite.

He was probably grown up, and perhaps married when Our Lord was born, for he evidently was not at Bethlehem, nor did he go down into Egypt. Later we may imagine his love for the little Jesus as "He advanced in wisdom and stature, and in favour with God and men."[1] If, as seems probable, S. Joseph died when Our Lord was still a boy, it may be that S. James became the protector and adviser to the widowed mother and her Son. This would have been natural for one who was to write, *pure religion and undefiled before our God and Father is this: to visit the fatherless and widows in their affliction.*[2] This supposition is strengthened by the fact that the Blessed Virgin depended in some sense on the sons of Joseph, for she brought them with her when she would have restrained the activity of Our Lord.[3]

That S. James always loved Our Lord may be taken for granted. The intimate relation between his spirit and the spirit of the Sermon on the Mount may be in part due to continual intercourse during those first thirty years. Our Lord had a work to do for His own family before He began His work for the world. The seed was sown secretly, but S. James, looking back down the vista of the years, recognized and wrote about *the implanted word.*[4]

How was it, then, that he did not believe on Him? We do not, of course, know the extent of his unbelief. He apparently followed Our Lord when He

[1] Luke ii. 52
[2] Jas i. 27
[3] Matt xii 46
[4] Jas i. 21

made His home in Capernaum. He probably believed in Our Lord being the destined Messiah, but his conception of the Messiah was inadequate. As the far elder *brother* he could not forget how Our Lord had been the submissive child. He and the others would have helped Our Lord, but it was hard for them to believe that He could stand alone. Our Lord seemed to make mistakes; He seemed to work too hard. He left Himself no time so much as to eat.[1] He seemed to be carried away by extreme opinions, and to be exciting unnecessary opposition from men whom He ought to conciliate. S. James had not yet learnt that *friendship with the world is enmity with God*,[2] and so in his anxiety he joined with the others in their effort to restrain Him. That effort was clearly inspired by affectionate solicitude for Our Lord's welfare.

Then came Our Lord's hard sayings, His tremendous and undreamed-of claim. The brethren were no doubt fairly puzzled. Was He beside Himself, or was the Jesus they had played with indeed the Son of God? To a devout Jew, with all a Jew's awful reverence for the divine transcendence, such an alternative must have been appalling. S. James, perhaps, had taught Him when a boy to know the Law and the Prophets; and he found it all the harder in consequence to receive the new Gospel. "A prophet," said Our Lord sadly, "is not without honour, save in his own country and among his own kindred";[3] but the brother also who loved Him must have known the torture which goes with a doubtful mind.

The brethren did not apparently accompany Our

---

[1] Mark iii. 20-21   [2] Jas. iv 4.   [3] Matt xiii. 57.

Introduction

Lord on His missionary tours, and this probably accounts for the lack of any reference to miracles in this Epistle. They heard tell, however, of His mighty works, and marvelled that they should be done in villages and out-of-the-way places. The time for the Feast of the Tabernacles was at hand, and so they urged Him: "Depart hence into Judea that Thy disciples may behold the works that Thou doest . . . Manifest Thyself to the world."[1] Both their faith and their lack of faith were alike pathetic. They wanted Him to succeed, but thought that they understood best the way to success. They wanted to believe in Him, but they needed for belief the support of the world's opinion. If only Jerusalem would acclaim Him, if only He would manifest His power, if only the rulers and priests would acknowledge Him, how happy would His brethren be with all their doubts dispelled.

Our Lord did not accept their invitation, and it was not until after the Resurrection that S. James was converted. In the Gospel according to the Hebrews the following story is related: S. James, when Our Lord was crucified, made a vow that he would neither eat nor drink until the Kingdom of God had come, and Our Lord appeared to him on Easter morning, took bread, blessed and brake it, saying, "My brother, eat thy bread, for the Son of Man hath risen from the dead." This story in its present form cannot be accepted; but no doubt S. James was overwhelmed with horror at the Crucifixion; no doubt as a Jew he fasted and prayed. It was, however, his love and not his faith which was rewarded when he saw the risen

[1] John vii. 2, 4

Lord. S. Paul, it will be noted, records first the appearance to the five hundred in Galilee,[1] and then the appearance to S. James, which would lead us to suppose that the meeting took place in the old home among old associations.

According to our argument, S. James was at the time of his conversion a man of fifty, or thereabouts. His habits and ways of thinking were fixed, and this accounts for much that we know about him, and for the form that his Epistle takes. Had he been a younger brother of Our Lord it is hard to believe that he could have resisted His influence, unless he had reacted against it altogether. A man evidently of strong character, he would have been His enthusiastic disciple or His determined opponent. If, on the other hand, he were fifteen to twenty years Our Lord's senior, we may believe that he had always loved Him, but had been unable to surrender himself wholly to One whom he had played with and helped as a little child.

Again, had he been converted as a young man under thirty, he would probably have been less loyal to his old traditions. The Gospel would have meant so much to him that he would have cared but little to study the Old Law. But a devout man of middle age, with definite habits of piety, may grow in knowledge and grace, but does not easily break with his past. He accepted the Gospel as the fulfilment of the Law; he accepted Our Lord as the promised Messiah, but he remained a Jew in his habits and a Jew in his outlook. So, in the providence of God, he was spared for thirty years to bridge the gulf between Judaism and Christianity, to

---

[1] 1 Cor. xv. 6, 7.

guide the Church in the way of continuity, and save her from the dangers which beset a revolution.

S. James was not merely *a hearer but a doer of the Word*,[1] and so directly after his conversion we find him associating with the Apostles in the Upper Chamber, a member of the little band who believed.[2] He was not, however, chosen to fill the vacant place left by the traitor Judas, for it was fitting, as S. Peter said, that someone should be selected "who had companied with us all the time that the Lord Jesus went in and out among us, from the baptism of John unto the day when He was received up from us."[3] But as time went on, he also was raised to the rank of the Apostolate. At least S. Paul calls him an Apostle, and the title was evidently very jealously guarded.

Clement of Alexandria, in his *Hypotyposes*, writes: "They say that Peter, James, and John after the Ascension of the Saviour . . . strove not after honour, but chose James the Just, Bishop of Jerusalem."[4] This perhaps is not exactly the way in which a contemporary would have written, but it more or less represents what occurred. Very early, probably, the twelve recognized that theirs was a missionary vocation, and that it was necessary to have someone to administer the affairs of the Church at Jerusalem. When S. Paul was introduced to the Church by S. Barnabas only S. Peter and S. James were present,[5] and when S. Peter fled after his escape from prison, he left word that it should be reported to "James and the brethren."[6]

[1] Jas. 1 22
[2] Acts 1 13, 14
[3] Acts 1. 21, 22
[4] Quoted Eusebius 11. 1-3
[5] Acts ix 27 , Gal. 1. 18, 19.
[6] Acts xii. 17.

From the Day of Pentecost until the death of Stephen, the Church had been composed of Palestinian Jews and Grecians, but the persecution which ensued seems to have been principally directed against the Hellenistic Christians, and their dispersion probably strengthened the position of S. James. At any rate, after this date it is clear that the Church at Jerusalem was Palestinian in character, and when S. Paul began disputing in the Synagogue of the Grecians, there was no longer any support to be hoped for from them.[1]

In A.D. 50 was the first Council of the Church. S. James presided. He spoke last, and his decision was final. On the first day S. Paul related his experiences, and the Christians who were Pharisees began disputing with him. On the second day S. Peter related his experience, and gave his voice for freedom. This secured S. Paul and S. Barnabas a second hearing, but their eloquence was received in silence. Lastly, S. James arose, saying ἐγὼ κρίνω,[2] and no form could be more pontifical. His decision was embodied in a letter which reads, "it seemed good to the Holy Ghost and to us."[3] The infant Church was authoritative and unashamed.

The dispute was as to the necessity of circumcision for Gentile converts, and it had apparently arisen from Jewish brethren misquoting S. James at Antioch. The letter says, "certain that went out from us have troubled you with words subverting your souls, to whom we gave no commandment."[4] At the same time it is noteworthy that S. James having listened to S. Paul's

[1] *Cf* Acts vi 1-10, ix 29
[2] Acts xv 19
[3] Acts xv. 28
[4] Acts xv. 24.

Introduction

pleading and approved S. Peter's argument for liberty, is careful to add certain restrictions which would safeguard the social life and customs of legally-minded Jews.

His decision was, in fact, a compromise, and illustrates that practical wisdom for which he urged men to pray.

The Gentile Churches were young, and S. James, we may assume, knew little about them. He was probably quite confident as to the ultimate triumph of a Christianity according to the Jewish type. "For," as he said, "Moses from generations of old hath in every city them that preach him, being read in the synagogues every Sabbath."[1] But he had patience, and he was not going for the sake of a party triumph to rend the Church in twain. S. Paul had spoken to an unfriendly audience, which looked to S. James as their leader. But S. James, whatever his private opinions on the question in dispute, admired the heroism of S. Barnabas and S. Paul, who had "hazarded their lives for the Name of the Lord Jesus Christ."[2] There was no bitter jealousy in his heart, the spirit of faction was hateful to him. He had not the temper which presses principles to extremes, and so it came to pass that, with the practical wisdom of an old man, he gave a decision which obviated the evils of the day. He left time to decide as to conflicting principles, being confident that truth would in the end prevail. The true principle has prevailed, and not in the way that S. James expected, but that is no reason why we should underrate his service to the Church. *The fruits of*

[1] Acts xv. 21. [2] Acts xv. 26.

righteousness are sown in peace of them that make peace,[1] and it was through his tolerance that S. Paul was enabled to go on his way unhampered by the racial restrictions of the Jewish Law.

So S. Paul and S. Barnabas returned to Antioch, accompanied by Silas and Judas, called Barsabas, as representatives of the Church at Jerusalem. Shortly afterwards S. Peter must have arrived at Antioch, and for a short time all went peaceably, Jews and Gentiles living together. Then "certain who came from James"[2] once more stirred up dissension. They no longer urged that Gentiles must be circumcized, but that Jews must not abandon their social exclusiveness. A Gentile by becoming a Christian was not in consequence a Jew's equal The same argument is heard to-day with regard to the converted members of coloured races. Religion was one thing, race another. S. Peter separated himself from the Gentiles; the Jews dissembled before these emissaries from S. James, and even S. Barnabas was led away by their dissimulation. But S. Paul stood firm for his great principle that "there should be neither Jew nor Greek," but "all should be one in Christ Jesus."[3] His was the true principle, and we can see now that the whole future of the Christian Church depended on its being accepted But we only have S. Paul's version of the quarrel, which was not of long continuance, and we do not know how far the men who came from James were acting on their own responsibility. Perhaps reports had reached Jerusalem that the decree as to "blood and things strangled"[4] was not being observed; and S. James, whether he believed this

[1] Jas iii. 18. [2] Gal. ii. 12. [3] Gal. iii. 28 [4] Acts xv 29

Introduction 25

or not, thought it advisable that the conduct of the Apostle of the Circumcision should not be open to this suspicion.

He may in consequence have sent a warning to S. Peter that his eating with Gentiles was imperilling the peace and impeding the progress of the Church at Jerusalem. We have to remember that for S. James the triumph of Christianity among the Jews was of the first importance. The Gentile converts were still so few in number, while the Church was growing rapidly among the Jews. S. James knew and sympathized with the difficulties of converts from among the Pharisees. He acted for the best on behalf of those whom he knew, and was only wrong because there were others whom he did not know, and wider interests which he did not understand.

For the next five or six years the Church at Jerusalem progressed in peace. There were thousands who believed, and they were all zealous for the Law.[1] The influence of S. James among his own people was probably at its height when S. Paul returned from his third missionary journey. The great Apostle was accorded an official reception by S. James and the presbyters. He made his report, and they glorified God for the fruits of His ministry.[2] But the time was critical, for thousands were coming to the Feast, and among the pilgrims would be all that was most fanatical in Judaism. Many libels and much scandal had already been retailed in Jerusalem to the detriment of S. Paul, and S. James was in consequence most anxious that he should be able to present him to the Church as an

[1] Acts xxi. 20. [2] Acts xxi. 18.

obviously orthodox Jew. Luckily S. Paul had taken a Nazarite vow, and when he shaved his head certain rather costly sacrifices had to be offered. Poor men were often bound for years through inability to pay the cost, and it was regarded as particularly meritorious to help poor Nazarites in fulfilling their obligations. S. James in consequence persuaded S. Paul not only to purify himself, but to be "at charges" for four poor men. In this way he hoped that the Apostle would not only prove his own orthodoxy, but also have grateful witnesses to testify in his favour.[1]

All would have gone well but for the Jews of Asia, who recognized S. Paul, and raised a tumult, alleging that he had brought Greeks into the Temple and polluted the Sanctuary. The riots occasioned by S. Paul's arrest, and the subsequent proceedings against him, proved a turning-point in the history of the Church. It embittered the relations between Jews and Christians, and split the Church in twain. We do not know how many of those thousands who were "all zealous for the Law" remained faithful, but the writer of the Epistle to the Hebrews evidently knew of many defections when he writes: "They were once enlightened and tasted of the heavenly gift, and were made partakers of the Holy Ghost, and powers of the age to come, and then fell away."[2] Not only was this so, but many who remained were "dull of hearing"[3] and slow of comprehension; miserable in their isolation, they despaired of the coming of the Lord. They had not grasped the idea of the Priesthood in the New Covenant,[4] nor understood the significance of the Cross

---

[1] Acts xxi. 21-26
[2] Heb. vi. 4
[3] Heb. v. 11
[4] Heb vii., viii.

Introduction

as a Sacrifice[1] nor of the Blessed Sacrament as taking the place of the sacrificial feasts.[2] They were not prepared to go without the camp to worship.[3] They neglected the assembling of themselves together.[4] They did not rightly value the New Covenant, nor perceive that the old was ready to vanish away.[5]

To the religious bitterness, to the defection of many, to the doubts and perplexities of those who remained, must be added the rising storm of fanaticism, inspired by the nationalist movement. During the last five or seven years of his life, S. James no doubt faced many difficulties, suffered many disappointments, and endured manifold trials. He needed, then, all his courage and patience, and perhaps found a new consolation in the lives of the Prophets.

Josephus[6] briefly records his end. Festus had died, and before his successor, Albinus, could arrive in Judæa, Ananus, the Sadducean High Priest, brought James and some of his companions, probably presbyters, before the Sanhedrin, and condemned them to be stoned. The act was no doubt popular with the mob, but many Jews who were not Christians resented this violation of the laws. Some travelled to meet Albinus at Alexandria and complain of the High Priest. Albinus wrote angrily threatening Ananus, and Agrippa deposed him.

Hegesippus gives many details as to his martyrdom, but the tradition had evidently become confused and was not always understood by the relater. A critical examination of his story would take many pages and

---

[1] Heb. ix. [2] Heb x., xiii. 10, 16. [3] Heb xiii 13.
[4] Heb. x. 25 [5] Heb viii. 13 [6] Antiq xx. 9, 1.

add very little to our knowledge of S. James. Let us end with the words of the author of the Epistle to the Hebrews, written shortly after the martyrdom of S. James and his companions: "Remember them that had the rule over you, which spake unto you the word of God, and consider the issue of their life, imitate their faith."[1]

VII.—THE DISPERSION.

The *Diaspora* dates from the time of Shalmaneser and Sargon who deported the Tribes of Israel to Mesopotamia. Then came the deportation of Judah under Nebuchadnezzar, and the flight of many into Egypt. A remnant returned on the decree of Cyrus, and subsequently under Ezra and Nehemiah. They probably included the most religious and also the least prosperous of the race. The Persian Kings settled many as far north as the Caspian Sea, as loyal subjects who would leaven conquered populations. Under Alexander the Great, the Jews acquired great importance and even citizenship in Alexandria and other new cities. Antiochus the Great (223-207 B.C.) founded Jewish colonies in Lydia and Phrygia. One of the Ptolemies transported thousands to Cyrene, and Pompey carried crowds of Jewish slaves to Rome. Wherever they went, and under whatever conditions, they managed to prosper. In Syria and Mesopotamia they were landowners; they were traders in every Greek city; with the Phœnicians they controlled the carrying trade of the world. They were, in Our Lord's time, most numerous in Babylonia; but Syria was full of them,

[1] Heb xiii. 7

and Josephus states there were at least ten thousand in Damascus alone. They occupied two quarters out of five in the city of Alexandria, and Philo estimates the Jewish population in Egypt at a million. They were probably a fourth of the people in Cyrene. The Trastevere at Rome was filled with Jews, and they were numerous in trading ports like Antioch, Ephesus, Puteoli, and Marseilles.

In the East they were rigidly conservative. They preserved their language and boasted about the purity of their race. They declared that when Ezra took back exiles to Palestine, he left the land behind him as "pure as fine flour." They affected to look down on the dwellers in Palestine as demoralized by the Gentile world, while the Jews of Palestine spoke of them as the Upper Barbarians.

The Jews of Syria naturally spoke Greek, and yet were in closer touch with Palestine than the rest of the Diaspora. The soil of Syria was declared clean, though the very dust of the lands was supposed to defile.

The Hellenistic Jews, on the other hand, were despised. When the Jews asked " Whither will He go, that we shall not find Him? will He go to the Dispersion among the Greeks, and teach the Greeks?"[1] they intended to express their contempt not only for the Lord but for their Hellenistic brethren. The Greek Jews, they thought, needed teaching, and were likely to be deluded by a false prophet. The Greek Jews had developed a new theology, and adapted themselves to Greek ways of thinking; they were not careful about Levitical customs, and treated their national history as

[1] John vii. 35.

material for allegory. Some had gone still further. Aristotle, three centuries before, claimed to have met a Jew with "a Greek soul." Many Jews had apostatized in the days of Antiochus; and many had adopted Greek customs under the Herods. When St. James wrote, the danger of apostasy was passed, but the dangers of syncretism were still imminent. It is, however, probable that Palestinian Rabbis exaggerated the differences which were due to environment rather than to creed. At any rate, the Hellenistic Jews as a body were attached to Jerusalem, and, like Jews in other countries, supported the Temple treasury. The hierarchy in Jerusalem, through their annual emissaries and collectors, were kept in touch with the whole Diaspora, while the pilgrims from many lands who came to the Feasts were the means of keeping race consciousness and national hopes alive. It was, we remember, at the Feast of Pentecost that the Church started on her way. There were at Jerusalem "Parthians, and Medes, and Elamites, and the dwellers in Mesopotamia, and in Judæa, and Cappadocia, in Pontus, and Asia, Phrygia, and Pamphylia, in Egypt, and in the parts of Libya about Cyrene, and strangers of Rome, Jews and proselytes, Cretes and Arabians."[1] Many of these carried home with them the tidings of the Christ; from the very beginning the sound of the Gospel went out into all the world.

But the infant Church was also to have its Diaspora. After the stoning of S. Stephen, the Hellenistic congregations were dispersed, but even before then there must have been a congregation of some importance at

[1] Acts ii 9-11.

Introduction

Damascus, or S. Paul would not have been sent to suppress it.[1] We read of the founding of the Church at Samaria,[2] and of Christian communities at Joppa and Lydda[3] and later at Cæsarea.[4] Antioch, too, had a flourishing Church. It was large enough to attract general notice, and the brethren were there first nicknamed Christians.[5] After the persecution of Herod, another dispersion took place, and, besides, there was always a constant coming and going, so that the Church expanded sporadically in all directions.

During the festival seasons S. James would be brought into contact with Christian Jews from all parts. He would listen to many stories of hardship and privation due to the acceptance of the Gospel. He would hear complaints of injustice in Jewish courts, and of how the Holy Name of Our Lord was blasphemed. He would also have brought before him local disputes as to faith and conduct, and find how many of them began with rash words, or were the result of petty jealousies. Teachers would strive to win his approval for themselves, or obtain his condemnation of their adversaries. It would be brought home to him how the Church was not only menaced from without, but weakened from within by the rival ambitions of those who belonged to her. He would note how the most zealous could not work together, and of how many misunderstandings arose out of heedless gossip. He had to do with a people who had been trained in controversy, and were apt to confuse religion with theological disputations. The Faith he wished to

[1] Acts ix 2.   [2] Acts viii 5.   [3] Acts ix. 32, 36.
[4] Acts viii. 40, xi. 11, xviii 22   [5] Acts xi. 26

promulgate was a Way of Life, and for him the Christian Creed was best expressed in conduct.

After some festival, with its many interviews, we may imagine S. James sitting down to write his letter. It is men rather than principles which concern him. He does not write to explain a theology or establish an ethical system, he has rather something to say to the kind of men whom he knows. He naturally dramatizes his thought, and writes each sentence to someone whom he conjures up before his imagination. Now it is a downtrodden labourer, now it is a theological disputant, now it is a wealthy merchant, and now a smug attendant in a synagogue. He is addressing not one correspondent but many. He visualizes them in turn. His point of view shifts as he thinks first of one and then of another, so that there is something paradoxical about the net result, which has puzzled his critics, and made them doubt the integrity of his work.

The letter so written was no doubt copied and distributed among the pilgrims who came up to the next Feast. The Jews were quite accustomed to this method of publication, for those who brought the Temple tribute often returned with letters, decrees, and advice from the hierarchy at Jerusalem. The letter was not primarily intended for Mesopotamia and Babylon, or it would have been written in Aramaic. Neither was S. James thinking chiefly of the Hellenistic Jews, or he would have chosen other topics. He was no doubt thinking chiefly of the Churches of Syria and Cilicia, so well known to him by report. The letter was carried further. From Cilicia, we may imagine, it penetrated to Galatia; from Antioch it passed to Corinth and

Rome. S. James intended his letter for all. It was disseminated far and wide; but it was written from a limited experience, from his personal knowledge of the Churches most intimately connected with Jerusalem and himself.

VIII.—EVIDENCE AS TO DATE. THE EPISTLES OF S. PETER AND S. PAUL.

For those who believe in the authorship of S. James, the possibilities as to date are confined within very narrow limits. He would hardly have written in so authoritative a tone while the Apostles remained at Jerusalem, so we may conclude it was written after the death of Herod in A.D. 44. It cannot be later than A.D. 62 or 63, for in one of those years he was martyred. The real question at issue is as to whether it were written before or after the Council at Jerusalem in A.D. 50.

Critics who see in S. James a literary dependence on S. Peter and S. Paul naturally conclude for the latest possible date, and interpret the famous passage as to Faith and Works accordingly. As will be seen in Lecture VIII., I am convinced that S. James was not writing a counterblast to S. Paul, and I think it most probable that both S. Peter and S. Paul had read the letter of S. James. Anyhow, on the literary question there is no consensus of opinion. Critics give priority to S. Peter and S. Paul, and critics decide for the priority of S. James, while some critics, and those not the least eminent, believe that all three writers wrote independently. No one in consequence can dogmatize on the subject, but, apart from these literary considerations, I think there are good reasons for assigning the Epistle to an early date.

First, there is no reference to the dispute about circumcision. After A.D. 50 this was a burning question among the Jews, and it is unlikely that S. James, when writing to his own people, should have nothing to say on the subject.

Secondly, there is no advice as to the social relations between Jews and Gentiles, and this is fatal to the suggestion that the letter was brought to Antioch by "certain that came from James"[1] after the Council. Such emissaries would scarcely have dared to treat the question of eating with Gentiles as a matter of the first importance, if they were bearers of an authoritative letter from their chief, which did not even allude to the subject.

Thirdly, the Gentiles are not mentioned at all. This is not surprising if the letter were written at a time when the Gentiles were an almost negligible factor in Church life, but it is strange if we date the letter after the return of S. Paul from his first missionary journey.

Lastly, there was, when the letter was written, no need to distinguish between *works*, *good works*, and *works of the Law*, but these distinctions became vital for subsequent controversialists. The word *justification* had evidently not acquired a technical sense, and the author shows no acquaintance with the doctrine of S. Paul.

It is probable, then, that the letter was written some little time before S. Paul and S. Barnabas concluded their first missionary journey; and if it have any reference to their teaching, this may be due to a misunder-

---
[1] Gal. ii. 12.

standing arising out of reports brought by S. Mark to Jerusalem.

It is easy to connect the Epistle with the subsequent controversy on circumcision. S. James had written: *If a man keep the whole law and offend in one point, he is guilty of all.*[1] The Judaizers no doubt tore these words out of their context, and argued: "Circumcision is commanded in the Law. Therefore, if you neglect to be circumcised, you are involved in guilt." Some such argument was clearly used, and the authority of S. James was claimed for it. He, however, repudiated the inference in the letter from the Council when he wrote: "Certain that went out from us have troubled you with words, subverting your souls, to whom we gave no commandment."[2]

IX.—S. Paul and the Three Pillars.

This brings us to the final questions, which need to be thought out before attempting to interpret the Epistle. Did Christianity develop as the result of opposed forces and contradictory views, or was there from the start one Body and one Spirit? Did the Apostles think of themselves as speaking in their own names, or regard themselves as guardians of a sacred deposit? Can the Faith be regarded apart from institutional Christianity? Is the Church Divine or human in its origin? Is it a convenient organization, or the Body of Christ and the family of God?

When we go to the New Testament the evidence seems clear. The Apostles only claimed to be loyal

[1] Jas. ii. 10. [2] Acts xv. 24.

witnesses. The Gospel for them was "by the Holy Ghost sent forth from heaven."[1] It was "the revelation of Jesus Christ." They only declared, in the words of S. John,[2] "what was from the beginning, that which we have heard, that which we have seen with our eyes, that which we beheld, and our hands handled concerning the Word of Life." So S. James appeals confidently to *the Faith of the Lord Jesus Christ*,[3] as to something which all the brethren knew and accepted, about which there was no dispute.

This definite body of Truth accounts for and justifies the dogmatic tone which is dominant throughout the New Testament. S. Paul writes: "If any man preach any other Gospel than that ye have received, let him be anathema."[4] We cannot imagine good men asserting such authority for their private opinions. They spoke as they did because the One Faith did not proceed from themselves. They believed that God had revealed what S. James calls *the Word of Truth*.[5]

But were the Apostles in essential agreement as to its content? I believe they were. S. Paul, in his most controversial epistle, claims for himself direct revelation from Jesus Christ, but he also tells us how he laid before his fellow Apostles the Gospel which he preached to the Gentiles, "lest by any means he had been running or had run in vain."[6] He tells us that they had nothing to object and nothing to impart, but gave him the right hand of fellowship. So when S. Paul wrote to the Galatians there was one Gospel common to the

---

[1] 1 Pet 1 12   [2] 1 John 1 1.   [3] Jas. ii. 1.
[4] Gal. i. 8   [5] Jas. 1 18.   [6] Gal. ii 2.

Introduction

"Three Pillars"[1] and himself. There was also a Church having authority in matters of Faith.

When we consider the sharply contrasted characters and varied genius of the Apostles, we may marvel that they should have professed one Faith and co-operated for one purpose, should all have been united in one Church. Nothing accounts for, or can account for this, but the One Lord who completely dominated them all, and the facts concerning Him which they all alike received. They did not organize a Church to maintain their Faith, their Master had founded a Church to which they belonged, and the Holy Spirit had informed that Church with a Faith of which they were the custodians.

The Apostles did not live isolated lives, they had continual intercourse, and acted and reacted on one another. Notwithstanding their diversified characters and different outlooks they each and all accepted that universal religion which appeals to men, women and children, of all times, of all races, at all stages of their development.

Regarding the facts in this way we are justified in illustrating S. James by other New Testament writers; we are also justified in maintaining that he believed many things which he had no occasion to state in this Epistle. In the following Lectures he will not be regarded as a writer apart, but as a member and representative of the Church, a man with his own character and his own point of view, but before all things a servant, nay a *bondslave of God and the Lord Jesus Christ*.

[1] Gal. ii. 9.

NOTE ON THE LORD'S BRETHREN.

It has been assumed in the Introduction that S. James was the son of S. Joseph, but was not the son of the Blessed Virgin. As this is much disputed at the present day, it is necessary to say something of the controversy, and of the reason for my assumption.

There are three theories commonly called the Hieronymian, the Helvidian, and the Epiphanian.

The first theory may be stated as follows: The term brother often implies no more than kinship and need not be taken literally, and so we have only to discover if Our Lord had any relation called James. Now in S. John xix. 25, we read: "There was standing by the Cross His mother, and His mother's sister, Mary the wife of Clopas, and Mary Magdalene." S. Matthew speaks of "Mary the mother of James and Joses,"[1] and S. Mark of "Mary the mother of James the Less and of Joses and of Salome."[2] S. Luke also speaks of "Mary the mother of James."[3] S. Jerome, putting these references together, decided that as Mary the wife of Clopas was the sister of the Blessed Virgin and the mother of James, that therefore when the people of Nazareth referred to Our Lord's brethren as "James and Joses and Judas and Simon," they intended to refer to His cousins.

Since S. Jerome many have identified Clopas with Alphæus and in consequence maintained that the James who was Our Lord's cousin was also one of the Twelve Apostles, first Bishop of Jerusalem, and the author of our Epistle.

Now, though it is no doubt true that relations might be sometimes called brethren, it is extremely unlikely that a cousin would be distinguished by the title *The Brother*. "Cousin" and "nephew" are both terms to be found in

---

[1] Matt. xxvii. 56 [2] Mark xv. 40, *cf.* xv. 47, xvi. 1.
[3] Luke xxiv. 10

Introduction

the New Testament.[1] Secondly, the text from S. John on which the theory hinges may be read differently: "His mother and His mother's sister; Mary the wife of Clopas and Mary Magdalene." The Peshitto Syriac so understands it and puts in an additional conjunction to make it plain. Thirdly, the identification of Clopas with Alphæus is exceedingly doubtful, while the fact that "neither did His brethren believe in Him" seems fatal to the theory which would include "the brother of the Lord" in the number of the Twelve.

The only merit that the theory has, is that it gets over the difficulty that Joseph had four sons named James, Joses, Jude, and Simon, while Mary the wife of Clopas had at least two, named James and Joses, while if Clopas may be identified with Alphæus, there was also a Jude, and, if Hegesippus is to be trusted, a fourth named Simeon, who became the second Bishop of Jerusalem.

But names were few in those days, and names at all times recur in allied families. Besides, it seems that Hegesippus regarded Clopas as the brother of S. Joseph, and it is possible to translate him as saying that Simeon was the cousin of James

(2) S. Jerome constructed his theory in opposition to a man named Helvidius, who had propounded the view that James and the Brethren were uterine brothers of Our Lord, the sons of Joseph by the Blessed Virgin Mary. Arguing from the text: "Is not this the carpenter, the son of Mary, and brother of James and Joses and Judas and Simon? and are not His sisters here with us?"[2] Helvidius would credit the Blessed Virgin with having given birth to at least six children after the Lord Jesus Christ.

This theory, which was repudiated by the whole Church in the fourth century, has been hotly contended for by Protestant writers in recent times; and they enforce their arguments by inferences drawn from the two texts: "She

[1] Luke i. 36; Col. iv. 10.   [2] Mark vi. 3, Matt xiii. 54-56.

brought forth her firstborn son"[1] and "Joseph . . . took unto him his wife and knew her not till she had brought forth a son."[2]

It has been replied that since Our Lord was known in Nazareth as the son of Joseph, it would have been quite natural for His neighbours to speak of the children of Joseph by a former wife as His brothers. Secondly, the inferences from the two texts cannot be pressed. *The firstborn Son* among the Jews had definite privileges and it was Our Lord's legal designation. It does not in consequence imply that there was a second-born son. The text of the second quotation is doubtful, and there are authorities for more than one reading. But should our text be the correct one, it would still be exceedingly precarious to deduce a fact from the grammar of the narrative, when it is clear that the writer was only engaged in establishing a fact of another kind. You may press an inference from a creed, a law, or a definition, but you cannot treat a story in the same manner. In dealing with a narrative you have only to ask yourself one question, What did the author intend us to learn? In this narrative the answer is clear. He intended us to learn that Jesus was born of a virgin.

(3) The third theory, called after Epiphanius, is simple. St. Joseph was a widower with sons and daughters before he became espoused to Mary the Virgin. So, as Our Lord was reputed to be the son of Joseph, James and the others were known as His brethren. It has been objected that if Joseph had an older family Our Lord would not have been heir to the Kingdom of David, but this does not follow, as Solomon himself did not succeed by right of primogeniture. Secondly, this theory does not free us from the difficulty of believing in two families of cousins with the same names, but neither does the Helvidian theory, and it is after all easier to believe in cousins with the same names than in two sisters called Mary.

Each of these theories has been ably defended by modern

[1] Luke ii. 7.   [2] Matt i 25

Introduction 41

critics, but it is quite clear that prejudice has been the determining factor in their decisions. Those who regard Our Lady as a very ordinary woman and are suspicious of anything which would exalt virginity at the expense of marriage naturally favour the Helvidian view. Roman Catholics are more or less pledged to the theory of S. Jerome, and champion it accordingly. Others incline to the Epiphanian solution. Long ages ago S. Basil wrote: " The lovers of Christ cannot endure to hear that the Mother of God ceased to be a virgin," and to me it is inconceivable. With this frank confession of prejudice, I will go on to state my reasons for believing the Epiphanian theory to be the most probable.

First the great majority of the Fathers held this view, which can be traced back to the early days of the second century. It is said, indeed, to be based on the fabulous legends in the Apocryphal Gospels, but it is possible that the legends have a certain significance.

The Protevangelium Jacobi, the Gospel of Peter, the Pseudo-Matthew, the history of Joseph, the Gospel of Thomas, and the Arabic Gospel of the Infancy are all in accord with the Epiphanian view. Some of these works are Ebionite and some Docetic in their tendencies, and neither to the Ebionites nor to the Docetæ was the virginity of Mary of any importance. The books were written in different countries; some of them are the wildest of romances, and yet they all preserve the same tradition as to the Blessed Virgin and the sons of Joseph. The tradition can only have arisen in Palestine, and among the Jews there was no tendency to exalt celibacy, while the mother of many was esteemed more honourable than the mother of one. In consequence there was no impulse at work to account for the invention of the legend; and the natural inference is that among the discordant details due to the imagination of various writers, these books have preserved one fact which is common to them all.

Secondly, the mother of Our Lord has ever been known

as "The Virgin." This, her pre-eminent title, is certainly as old as the Epistles of Ignatius, and it seems wellnigh impossible that she should have received or retained this title had she ever been known as the mother of at least seven children. We may go further and maintain that had the mother of Our Lord been known as the mother of six other children born in the course of nature, it is extremely unlikely that the doctrine of the Virgin Birth would ever have been accepted by the whole Church.

Thirdly, very early marriages were the rule among the Jews. The Talmud says: "Any Jew who has not a wife is not a man." But Joseph was apparently a man of mature age. He is called $\delta\iota\kappa\alpha\iota\sigma$,[1] which is hardly the epithet which a Jew would confer on a boy who had recently arrived at the age of puberty. It is to be noted that he acts as a mature man. He keeps his own counsel and resolves "to put her away privily"; and after being reassured by the angel, he takes Our Lady with him to Bethlehem out of the way of slanderous tongues. That he was of some age is also to be inferred from the fact that he is not mentioned after the visit to Jerusalem, when Our Lord was twelve years old. It is supposed that he died, and had he died in the flower of his age the fact would probably have been noted. Again, S. James who was martyred in A.D. 62 or 63 is represented in tradition as a man of such age that he was venerated even by the unbelieving Jews, and this agrees with the evidence of Josephus as to the resentment felt at his death.

Fourthly, had Mary been the mother of six little children it is unlikely that she would have been able to accompany her husband when they went with Our Lord to the Temple. A prudent mother would not have taken them with the caravan even if it had been possible to do so. Besides, if we suppose her to have done so, it seems inconceivable that both parents would have hurried back to Jerusalem at the end of a long day's march, when they found Jesus to be missing.

[1] Matt. 1. 19

Introduction 43

Fifthly, when the people of Nazareth said: "Is He not the brother of James and Joses and Judas and Simon?" the natural inference is that they were older than He. They were well known, and had some position in the town. Our Lord was only known as their brother. The same inference is to be drawn from their coming to restrain Him at Capernaum. It was the act of those who felt that they had a duty towards one less experienced than themselves.

Sixthly, upon the Cross Our Lord especially entrusted His mother to S. John the Divine, who took her to his own home, and we naturally ask, Is it conceivable that He would have done so had she had four natural protectors? Would He have been justified in disregarding their rights? They were good men, even if at the time they did not believe in Him, and a failure of faith does not abrogate the Fifth Commandment. It is said, they were all probably married, but there is a tradition that S. John also was married. It is suggested that they may not have been at Jerusalem, but if they were not there, that would hardly justify the words: " Woman, behold thy son. Son, behold Thy mother."[1]

Lastly, S. James himself did not claim the title. Others might call him "the brother of the Lord," but he, who knew, writes of himself simply as *the bondslave of the Lord Jesus Christ*. Still more remarkable is it that S Jude calls himself "the brother of James,"[2] because the words are so obviously inserted with a view to claiming authority He, too, felt that he could not make the more tremendous claim

[1] John xix. 27, 28.   [2] Jude 1.

LECTURE II

TRIALS

"Count it all joy, my brethren, when ye fall into manifold temptations, knowing that the proof of your faith worketh patience And let patience have its perfect work, that ye may be perfect and entire, lacking nothing But if any of you lacketh wisdom, let him ask of God, who giveth to all liberally and upbraideth not, and it shall be given him But let him ask in faith, nothing doubting for he that doubteth is like the surge of the sea driven by the wind and tossed. For let not that man think that he shall receive anything of the Lord, a doubleminded man, unstable in all his ways. But let the brother of low degree glory in his high estate and the rich, in that he is made low, because as the flower of the grass he shall pass away For the sun ariseth with the scorching wind, and withereth the grass, and the flower thereof falleth, and the grace of the fashion of it perisheth so also shall the rich man fade away in his goings Blessed is the man that endureth temptation for when he hath been approved, he shall receive the crown of life, which the Lord promised to them that love Him."—JAS. 1 2-12

I.—INTRODUCTION.

IN the passage before us S. James deals with the problem of Temptation. He does not pretend to review the whole subject. He is writing a letter and not a treatise. He deals with such points as apply to his correspondents. He does not argue, and his tone is not persuasive. He is the master writing to disciples, and he writes as one having authority, as a strong man anxious to sustain the weak, as a practical man quick to condemn those guilty of unprofitable speculation.

II.—THE LIFE OF TRIAL.

His first words are startling and abrupt. They are like an unexpected bugle call, and the bugler sounds an heroic note. These converts had probably joined the Church in the enthusiasm of Pentecost,[1] expecting the immediate coming of the Kingdom,[2] and the restitution of all things. Now they are disillusioned and disspirited. They find themselves a despised minority in the scattered synagogues of the Dispersion. They are looked on as an heretical sect, meriting persecution and oppression, and they have come to look upon themselves as objects of pity. Surely S. James will feel compassion, and write with tender solicitude a letter of consolation? No! S. James does better. He neither weeps with them nor expects them to weep. There is rather a note of congratulation in his call to courage. *My brethren, count it all joy when ye fall into divers temptations.* He appeals to their manhood. They are soldiers of Christ, and in consequence for them the post of danger is the post of honour.[3] Crowns of victory are not to be won in ease and security, they are for those who jeopard their lives in the high places of the field.[4] S. James is republishing Our Lord's reiterated beatitude: "Blessed are they which are persecuted for righteousness' sake: for theirs is the Kingdom of Heaven. Blessed are ye when men shall revile you and persecute you, and shall say all manner of evil against you falsely for My sake. Rejoice and be exceeding glad, for so persecuted they the prophets which were before you."[5]

[1] Acts ii. 9-11, 41.   [2] Acts iii. 21   [3] Rev. iii. 11, 12.
[4] Judg. v. 18.   [5] Matt v. 11, 12.

But here we pause to consider what S. James means by *Temptation*. In this opening verse he is obviously referring to external trials hard to be borne. For Christians all life is a probation, but probation does not necessarily involve suffering. S. James admits that a man may be tried by prosperity as well as by adversity, but it is in adversity that he calls upon his converts to rejoice. S. Paul was to tell how we are under a God, "who will not allow us to be tempted beyond what we are able to bear"[1]; and such a God, in calling on us to suffer, assures us that He knows we are capable of a severe test. *Count it all joy*,[2] says S. James. Refuse to consider it in any other way. But this joy is only to be reckoned when we *fall into manifold temptations*, not when we rush into them of our own accord. A natural diffidence as well as a Divine command makes us pray: "Lead us not into temptation."[3] We are right to fear the hazard, but we are also right to rejoice when God makes proof of us in dangers and difficulties not due to our own presumption.

III.—The Uses of Adversity.

S. James, having called upon his converts to rejoice, sums up in a few pregnant words the uses of adversity: *Knowing that the proof of your faith worketh patience, and let patience have its perfect work, that ye may be perfect and entire, lacking nothing.*

Inasmuch as Christians look on this life as a preparation for another, so the one thing important for the individual is the formation of character. Faith, in the

---
[1] 1 Cor x 13.   [2] *Cf* 1 Pet. iv. 12, 13   [3] Matt. vi. 13

sense of submission to God's will, must be repeatedly tried if any progress is to be made. In this way not only is our faith tested by God, but our faith is confirmed for ourselves. God does not test our faith to satisfy His own curiosity, for He knows. He does not merely test our faith, that we may witness to His power. He also tests our faith that we may learn its value: His purpose is educational. We become stronger as we learn to endure and endure cheerfully, *counting it all joy*. This temper of endurance is not acquired all at once. That is well known in physical culture, and the same law holds good in spiritual progress. And why, we ask, may the power of endurance have such splendid results, as to make a man *perfect and entire lacking nothing*—that is, a man without blemish, no longer halt or maimed? Because such training endured in the right spirit corrects and purges what is weak in us, deepens our knowledge and awakens our sympathy, makes us look forward to the future instead of resting in the present—we become free from the shameful shackles of enervating ease. But beyond all this " love by suffering entereth"; we become one with Him who was " made perfect by suffering "[1] and share His spirit. So S. Paul, having this Epistle probably before him, amplifies the words of S. James. " We glory in tribulation, knowing that tribulation worketh patience, and patience experience, and experience hope, and hope maketh not ashamed, because the love of God is shed abroad in our hearts, by the Holy Ghost that is given unto us."[2]

[1] Heb ii 10   [2] Rom. v. 3-5.

IV.—Prayer for Wisdom to Understand Them.

Having reached so far, S. James, as it were, pauses to listen to the murmur of his disciples. He hears one say: 'Yes, that is of course true, but this view of temptation does not apply to my particular case. I hope I should have the courage to face the Sanhedrin like S. Stephen, and like him be stoned.[1] The report of his martyrdom thrills me, and the results of his martyrdom have been great. But my trials are not of that sort: my life is a series of petty persecutions and injustice. My relations are unkind to me. I have lost my rightful place in the synagogue, my business has been wellnigh ruined, and my children are handicapped from the start. Now the Faith is not advanced by any of these trials, what is the good of them? I am sure I am none the better for them. Indeed I grow worse. My mind is more and more distracted. I can no longer attend to spiritual things. The pressure of these petty worries is crushing the life out of me. I am surely not to blame if I fail to see—and I have tried—how God through these temptations is bringing me to perfection. You may be quite right. But perhaps I lack the soldier spirit on which you call. I can't help it if I do.'

And how does S. James deal with this position? He does not try to convince them that they are wrong. He accepts as truth the plea that they cannot understand God's purpose. He meets them with a practical suggestion: *Pray for the wisdom that you lack.* For the author of "Wisdom" says, "I called upon God, and the Spirit of Wisdom came to me."[2]

---

[1] Acts vi. 9, and vii.   [2] Wisd. vii. 7; *cf.* viii 21.

To understand the idea of Wisdom in the mind of S. James, we must seek the Wisdom literature of the Old Testament and Apocrypha. It is neither reasoning power nor an apprehension of intellectual problems. It has nothing to do with the questions *why* or *how*. It implies a practical insight into life as it is. It is a perception of facts in their true bearings. It enables us to seize the good in things seeming evil, to act aright amid unsolved problems.

V.—Encouragement and Warning for those who Pray.

To this advice S. James adds encouragement and also warning. First he tells them that God will hear and answer—*He giveth to every man.* Giveth what? *The wisdom that they lack.* And how does He give? Generously! *Liberally!* without condition, *and upbraideth not.* These last words are necessary for men's encouragement. Too many will not pray because they fear to obtrude their doubts and feelings of rebellion. Yet God will hear the sceptic's prayer if said in sincerity: "O God, if there be a God, save my soul, if I have a soul!" He will hear our anxious supplication: "Lord, I believe, help Thou my unbelief."[1] He knows our sincerity and our limitations. He is conscious that our inclinations are in opposition to His will. Yet He hears and does not upbraid.

So much for encouragement; but S. James goes on to warn. He says that such a man must *ask in faith, nothing wavering;* and for a moment it may appear that

[1] Mark ix. 24.

this is in flat contradiction to what has been said above. But *faith* is here used in the sense of moral submission, and not of intellectual assent. A man must not come to God like a petulant child, asking *why* out of sheer impertinence. Neither must he approach God with the superiority of a critic ready to quibble over the answer and reject it. Nor must he come asking in the spirit of idle curiosity. He is to ask in faith—that is, in the spirit of one who humbles himself before a superior, who feels the need of help and seeks it, longing for enlightenment.

This view of what faith here means is borne out by the words *nothing wavering*. The Revisers have altered them into *nothing doubting*, and have spoilt the rhythm of the passage without interpreting S. James any the better. It is true that in the Greek there is nothing to justify the metaphor nor the play upon words, but neither is διακρινόμενος correctly translated by a word that implies intellectual perplexity. The doubting is moral and not mental, the attitude of indecision which is rendered admirably and pictorially by the word *wavering*. *Let him ask in faith, nothing wavering*, is a warning to come to God in a spirit of submission, sincerely wanting what is asked for. There are any number of people who complain bitterly of their woes, but are not sincere in their wish to have them removed, and still less sincere in wishing to find that they have a reason and a use. They hug their grievances, are proud of their misery, and find a perverted pleasure—nay, a distinction—in fancying themselves the victims of injustice. Their prayers for wisdom would be unreal, for they would not wish them answered. For them

Trials

complaint is a luxury which they will never relinquish. They could not be satisfied, for they know not what they want.

Such people S. James compares to *a wave of the sea driven by the wind and tossed.* He is no doubt thinking of many a sudden squall in the dangerous Lake of Galilee, when the wind, having swept down the gorges, stirred up great waves that were driven before it, to break in what seemed like purposeless fury on the shore. *Let not that man think that he shall receive anything of the Lord: he is a double-minded man, unstable in all his ways.* That man, ὁ ἄνθρωπος ἐκεῖνος, is contemptuous, and so perhaps is διέσθω. It might be rendered *fancy*,[1] and then we immediately understand how faith and fancy do not agree. S. James coined the word δίψυχος, but it has a marked resemblance to the double heart (*lit.*, a heart and a heart) of Psalm xii.[2] "I am not quite at union with myself," says the Dipsychus of Arthur Clough. It is the lack of simplicity in the asker, says S. James, that accounts for so many unanswered prayers. It is duplicity that accounts for so many failures, for so many futile lives. There are men of whom it can be said:

> "You are this and that
> And here and there, and nothing flat."

Before they can ask for wisdom to understand the woes of life, they have to ask for single-mindedness, which will enable them to approach their woes as trials. They are really outside S. James's argument, for they have no anchorage to be tested or from which they can be driven.

[1] *Vide* Knowling *in loco.*   [2] Ps. xii. 2

VI.—How Trial affects Rich and Poor.

S. James has called on men to rejoice in trial. He has summed up the uses of adversity. He has given practical advice as to how an objection may be met, and added to his advice both encouragement and warning. He now goes on to consider special trials, like poverty, riches, and loss, and how they may be regarded in the light of that practical wisdom which he has counselled men to pray for.

He calls on all men, rich and poor, to *glory* in their condition. This glorying was for S. James the best corrective for the double-mindedness he has just reproved. The double-minded man could glory in nothing, for neither way was he content. But for S. James both riches and poverty might fill men with Christian exultation, as providing opportunities for the exercise of virtue and the attainment of a crown.

The brother of low degree is to glory *in his high estate*, and this exhortation is no doubt due to the first Beatitude, which assures the Kingdom of Heaven to the poor. S. James, it will be noted, does not in this case assume that external conditions are unimportant, he insists rather on their importance. Poverty enables a man to concentrate his hopes on the future, and aids him to find his true exaltation in being a son of God. It should in consequence cease to be a trial, and be accepted as a blessing.

But all the Christians were not poor. We know of Joseph of Arimathæa, Nicodemus, Barnabas, Mark, and others who were rich. Rich Jews, become Christians, had no doubt to suffer from many unaccustomed humiliations. S. James calls on them to glory in these also. *Let the rich man glory in that he is made low.* The deference, respect, position, readily accorded to the rich, S. James aptly compares to the brilliant wild flowers in the grass of Galilee.[1] These lost, the charm of wealth disappears. Let the rich man in consequence rejoice. He is learning the true value of his possessions. He is no longer tempted to trust in riches. He ceases to glory in them. He obtains a power of detachment, and, becoming poor in spirit, inherits the beatitude, and finds his value as a man.

Then, with unbounded optimism, S. James goes on to consider the actual loss of wealth as a new theme for glory. He is led thereto by his reminiscence of Isaiah, which seems at first sight to divert his thoughts from the direct line of his argument. Isaiah had proclaimed that "all flesh is grass . . . the grass withereth, the flower fadeth, but the word of our God shall stand for ever."[2] S. James, on the other hand, would teach that, though the fine gold becomes dim, though riches melt away, though the bloom of the fairest fades and desire fails,[3] though with age all things wither, yet man is no part of his transitory possessions, but by union with the everlasting word, *the word of Truth*, he escapes from the sphere of mutability, and in union with God saves his soul. The rich man, *qua* rich man, may be no more. But he has attained a position where nothing can harm him. Having endured his trial, he also is blessed and his life crowned.

[1] *Cf.* 1 Pet. 1 24   [2] Isa. xl. 6-8   [3] Eccles. xii. 5.

The way in which S. James writes his parable reveals the man. *The sun ariseth with the scorching wind and withereth the grass; and the flower thereof falleth, and the grace of the fashion (τοῦ προσώπου) of it perisheth: so also shall the rich man fade away in his goings.* He is thinking of Galilee, of the sun's scorching heat and the south-west wind from the desert withering the flowers. But he sympathizes with the flowers. For him each flower has a face. He notes its tender gracefulness. He feels the pathos of decay, and sighs over the falling petals. By taking his simile from nature, he is betrayed into a sympathy with the ruined rich man which he might not otherwise have expressed, for he loves the lily of the field and cares but little for the gorgeous raiment in which the rich are clad. The stern ascetic, through kinship with nature, is led to understand the ways of men, and what burning injustice and withering scorn may mean to those who have lived delicately in gracious surroundings. "Their flowering pride, so fading and so fickle," is gone; and while we accept the bracing creed of the moralist, we rejoice to find him capable of tenderness, of feeling the reality of the loss.

VII.—The Reward of Endurance.

But S. James still prefers to look forward and not backward, to inspire hope rather than to minister consolation. So he tells the rich man: *Blessed is the man that endureth temptation; for when he hath been approved he shall receive the Crown of Life, which the Lord promised to them that love Him.* There is both a

Trials

recompense and a reward. Men are not merely made perfect by trials, but are to be more than compensated for losses. A Crown of Life is the promised reward. It is not for Christians to say: "Let us crown ourselves with rosebuds before they be withered."[1]

Three crowns were known to the ancients, and three are mentioned in the New Testament. The Crown of Victory bestowed on athletes answers to the *Crown of Life*[2] bestowed on those who endure to the end. The Crown of Merit voted by the State to benefactors answers to the Crown of Righteousness expected by S. Paul as the fruit of his many labours.[3] The Crown of Sovereignty assumed by Kings answers to the Crown of Glory conferred on those rulers of the Church who have not been lords over God's heritage in their own selfish interest.[4]

The Crown of Victory was composed of laurel, a symbol of the fame that would not fade. The Crown of Life is the abiding reality conferring what it symbolizes, no mere adornment, but an everlasting possession. And who is it for? For them that love the Lord. And how have they shown their love? By not being double-minded, wavering between allegiance to Him and love of the world. It is for those who have counted all things well lost if only they might win Christ.[5]

The conquered die; the victors live—by their tenacity they have proved their right to survive. This is commonplace, but the Christian idea of a communicated life was original. It springs from the doctrine of

[1] Wisd. ii. 8. [2] Rev. ii. 10. [3] 2 Tim. iv. 8.
[4] 1 Pet v 4 [5] Phil. iii. 8

the Resurrection and the belief in sacramental union with Him who is the Lord of Life. He came into this world neither promising cessation of effort nor any Nirvana. He brought no anodyne for pain. He came announcing an extended life, an intensified liveliness, a perfected sensibility. He who was crowned with the live thorns says: "I am come that ye may have life, and have it more abundantly."[1]

So S. James, *the servant of Jesus Christ*, proves himself no Stoic, counselling endurance as the way to peace, and detachment from one's surroundings as a way to self-perfection. He speaks with an accent of triumph. His crown is a Crown of Life, and he looks confidently to a future for a wider world in which life and liveliness will result from the eager spirit of joy.

[1] John x. 10.

LECTURE III

TEMPTATION

"*Let no man say when he is tempted, I am tempted of God for God cannot be tempted with evil, and He Himself tempteth no man but each man is tempted, when he is drawn away by his own lust, and enticed. Then the lust, when it hath conceived, beareth sin and the sin, when it is full grown, bringeth forth death Be not deceived, my beloved brethren. Every good gift and every perfect boon is from above, coming down from the Father of Lights, with whom can be no variation, neither shadow that is cast by turning. Of His own will He brought us forth by the word of truth, that we should be a kind of first fruits of His creatures.*"—JAS 1 13-18

I.—DIFFICULTIES AS REGARDS TEMPTATION—

HERE S. James again pauses to consider objections. Temptation does not only mean trial, it also means inducement to do evil. Few people are probably such confused thinkers as not to be able to distinguish between these uses of the word, but it is perfectly simple to pass from the one to the other. Failure under trial often entails a falling into sin, and the trial that leads to sin may naturally, if not logically, be looked on as the cause of sin by the sinner. *Post hoc, propter hoc* is a fallacy dear to many! So the objector argues: "The God who made me tries me, and I fall into sin. The God who made me knew my power of resistance, and that I should fall into sin. Therefore God tempted me to sin, and I am not responsible!" This line of argument started when Adam said: "The woman whom *Thou* gavest to be with me, she gave me of the tree and I did eat."[1] This argument was reproved by Jesus, the son of Sirach: "Say not thou it is through the Lord that I fell away . . . say not thou He has caused me to err."[2] Age after age, moralists have to preach the same truths and meet the same objections. This objection was well known to S. James; and it is well known in our day, when men and women talk a jargon about heredity and environment, asserting their right to do as they please without incurring any responsibility for so doing.

The objection has its source in two insoluble problems, the mystery of evil and the freedom of the will. Men have speculated on these problems since thought began, but their speculations do not concern us here; we have only to see how S. James deals with the man who says, when he is tempted, *I am tempted of God*.

He first argues from a dogmatic assumption as to God's nature. He next analyzes the nature of temptation as we know it. He then appeals to the experience of his converts who had received grace from God.

II.—S. JAMES'S ARGUMENT: (A) FROM NATURAL RELIGION.

God cannot be tempted of evil, and He Himself tempteth no man. The assumption is necessary if we believe in God's perfection, His goodness and changeless Being. And, the assumption once made, the conclusion is inevitable. He who cannot even know inducement

[1] Gen III 12. [2] Ecclus xv 11, 12.

to evil cannot revolt against His own nature by tempting others. So Plato, before S. James, had been able to sum up a lengthy argument, which covers somewhat the same ground, by saying, "God is perfectly simple and true both in word and deed; He changes not, He deceives not, either by word or deed, by dream or waking vision."[1] So Marcus Aurelius, independently of S. James, was to write: "The Reason that governs the universe has in itself no cause for doing evil, for it has no malice, nor does it do evil to anything, nor is anything harmed by it."[2]

So if S James appeals to a dogma in this case, it is to a dogma recognized by Natural Religion, and which may be maintained as reasonable. He then goes on to analyze human experience as to how each man is tempted.

III.—(B) From the History of Temptation.

A man is tempted by his own lust, being drawn away by it and enticed. So our Blessed Lord had taught that "there is nothing from without a man that, entering in, can defile him"; but that all evil "comes from within and defiles the man."[3] Man's natural desires are good, for they are God-given, but in the hierarchy of man's nature Reason, and not Desire, was to dominate. Man's harmony and perfection necessitates self-control. When any lust is undisciplined and drawn away from the power of the directive Reason, man offers himself as ripe for temptation. Such temptation may come through suggestions received by the senses, those

[1] Rep. II 383. [2] De Suis Rebus vi 1. [3] Mark vii. 15-21.

portals of knowledge; or it may come as opportunity, protesting there is no time for consideration. But we must note that S. James uses the word *enticed*, and *enticing* is a word proper to persons. It is probably of the devil he is thinking, who appeals through the senses, acts by his instruments and servants, or, being a spirit, whispers apart from the senses directly to the soul. The words suggest the fisherman and his bait and the fish to be drawn out. But, finally, it is not the skill of the fisherman or the attractiveness of the bait which insures the catch. It is the appetite of the fish —*the lust within*.

Then, when lust hath conceived it bringeth forth sin: and sin, when it is finished, bringeth forth death. These words have become vital for us, thanks to the dramatic imagination of John Milton. In the second book of *Paradise Lost* is the loathsome scene at the Gate of Hell, when Sin deformed, and shapeless Death, trace their ultimate origin to the lustful imagination of Satan's brain.

The natural history of Temptation as described by S. James is a tragedy complete in five acts. In the first we see a man with desires as yet innocent but undisciplined. In the second we see the Tempter with his enticements. In the third the man has deliberately begun to take pleasure in receiving the suggestions of evil; his imagination is at work, he broods: Lust has conceived. In the fourth intense excitement has become painful, the pressure of imagination unbearable, relief has become necessary, and relief is found in action. The deed is brought forth. Sin is born. In the last act are the consequences:

Sin working itself out, Lawlessness leading to disruption, and ending in death.

There, says S. James, is the history of man's temptation and fall, and in this awful drama God plays no part—man is responsible.

IV.—(C) FROM THE DOCTRINE OF GRACE.

'But,' say the objectors, 'you evade our main difficulty: who is responsible for man's nature?' To this question S. James is not bound to reply. When once we have acknowledged that God cannot tempt, and that we are personally conscious of our own responsibility for our falls, the further question is only one of speculative importance, and S. James is averse from speculation. It is not that speculation is wrong, but these Jews were apparently speculating in a wrong spirit. We may speculate as hardily as S. Paul; but we must not deny, disregard, or explain away facts which we know, and truths which we have tested, in order to establish our own system of thought, or magnify the cogency of our own doubts. We have no right to reject the Faith because some particular problem is not solved, when plentiful reasons both for faith and practice are obviously at hand.

So S. James turns on the objectors with affectionate entreaty, *Do not err, my beloved brethren.* How do men err? By wandering out of the way, deserting the facts they know, and the reasoning they have tested, in search of a wider view to which they have no guide. They pay the penalty of their folly "in wandering mazes lost."

But though S. James will not speculate, he has a further argument which is at least valid for those to whom he is writing. He appeals once more to their experience. God has helped them in past trials. He has aided them to overcome temptation, and no being could both tempt and resist the temptation at one and the same time. Moreover, although there may be no answer to the question as to why man has come into the world with an imperfect nature, his converts know that God has willed their regeneration, and *begotten* them again *by the Word of Truth*. They complain of the old nature, let them rejoice in the new, regarding themselves as first-fruits of God's creatures.

So he begins, *Every good gift and every perfect boon is from above*. They have no blessings that they do not owe to God. *The good gift* or giving indicates the nature of a person, lavish in his generosity, while *the perfect boon* represents the value of the gift received. The opening words may be a quotation from a Christian hymn: πᾶσα δόσις ἀγαθὴ καὶ πᾶν δώρημα τέλειον forming an hexameter line. If this be so, we may note the skill with which S. James enforces his argument, by a quotation that will waken in the minds of his readers the memories of grace received.

And who is this God who helps and is above us? He is *the Father of Lights*. S. James uses this splendid title to reassure those in the darkness of error and gloom of doubt. The title suggests to our minds the thought of sun, moon, and stars, but a Jew would naturally pass from them at once to the angels,[1] those happy beings of pure intelligence who serve God con-

---

[1] Job xxv. 5, xxxviii. 7, Rev. i. 20.

tinually and are His ministers to the sons of men. But the *Father of Lights* must Himself be light—" in Him is no darkness at all,"[1] for Him there is *no variation* (παραλλαγή), *neither shadow that is cast* (ἀποσκίασμα) *in turning* (τροπῆς).

All the words are of a technical character, and it is not certain that S. James uses them in their recognized sense. His aim, however, is quite clear. He would distinguish between the earthly and the heavenly, between the science of this world and the mind of God.

Other lights rise and set, wax and wane and suffer eclipse, but God is incapable of change, for how could the Almighty and the Perfect suffer change except by ceasing to be almighty and perfect? Still less can He be changed by any other. None can overshadow Him. In the sunshine which we know there is always shadow, life as we know it is composite and made up of contrasts, in God and God alone is pure light. Therefore, through believing in the simplicity of God, we learn that the source of many perfect boons cannot also be the source of evil.

V.—God's Grace and Man's Freedom.

But the objector still pleads the infirmity of his own nature as a sufficient excuse for his sinning. He forgets grace, even the grace he has himself experienced, and S. James reminds him how God, of *His own will, hath brought us forth by the Word of Truth*. How silly men are to grumble about that for which a remedy has been supplied by the very God they grumble at. He has

[1] 1 John 1 5

provided them with a means of escape, and so has deprived them of the excuse some would rather retain. Granting the infirmity of the old nature, there is the new nature due to *the implanted word*.

This new nature is not of merit, nor of man's desire. It is of God and His grace. " Ye have not chosen Me, but I have chosen you," said our Blessed Lord.[1] " By the grace of God I am what I am,"[2] said S. Paul, and S. James is entirely at one with him when he emphasizes the fact that it is God *of His own will* who insures our regeneration. We cannot find God of ourselves, we must be found of Him. It should be obvious that we have no part in our own regeneration. As we were born first into a human family without being consulted, so God begets us anew, and we are born into His family of His own will, not ours.

This teaching is not inconsistent with the freedom of man's will; it merely defines the sphere of its operation. An illustration may help us to understand this. A child of five is watched over by a careful mother. He does not choose his hour for rising or going to bed. He does not choose what he should eat or what he should wear. He does not choose when he should go out or where he should play. He does not choose his nurse or his companions. The sphere of his liberty is very narrow, but his mother is perfectly aware that he has a will of his own. He can be obedient or disobedient, sweet-tempered or sulky, a fountain of joy or, oh, so troublesome! And the mother, who feels herself responsible for his well-being and his training, never doubts that the child is responsible also, and rewards or punishes him accordingly.

[1] John xv. 16   [2] 1 Cor xv. 10.

Temptation

It is not, then, of our own will we become children of God. It is God's Will, and He has chosen us, just as He had chosen those Jews to whom S. James is writing. They had received God's grace, and in becoming Christians had acknowledged the same. Therefore for them there was no way out of S. James's argument. They could no longer cast the responsibility of their sins on God, for they had been regenerated *by the Word of Truth*, and received power to overcome temptation.

VI.—THE WORD OF TRUTH.

But what, it may be asked, is meant by the *Word of Truth?* S. James was probably thinking of our Blessed Lord's parable of the Sower;[1] but in other places regeneration is attributed to Baptism, both by Our Lord and His Apostles, and we may not interpret one passage of Holy Scriptures in such a way as to contradict another.

A systematic theologian, however, need find no difficulty. He may assume that the Word is here identical with the Personal Logos of S. John,[2] who declared Himself to be Truth,[3] and conclude that men are regenerated in Baptism because they then enter into His nature. Secondly, he may assume that the *Word of Truth* stands for the threefold Name of God into which men are baptized, which is the earliest and divinely revealed summary of the Gospel.[4] Both explanations express what is true. Either of them, as

[1] Matt. xiii 3; Mark iv. 3; Luke viii. 5. [2] John i. 1.
[3] John xiv 6   [4] Matt. xxviii. 19.

statements of doctrine, would no doubt have been assented to by S. James, but neither of them may have been consciously in his mind at the time of writing. God, he tells us, is the sole author of regeneration; and it is the *Word of Truth* implanted within us that constitutes the new life. By the Word of Truth he probably understood the potentiality involved in the whole Gospel of Jesus. Had anyone asked S. James how God, the author of regeneration, implanted the Word of Truth, there is no reason for supposing that he would have differed from other writers of the New Testament. He would have answered that God worked by means of Baptism.

VII.—The Firstfruits for Sacrifice.

Finally, S. James reminds his converts that through regeneration *we should be a kind of firstfruits of His creatures*. The words at first sight seem to have nothing to do with the argument we have been pursuing, but they are really exceedingly suggestive. *The firstfruits*, as a Jew would instantly remember, were offered to God in sacrifice.[1] So S. James, looking back on the whole course of his argument, finds a new way in which his converts may regard their trials. Let them find in them an opportunity for sacrificing to God, that the full harvest to be reaped from the proclamation of *the Word of Truth* may be enjoyed. Secondly, S. Paul was afterwards to speak of Our Lord as "the firstfruits of them that slept."[2] So the idea of the firstfruits contained the promise of the future. These

---

[1] Exod xxiii 16, Lev. ii. 12. [2] 1 Cor xv 20

Jews might not consider their position as hopeless. Offered to God, they belonged to Him, and with Him were safe. Thirdly, perhaps we may see in these words an implied answer to a final objection. Granting we may not plead the infirmity of our nature as a reason for sin because of the grace at our disposal, yet there are multitudes to whom that grace is unknown. What of them? The answer to this question may seem to us, in the light of what S. James has written, to be as follows: 'Be true to your own experience, and do not speculate on the condition of others, about whom you are imperfectly informed. You have known God's goodness to yourselves, and knowing that goodness, cannot you trust Him to do what is right for others? Somehow, somewhere, and at sometime, each soul must have an opportunity of salvation.' But here S. James makes no such answer. It is a practical instinct that makes him write that they are *firstfruits of God's creatures*. They are, indeed, the elect, dedicated to God, but not for their own sakes. They are dedicated to God that others may be won.

VIII.—CONCLUSION. ST. JAMES'S REPLY TO ARGUMENTS FROM DESTINY, ENVIRONMENT, AND HEREDITY.

It may be said that S. James has not solved the problem of evil or the problem of man's responsibility, but he did not set out to do so. His aim was practical, and he has fairly met man's three favourite excuses for yielding to temptation—"It was destiny," "I am the sport of circumstances," "I am the victim of an inherited frailty." *Destiny*, says S. James, is another name for God, and God can neither be tempted nor tempt. *Circumstances*, says S. James, would not entice you but for the lust that is within. *Heredity*, says S. James, may predispose you to evil, but God's grace is freely offered to counteract its influence.

LECTURE IV

HEARING AND SPEAKING

"Ye know this, my beloved brethren. But let every man be swift to hear, slow to speak, slow to wrath for the wrath of man worketh not the righteousness of God Wherefore putting away all filthiness and overflowing of wickedness, receive with meekness the implanted word, which is able to save your souls"—JAS. 1 19-21

I.—REPENTANCE, FAITH, AND OBEDIENCE.

S. JAMES is writing a letter to people he knows and who know him ; and if we are to understand his epistle, this fact must be kept perpetually in mind. Those to whom he is writing are not heathen ; they have been instructed in the Gospel : they are his *beloved brethren*. He refutes a sophistry by alluding to their regeneration, and says confidently, *ye know this*. There is no need for him in consequence to speak further on the subject. But then he immediately thinks how his argument might be misapplied by Jews, naturally inclined to take their privileges for granted. Those who once boasted that Abraham was their father, without feeling called on to do the works of Abraham,[1] might easily find a source of complete satisfaction in the boast that they were members of Christ. He thinks how the time may come when they will say, "Your argument is true. Our salvation is of God's Will, not ours. He has chosen

[1] Luke iii 8, John viii. 39

us, redeemed us, done everything for us; there is nothing for us to do but to be the passive recipients of His indefectible grace. We are saved." To counteract this tendency, S. James goes on to assure them that they are responsible for the use that they make of God's good gift, that they must renounce *the malice* of the Devil, must *receive with meekness the implanted word*, and must be active in fulfilling the *new law of liberty*. Repentance, faith and obedience [1] were, no doubt, the commonplaces of their catechetical instruction. They were insisted on by S. Peter in his first address at Pentecost. S. James, in consequence, does not deal with them directly. He speaks rather to men who may delude themselves as regards their repentance and faith, who may interpret obedience as a merely passive quality, or limit it to ritual conformity. A Christian must listen and speak and do, but he must be careful how he hears, when he speaks, and what he does. He will convert no one by abusing him, and above all he must beware of self-deception. It is interesting to compare this teaching with a saying of Shammai's: " Make thy Torah a fixed thing, say little and do much, and receive every man with a cheerful countenance." [2]

II.—BE SWIFT TO HEAR.

Jesus, the son of Sirach, had written, " Be swift to hear," and also that " a wise man will hold his tongue till he see opportunity ", [3] while the Book of Proverbs

---

[1] Acts ii. 38.
[2] M Aboth i. 15, quoted in Hastings' *Dictionary of the Bible*, v 58
[3] Ecclus. v. 11, xx. 7.

Hearing and Speaking

assures us how "he that is slow to wrath is of great understanding."[1] But these are general maxims, and the teaching of S. James in this place has reference to the Word of Truth, how we are to hear it, when we are to speak of it, and in what way we are not to contend earnestly for it.

Again and again our Blessed Lord reproved those who were dull of hearing,[2] and S. James, remembering his own past doubt and hesitation, implores his disciples, *Let every man be swift to hear*. By the single word *swift* he conveys a wealth of meaning. To be *swift to hear* implies a readiness to receive instruction, an interest in what is being said, a liveliness of apprehension, and a keenness in pursuit of fresh knowledge. Those who have minds blocked with prejudice are slow to hear, and when S. James was writing *the Word of Truth* seemed new, original and revolutionary, and so could only by slow degrees make its way. Secondly, those who are uninterested are also inattentive; they need to be told more than once, and then having heard with difficulty forget with ease. Thirdly, there are those who are naturally of a sluggish temperament. They are well-meaning folk who cannot or will not concentrate their minds. They listen politely, and dimly comprehend the importance of what is being said. They resolve to meditate upon it at a more convenient season. Lastly, there are those who hear with pleasure, and then wait with great complacency for fresh instruction. They are receptive but inert. They leave to someone else the task of thinking for them.

There never was a time when we needed more to

---

[1] Prov. xiv. 29. [2] Matt. xiii. 15; John xii. 40 *et seq*

reiterate this maxim. Attention of the soldierly sort is almost a lost attitude with Christians. We may indeed listen to the outward proclamation of the Gospel, but we do not wait upon the Spirit within, dictating its application to our own souls. God refuses to compel our attention. He speaks with "a still small voice,"[1] and only those who are alert for the Word of the Master hear and understand.

And in place of servants waiting on and attentive to a master, we have many busybodies bustling about what they think should be the Master's business. There are also plenty of lazy dreamers who will hear of nothing definite, and still less of anything actual. There are plenty of adventurous speculators who will not wait to hear anything at all, and there are plenty of self-opinionated controversialists seeking a personal triumph. They begin to contradict and criticize what they have only half heard, or to maintain with fury what they have not given themselves time to understand. None of these classes were unknown to S. James, but it is to the last especially that he says, *Be slow to speak, slow to wrath.*

III.—BE SLOW TO SPEAK.

Let us at once note that S. James neither counsels silence nor condemns anger. It is "with the mouth confession is made unto salvation,"[2] and there is a time when we may "be angry and sin not."[3] Our Lord refused to silence His disciples on Palm Sunday, declaring, "If these should hold their peace, the very

---

[1] 1 Kings xix 12   [2] Rom x. 10   [3] Eph. iv. 26

Hearing and Speaking 73

stones would immediately cry out;"[1] and no man ever spake on occasion with such burning indignation as the meek and lowly Jesus. He spoke from the awful wrath of a perfectly loving heart.

Being slow to speak makes for thoughtfulness, and is a safeguard against insincerity and irreverence. It helps a man to say what he means, prevents him from assuming untenable positions, and saves him from the wickedness of attempting to maintain them. We may imagine S. James himself to have been slow to speak. Certainly he was slow in writing. No one can imagine that his aphorisms were penned with speed. They were patiently hammered out, until every word was significant, and they strike us with the gravity that comes of deliberation.

We are all in great danger of talking away our religion. The repeated affirmation of a Creed said slowly will no doubt stamp upon our minds the proportion of the Faith; but a Creed is said to God. On the other hand, a constant flow of pietistic talk is a form of dissipation that is apt to end in spiritual bankruptcy. The religious phrase is so convenient for the man who talks much and thinks but little; but it may destroy the sincerity of the talker and render religion odious to the man who listens.

The Word of Truth is so precious that it should be jealously guarded against profanation. It is Our Lord who says, "Cast not your pearls before swine."[2] The fluent talker on religious topics is sometimes betrayed into irreverence, and still more often the cause of flippancy in others. There is also a peril when our

[1] Luke xix. 40   [2] Matt vii. 6.

tongues run away with us, that we assume an over-familiarity with the ways of God, and assert in His Name things for which we have no warrant. We need to remember the words of the Preacher: "God is in heaven, and therefore let thy words be few."[1]

Heedless talking, rash assertion and overstatement, lead to controversies that obscure the Truth. She cannot win her way because her advocates have asserted more in her name than they can prove. Error maintains her position as long as she can prove that all the Truth is not on the other side. Men hate to retract what they have said in a hurry. They prefer if possible to justify it, and become angry when their explanations are not accepted or forgotten. Hence arise those misunderstandings and recriminations that minister to a wrath against which S. James warns us.

IV.—BE SLOW TO WRATH.

The words, *be slow to wrath*, might lead us too far afield, unless we remember their reference to *the Word of Truth*. S. James is thinking of the synagogue and the impatient controversialist who loses his temper the moment he is contradicted; who mistakes his own cause for God's, and with the blindness of human passion thinks to forward God's righteousness.

The history of Christian controversy and religious persecution illustrates S. James's declaration that the *wrath of man worketh not the righteousness of God*. We profess a religion of love, and the *odium theologicum* is a by-word with our enemies.

[1] Eccles v. 2.

Hearing and Speaking

The reasons are fairly apparent. Zeal for truth is almost inseparable from hatred of error; but whereas zeal for truth should cause men to set forth its attractiveness to others, hatred of error often passes only too surely into hatred of the erring. Directly human malice enters in, the cause of God's righteousness is sacrificed.

Secondly, we are bound to remember that religion is man's most important possession, it penetrates to the very seat of personality. We are in consequence sensitive about it, and we act in self-defence while we delude ourselves into believing that we are jealous for the honour of God. It is not religion that makes men ill-tempered fanatics, but man's natural egotism. A man's wrath flames forth when his feelings are outraged and his inmost thoughts called in question. He feels identified with the Faith that is attacked. It is his, although he has not apprehended it perfectly, nor does he know its strength. He cries out that *the* Faith is in danger when he ought to cry *my* faith. It is terror that accounts for much cruelty. Passion and persecution are the fruits of little faith.

There are indeed times when we do well to be angry —at blasphemy, profanity, and flippancy. Sophistry, deliberate misrepresentation, and the cynical falsification of an opponent's position, merit the wrath that they incur. But even then we may be slow to wrath. It is necessary to remember whom we serve and in whose Name we are about to speak or act. The dignity of the universal Sovereign is not enhanced or His Name hallowed by the uncontrolled fury of His servant. *The wrath of man worketh not the righteousness of God.*

It is well to note the antithesis in S. James's mind. The righteousness of God is contrasted with the wrath of man. God's righteousness may be very terrible, but in it there is no malice, no selfishness, no mixture of motive. He is just. In man's wrath there is much ignorance and a great deal of blindness. When we have lost our tempers we think only of one thing—how we may hurt.

The wrath of man was shown by those who shouted at Pilate, "Let Him be crucified."[1] They were patriots, proud of their race, proud of their Temple, and jealous for their Law. So long as they could prove their patriotism to themselves and one another, they were reckless as to any injustice. They cared very little whether Our Lord was condemned for sacrilege,[2] for blasphemy,[3] or for treason against Cæsar,[4] so long as Judaism, as they understood it, was triumphant. Their prejudices were excited, and they became furious.[5] Their determination was fixed as soon as they found that there was an opposition to be overcome. In the end they were more intent on thwarting a Roman magistrate than in punishing Him whom they denounced.[6]

And God's righteousness is manifested by Our Lord. He met man's hatred with the dignity of silence[7]; but there is no unreal sentiment about His end, and no acquiescence with the evil He was fighting. He reproved Pilate,[8] while acknowledging that others had the

---

[1] Matt. xxvii. 22
[2] Mark xiv. 58
[3] Mark xiv. 64; John xix. 7.
[4] John xix 15
[5] Mark xv. 11
[6] Matt xxvii 24
[7] 1 Pet. ii 23: Matt. xxvii. 14.
[8] John xix. 11.

greater sin. He pitied the women of Jerusalem[1] as He thought of the inevitable consequences of the national spirit. He refused the myrrh[2] that would have rendered Him unconscious of the pain men were determined to inflict. With absolute justice He prayed for the soldiers, for they knew not what they did.[3] With infinite mercy He forgave the thief the instant the thief was penitent.[4] With calm conviction He announced that His work was finished—finished in spite of men and in spite of the Devil.[5] With perfect faith He surrendered Himself into the Father's hands.[6] Man's wrath brought the Son of God to die: by God's righteousness mankind was redeemed.

V.—MALICE.

Wherefore, says S. James—because the wrath of man worketh not the righteousness of God—you are to be among those who, *putting away all filthiness and overflowing of malice, receive with meekness the implanted word which is able to save your souls.*

These words bring out very clearly what is amiss with the wrath of man. It is impure, filthy, it clouds the brain, darkens the countenance, and defiles the conduct. It is not the result of mere zeal, but of mixed motives. There is in consequence an effervescence of malice, a boiling over or coming out of what cannot be contained or hid.

It is noteworthy that S. James uses the aorist parti-

---

[1] Luke xxiii. 27 29.
[2] S. Mark xv. 23
[3] Luke xxiii. 34
[4] Luke xxiii 43.
[5] John xix. 30.
[6] Luke xxiii. 46.

ciple, because the putting away must precede the reception of *the implanted word*. The metaphor is taken from the stripping off of clothes, as if human wrath were a filthy garment, whereas humility is "the ornament of a meek and quiet spirit."[1] From this it may be objected that S. James is only dealing with the outward expression of wrath and not with the malice implanted in the heart. But it is true that wrath is just one of those passions which is most successfully fought by denying it an outlet. Some vices when indulged produce an immediate reaction; but wrath indulged soon foams into fury, and waxes until it assumes an utter recklessness in seeking for its satisfaction.

VI.—Meekness.

The robe of wrath being put away, the robe of meekness may be put on. Then instead of the instigations of the Devil to a malice that destroys, a man may receive *the implanted word* which is able to save his soul. But he must do it with meekness, and the order of the words in the Greek emphasizes this: "*With meekness receive ye the implanted word.*" The proud are not amenable to instruction, and the angry can receive neither wisdom nor truth. It is necessary, too, that men should be meek in order to be taught of God, for communion with God is only possible when men realize their right position face to face with the Almighty.

[1] 1 Pet. iii. 4.

VII.—THE IMPLANTED WORD.

And what are men to receive? *The implanted word.* Our minds are carried back to the verse which tells that God of His own will brought us forth by *the Word of Truth;* and the difficulty at once arises, How can we be said to receive what is already ours? The same difficulty may be stated as regards the Sacraments. We are born again and made members of Christ in Baptism; but we are told to go and receive His Body and Blood in the Holy Communion. And the same solution may be found in Jesus. We are not dealing with a thing, but with a Person giving Himself to us without ceasing, acting and reacting on our natures with the insistence of Love.

As in the former passage it seemed clear that S. James had not Baptism in his mind, although he would have acknowledged that Baptism was the efficient cause of regeneration, so here we must not expound these words as directly referring to the Blessed Sacrament, nevertheless, S. James would certainly have acknowledged that the new life implanted in us was nourished and refreshed in the Holy Communion. The time had not yet come for the Logos doctrine of S. John to be formulated, but it is obvious that S. James's conception of a Living Word would ultimately have to be interpreted in terms of personality. The doctrine was already implicit in his mind. Words indeed deepen in their significance, they may be said to grow and be spoken of as living, but we receive them once and for all. Repetition only reminds us of our reception of them. It is in union with a Person that there is a specific moment of first contact and a constantly fresh reception of influence. The implanted word received with meekness, says S. James, *is able to save your souls.*

VIII.—REGENERATION AND SANCTIFICATION.

Here it will be noted that he does not confuse regeneration with sanctification. The regeneration of his converts was in the past, and to their knowledge of it he can confidently appeal, saying, *ye know this.* Their sanctification was in the future. They were only on the road, and there were many hindrances to their progress, such as stopping to talk too much, or falling out by the way with those who should have been their companions. He warns them not to delude themselves into mistaking the violence of their emotions for an advance in righteousness. For such an advance they must await the direction of the Spirit and be swift to hear, while to sustain them in their progress they must *receive with meekness the implanted word which is able to save their souls.*

Lastly, just as S. James had emphasized the truth that regeneration was God's act and not man's, so here it is *the implanted word* which saves. We cannot save ourselves, but we have wills which can respond to God's grace and co-operate with His working. S. Paul was subsequently to sum up this teaching by recounting his own experience: "By the grace of God I am what I am: and His grace which was bestowed on me was not found vain; but I laboured more abundantly than they all: yet not I, but the grace of God which was in me."[1]

[1] 1 Cor xv. 10.

LECTURE V

HEARING AND DOING

"But be ye doers of the word, and not hearers only, deluding your own selves For if anyone is a hearer of the word, and not a doer, he is like unto a man beholding his natural face in a mirror for he beholdeth himself and goeth away, and straightway forgetteth what manner of man he was. But he that looketh into the perfect law, the law of liberty, and so continueth, being not a hearer that forgetteth, but a doer that worketh, this man shall be blessed in his doing. If any man thinketh himself to be religious, while he bridleth not his tongue but deceiveth his heart, this man's religion is vain. Pure religion and undefiled before our God and Father is this, to visit the fatherless and widows in their affliction, and to keep himself unspotted from the world."—JAS. i. 22-27.

I.—DOERS OF THE WORD, AND NOT HEARERS ONLY.

WE saw in the last Lecture how S. James exposed the delusion of the bitter controversialist, who " put on the garments of vengeance for clothing, and was clad with zeal as a cloke "; [1] who worked no righteousness while he prided himself as appearing in the very panoply of God. It is better, says S James, to be swift to hear than swift to speak, but those may also delude themselves who are swift to hear but averse from action. So he writes: *Be ye doers of the word and not hearers only, deluding your own selves;* or, as it might be rendered, *Become doers of the word,* for the Christian life is one of progress. An ideal is proposed to which we can by degrees approximate, and

[1] Isa. lix. 17.

it is often consoling for us to remember that God sees us as we are becoming, and not merely as we are.

Our Blessed Lord had ever insisted on action. He had taught that men would be known and justified by their fruits.[1] He had warned men that it was not sufficient to cry, "Lord, Lord,"[2] or even to preach and prophesy in His Name. His promises were for "whosoever heareth these sayings of Mine, and doeth them." The man who was content with hearing and not doing was likened to a fool.[3]

The Jews, to whom S. James was writing, were accustomed to the spirit of the Synagogue. There they were strict to mark each word and letter of the Law, and everyone was exceeding zealous in maintaining the interpretation proper to his school or party. There are people to-day who delight in hearing good sermons, and find pleasure in the study of devotional classics, who are genuinely shocked at any criticism of the Faith; yet they have never obeyed the call to action. For them preaching is the one ministry that they recognize, and listening to sermons is the practice of religion.

This inconsistency is not so strange as it seems, for Christianity appeals not only to the will but also to the reason and to the emotions. It is in consequence quite possible to be an exact theologian without any fellowship with God, or to labour over vexed questions of morals while breaking elementary commandments. It is possible for a man to speculate with the same mental detachment on the Kenosis as on the problem of Natural Selection. It is possible for a man to shed

[1] Matt. vii 16-20   [2] Matt vii 21, 22.   [3] Matt. vii. 26.

tears, genuine if idle tears, as he listens to a preacher of repentance, according him the same ready sympathy that he offers to a tragedy queen upon the stage. He likes having his feelings touched, he is pleased to think of his own sensibility, and he has a thrilling experience to remember as he returns to the daily round of a life lived in sin.

And so it comes to pass that an eloquent preacher may be sure of an attentive crowd, but he may have an audience without having disciples. How many from those multitudes who surrounded Our Lord, and marvelled at His teaching, followed Him to the end, and embraced the shame of the Cross?

II.—THE MAN WHO ONLY HEARS COMPARED TO A MAN PASSING A MIRROR.

S. James, considering the hearers who are not doers of the word, proceeds: *If any be a hearer of the word, and not a doer, he is like unto a man beholding his natural face in a mirror: for he beholdeth himself, and goeth away, and straightway forgetteth what manner of man he was. But he that looketh into the perfect law, the law of liberty, aud so continueth, being not a forgetful hearer, but a doer of the work, this man shall be blest in his doing.*

The illustration at first strikes us with some surprise. It forces us to pause and think. In a modern writer we should imagine that it was an afterthought scribbled into the margin, or a quotation from one of the writer's old note-books. But it was intended for Jews accustomed to the gnomic sayings of the Rabbis. It agrees well with the kind of shorthand adopted by S. James. His style has the merit of making us linger over his words. We learn the more because we have to do much of the thinking for ourselves.

We are not prepared for the sudden analogy between sight and hearing, but it is obvious that a man who bestows only a fleeting glance upon an object may be compared with one who hears something to which he pays no heed. The introduction of *the mirror* is not so obvious. The man is presumably not condemned for lack of attention to his own echo—why, then, should he be compared to a man who is indifferent as to his own reflection? Hearing, however, depends not merely on the mechanism of the ear, or on the distinction of the sounds; it depends also on how far the person can appreciate or interpret the significance of what he hears. It is the same with sight. There is the thing seen, the physical condition of the eye, and the perceptive faculty. Our Lord spoke of those who, "seeing, see not; and hearing, hear not,"[1] for the soul within could not understand. So the whole world of sight and sound is in reality a mirror by means of which we realize ourselves. That to which nothing within corresponds has no meaning for us. We hear and take no notice; we see, but do not perceive.

We understand how a man seeing himself in a mirror will not feel called to action unless the glance reveals that there is something disordered in his appearance. We do not expect a man to brood over his own reflection, and we find it hard, perhaps, to believe that he can ever forget what he is like. The first point that

[1] Matt xiii. 13.

Hearing and Doing 85

S. James would make is that the mirror of metal only shows a surface, and he is about to contrast it with another mirror which he calls the law of liberty. The metal mirror only shows the outward man (τὸ πρόσωπον τῆς γενέσεως), and γένεσις here, as in Philo, stands for that which is seen and temporal as opposed to that which is not seen and eternal.[1] The mirror is a material thing and can only record a material fact. It has no power of interpreting that fact, and the man by a casual glance does not even learn all that the mirror has to tell. But he learns as little from the words casually heard, even though the truth they express be as exact as the reflection of a mirror. He knows the words. He has no difficulty about their meaning, but they do not penetrate into his soul or control his will, because he neither applies them personally nor remembers them for any length of time.

He is like the man with the mirror, *for*, says S. James (and in the Greek there is a subtle variation of the tenses), *he beheld himself and hath gone away, and straightway forgot what manner of man he was*. By the aorists he shows that the impression was momentary, and the oblivion instantaneous; by the perfect he implies a continuing condition of absence from the mirror. Now few men and fewer women can pass a mirror without a glance, and only a few wish to pause for a closer scrutiny. A man takes himself and his appearance very much for granted. He has an idea of himself with which the mirror does not always correspond, but he forgets the mirror. He likes to imagine how other people regard him, and he is not always pleased

[1] *Cf.* iii 6

when he knows. He forgets with ease such judgments as he hears, or solaces himself by attributing blindness to those who made them. So when he hears the word of the preacher, and the voice of conscience says, "Thou art the man,"[1] he moves hurriedly away, he seeks distraction, and is happy to forget, being convicted of sin. There is no repentance, and therefore no fruits of repentance. The man has heard, not heeded, and in consequence done nothing.

III.—THE MAN WHO HEARS AND DOES: HIS RELATION TO THE LAW OF LIBERTY.

S. James goes on to contrast such a man with one who *looketh into the perfect law*. The word παρακύψας gives the idea of bending over a mirror, and the *perfect law* reflects more than any burnished plate of metal. It is the Will of God. Peering into it a man learns why and wherefore he was created and what he should be like. He sees dimly, as in a glass darkly,[2] the image in which he was created, and finds God's reflection, however blurred and distorted, in his own nature. The perception is everything. It is a matter of no importance as to whether the perfect law is received through the eye or through the ear, whether it comes from watching the life of a saint or listening to his instructions. The meaning once grasped, the reflection once found, there is only one desire that the meaning may be clearer and the reflection more perfectly focussed. A man seeks for conformity with the God who works, and in acting will be blessed in his deed.

---

[1] 2 Sam. xii. 7. [2] 1 Cor xiii 12

Hearing and Doing

But what is the perfect law? S. James calls it *a law of liberty*, and to our minds law is so associated with coercion and restriction, that at first sight the words appear as a contradiction in terms. True liberty, however, is only the opposite of law; and opposites, unlike contradictories, do not exclude one another.

There had, indeed, been a law, formal and fixed, with definite penalties and powers of compulsion. It was suitable for a nation in its infancy. It was " a schoolmaster to bring men to Christ."[1] The Psalmist was able to say, "the law of the Lord is perfect,"[2] but he could not say that it was a law of liberty, because to most men it was felt as a burden. Jeremiah[3] had prophesied in the Name of God, saying: "I will put My law in their inward parts, and write it in their hearts." Then when man's desires correspond with God's Law, the law only exists to safeguard man in doing what he wishes: "Where the Spirit of the Lord is there is liberty."[4] In this world, it is true, correspondence with the Will of God is never complete. We admit, " God and God alone is perfectly free, for God alone is in perfect harmony with His own law." At the same time we can pray, "Not my will, but Thine be done,"[5] and so praying we become godlike, and are free by intention. So we affirm constantly, " In Thy service is perfect freedom," though by placing too much emphasis on the last word we sometimes reduce " the service " to a perfunctory compliment, and show that for us the law of liberty is not a command to work.

[1] Gal iii 24 [2] Ps xix. 7. [3] Jer xxxi. 33.
[4] 2 Cor iii 17. [5] Luke xxii 42.

Now God's promise to Jeremiah was fulfilled in our Blessed Lord. He came with the perfect law and translated it into action. It is to be studied in the mirror of His perfect life, and will only be learnt by continuous contemplation. So S. James contrasts the man who gave but a passing glance at his own unsatisfactory reflection with the man who bows down in the earnest contemplation of the Divine Word made manifest. Here again we are reminded how naturally the Word became personified. The man is *to be not a forgetful hearer, but a doer of the word*, and it is through contemplation of Our Lord in all His acts that the law is learnt, which shall be a law of liberty written by the Holy Spirit on the tables of man's heart. It is not an enactment from without: there is no compulsion. Throughout His ministry Our Lord refused to compel. It is an impression received within the heart, from the Lord who fills the heart and sets the heart free from the bondage of conflicting desires. The Psalmist, looking forward, had said: " I will run in the way of Thy commandments, when Thou hast set my heart at liberty."[1] The heart has been set at liberty and the way is open. We must hasten and run if we would be with Him who went about doing good. He passes on before us, and we must follow in His footsteps, or the impression of His glance, like the impress of His feet, becomes ever more dim. When it is lost, we are lost indeed.

But here we must remember that the command to follow can only come from Him. Until He calls it is for us to watch and wait, and this accounts for the fact

[1] Ps. cxix 32.

Hearing and Doing

that the best and most enduring work for Our Lord has been done by Contemplatives. The people in a hurry to accomplish, the fussy workers and strenuous busybodies, make more noise and more show, but their work does not last. S. James, we are told, was first of all a man of prayer. S. Paul made a long retreat in the wilderness:[1] S. John was "in the Spirit on the Lord's Day."[2] It is men like them who have been gifted with a vision of the Truth and turned the world upside down. They have been *blessed in their deeds*, because they reflected Him whom they continuously adored. They had contemplated Him until they could say: "I live, yet not I, but Christ liveth in me."[3]

Lastly, consider S. James's conclusion—*this man shall be blessed in his doing*. "God is pure Act," said the Schoolmen." "My Father worketh hitherto, and I work,"[4] said Our Lord. Man, too, was meant to work; it is the law of his nature; and to the man in harmony with God it is a law of liberty. Doing is the secret of happiness; the results of doing right will ultimately justify the action; but the crown of all is the commendation of the Master: "Well done, good and faithful servant: enter thou into the joy of thy Lord."[5]

IV.—Imperfect Doing: the Formalist who is Censorious.

Here S. James pauses once again. He considers his command, *Be ye doers of the word*, and remembers how men might delude themselves into thinking that they were

---

[1] Gal. i. 17, 18 [2] Rev. i. 10 [3] Gal. ii. 20.
[4] John v 17 [5] Matt xxv 21.

obedient to a perfect law while they were only formalists. There are many who delight in keeping rules, who never consider why the rules were framed. So S. James, after reproving the intolerant dogmatist and the lazy pietist, goes on to deal with the mere ceremonialist.

Coming from S. James, his words under this heading have a very special value, for he was himself an enthusiast for the Law and for the Temple worship, naturally a conservative, and even the unbelieving Jews called him "the Just." He had remained at Jerusalem, he cared for his own people, and at a later period we find him persuading S. Paul to fulfil certain ritual conditions of purification.[1] He was undoubtedly regarded by the Judaizing Christians as the head of their party, and yet it is from him that the warning comes: *If any man thinketh himself to be religious, while he bridleth not his tongue, but deceiveth his heart: this man's religion is vain.*

The words $\theta\rho\hat{\eta}\sigma\kappa o s$ and $\theta\rho\eta\sigma\kappa\epsilon\acute{\iota}a$ are, unfortunately, translated by "religious" and "religion." Since the sixteenth century we have come to use these words in a wider meaning, and they no longer represent the Greek. The passage refers to the external practice of the Faith; and perhaps the nearest words we can suggest are *devout* and *devotion*, but even they have a too extended significance.

The Jews made broad their phylacteries and enlarged the borders of their garments.[2] They sounded the trumpet when they gave their alms;[3] they stood praying at the corners of the streets;[4] they were ostentatious in their fasting, and strict as to meats and drinks.[5]

[1] Acts xxi 18-25 [2] Matt xxiii 5 [3] Matt vi. 2.
[4] Matt vi. 5. [5] Matt. vi. 16

Hearing and Doing

They were most particular not to incur ceremonial defilement; they kept many rules as to washing both themselves and pots.[1] They observed the Sabbath and celebrated holy days.[2] They quoted many texts, and regarded the people who knew not the Law as cursed.[3] Such people were very liable to esteem themselves too highly, to think themselves devout, and to say with the Pharisees, "God, I thank Thee, I am not as other men are."[4] They boasted overmuch, having no bridle upon their tongue.

Now, men such as these, who had been brought within the Church, did not need to be told that they must worship God, neither did they need to be told their duty towards their neighbours; but they did need to be warned as to the spirit in which they should worship God, and as to the motive that should inspire all service to their neighbour. They needed, too, that it should be made clear how the duties were allied, that they could not choose between them, that the wider ritual—the service of their neighbours—was an outcome which proved the sincerity of their devotion.

Remembering this, it will be clear that S. James is not condemning men for ritual propriety any more than in previous verses he condemns all wrath, or all listening to sermons. He sees the danger of formalism, and first proposes to the ceremonialist a test of his sincerity, and then points out to him the overwhelming importance of duties which he may be tempted to overlook.

A punctual regard for ritual may gain a man a

[1] Mark vii. 4
[2] Mark ii. 24; iii. 4.
[3] John vii 49
[4] Luke xviii 11.

reputation for devotion. He may *seem* religious, but the Revised Version is undoubtedly right when it translates δοκεῖ in this place by *thinks*. That the man thinks himself to be religious is clear from the immediate comment, that he is *deceiving his own heart*. S. James is not asking others to judge the man, he is asking the man to examine himself. And the test that he suggests is a simple one—Does he bridle his tongue? Is he free from boasting? Is he censorious? Does he thank God that he is not as other men?

The test proposed was the right one, and shows a profound insight into human nature. No one is tempted to such licence in speech as the zealous ceremonialist. We know this in our own day if we read the correspondence columns of religious newspapers. It matters little whether the writer be an enthusiast for Eucharistic vestments or an enthusiast for celebrating the Holy Communion at the North End of the Holy Table. He may be a "good Catholic" or a "sturdy Protestant"; but he is often spiteful, censorious, and scornful; he is apt to impute the worst motives, and to be suspicious without occasion. S. James assures him, *if he bridles not his tongue, his religion is vain*.

Now S. James was the last man to minimize the importance of such controversies. He himself, sometime later, presided over a council and settled the first ritual crisis.[1] He knew quite well that there is always a right and a wrong in matters which excite men's passions, that little acts of ceremonial which make the outsider smile are for those within the symbols of great doctrines and far-reaching principles. Men are

[1] Acts xv. 1-31.

Hearing and Doing

sensitive about them, as men are sensitive for the honour of the flag. What is the Union Jack but a bit of coloured bunting? and yet it is a symbol for which men gladly die.

In this place S. James is not concerned with any particular ceremonial. He is thinking of the man who rests in forms, and thinks himself devout because he observes them. He asks but one question—Does he bridle his tongue? If he do not, his devotion is vain. The form for him is an end in itself—an empty thing. He is not filled with the Spirit, which his forms are meant to embody and symbolize.

V.—WORKS OF MERCY AND THEIR MOTIVE.

A ceremonial law is capable of being kept, and therein lies its danger. Those who exactly fulfil its requirements are apt to be self-satisfied, and the moment a man becomes self-satisfied he is tempted to be censorious. He has his little standard by which he can gauge the demerits of others, and he naturally resents the action of anyone who sets up another standard by which he is himself condemned.

To counteract the self-satisfaction resulting from the observance of law, and to teach the true love of mankind for whom Christ died, S. James goes on to remind his disciples that *pure religion (θρησκεία) and undefiled before our God and Father is this, to visit the fatherless and widows in their affliction, and to keep himself unspotted from the world.*

Here are duties to be done that never can be finished. The doer of this word has no time for self-satisfaction.

The man engaged in this service must needs learn the difference between pedantic observance of the letter and loving correspondence with the spirit. In this service also a man will find not only a means of linking himself with others, but he will find also that it separates him from no one, and if his ritual was not a vain thing he will learn to love it better as he comprehends more perfectly who is the God whom he worships, and why he worships Him.

For this service too is part of the outward practice of religion. It also is θρησκεία. Our Lord says, "Inasmuch as ye do it unto one of the least of these My brethren, ye do it unto Me."[1] Moreover, it is through becoming a father to the fatherless that a man begins to understand what is meant by the Fatherhood of God; through the humiliation of failure, he will learn his need of God's help; and through the consciousness that he has neglected opportunities for helping, he will learn to approach God as an erring child. Formalism is only possible where a man neither knows his own needs nor God's love. God is to be known through the service of those whom God loves. "He that loveth not his brother whom he hath seen, how can he love God whom he hath not seen?"[2] And it is in the same service of his brother that a man gets to know himself. No one properly understands his limitations until he tries to help the unfortunate.

In the Old Testament there is no higher conception of the Almighty than that "He is the Father of the fatherless, and the judge of the widows."[3] In the Law of the Covenant the Israelites are forbidden to "afflict

[1] Matt xxv 40   [2] 1 John iv 20.   [3] Ps. lxviii. 5.

Hearing and Doing

any widow or fatherless child."[1] In this passage the command becomes positive—*to visit the fatherless and widows in their affliction*. God is no longer merely protecting those who are His, but He is calling on His sons to co-operate in His work—a work dear to His heart.

But while S. James calls men to this wider service, he is quite careful to avoid misunderstanding, and he has been most unjustifiably misunderstood. Men have used this text to prove that true religion and mere morality are convertible terms, that faith is of no importance, and that philanthropy is everything. This may be partly excused by the fact that $\theta\rho\eta\sigma\kappa\epsilon\acute{\iota}a$ is translated religion, and is partly due to forgetting the force that the words *pure and undefiled* would have for a Jew, and is mostly due to ignoring the words *before our God and Father*, and the condition at the close that the worker must *keep himself unspotted from the world*.

In all ritual known to the Jews there was always a danger of ceremonial defilement, and the service of the afflicted is only *pure and undefiled* when done in the sight of *our God and Father*, by one who *keeps himself unspotted from the world*.

Just as worship in church or temple may be a self-regarding action, done for one's own exaltation, so good works may be self-regarding actions done for the sake of one's own repute. Good deeds may be done to be seen of man, and not for love of the Father who searches the heart. They may be done with a view of storing up merit for oneself, or as a set-off against indulgence in some pleasant sin. They may be offered as a substitute for faith in God, or they may be done

[1] Exod. xxii. 22

in flat rebellion to God as a proof that the things seen are of more importance than the things unseen as yet. Corporal acts of mercy are sometimes the manifesto of the materialist, his way of asserting that the body is all.

But when a mere morality is opposed to religion, it is morality that in the long run suffers most from the opposition. It becomes cold and dead, a matter for rhetoric, an affair of sentiment, or a counsel of prudence; it has ceased to be animated by the Spirit of God; it is contaminated by the world.

The *world* in this passage, as often in the New Testament, stands for society as organized apart from any consideration of God, and the word *unspotted* carries on the metaphor from Jewish ritual. All sacrifices had to be without spot or blemish.[1] As the worship of the formalist was defiled by his unbridled tongue, so the service of men may be defiled by worldly motives. God ever requires a pure offering.[2]

VI.—The Conclusion of the Argument.

To sum up, S. James in the whole passage is writing, as it were, notes and comments on duties already known to those who had been instructed as *doers of the word*. There is first of all the recognized duty of worshipping God. Let a man see that in performing the duty he does not become a mere formalist. Let him examine himself as to how far he bridles his tongue. Secondly, let a doer of the word remember his duty to others, and as a follower of Him who was

[1] Lev. xxii. 20, 21, Deut. xv. 21. [2] Mal. i. 11

Hearing and Doing

made perfect by suffering, let him minister to His suffering members. In fulfilling this duty let him examine himself, whether his work is done as *before our God and Father*, for there is much so-called philanthropy inspired by other motives for other ends. Lastly, a doer of the word must be careful to *keep himself unspotted from the world*. He must not imagine that any number of good works will compensate for lack of faith or for indulgence in any sin.

LECTURE VI

RESPECT FOR PERSONS

"*My brethren, hold not the faith of our Lord Jesus Christ, the Lord of Glory, with respect of persons. For if there come into your synagogue a man with a gold ring, in fine clothing, and there come in also a poor man in vile clothing, and ye have regard to him that weareth the fine clothing, and say, Sit thou here in a good place, and ye say to the poor man, Stand thou there, or sit under my footstool, are ye not divided in your own mind, and become judges with evil thoughts? Hearken, my beloved brethren, did not God choose them that are poor as to the world to be rich in faith, and heirs of the Kingdom which He promised to them that love Him? But ye have dishonoured the poor man Do not the rich oppress you, and themselves drag you before the judgment-seats? Do not they blaspheme the honourable name by the which ye are called? Howbeit if ye fulfil the royal law, according to the Scripture, thou shalt love thy neighbour as thyself, ye do well but if ye have respect of persons, ye commit sin, being convicted by the law as transgressors*"—JAS ii 1-9

I.—CONNEXION OF THOUGHT.

THROUGHOUT this Epistle S. James shows himself to be a practical man. When he states a general principle, he goes on to apply it to a particular case, or considers how it might be perverted or evaded. So he not only says that a man must *keep himself unspotted from the world*, but he immediately proceeds to explain how, through *respect of persons*, a worldly standard may contaminate and corrupt those who *hold the faith of Our Lord Jesus Christ*.

II.—RESPECT OF PERSONS.

Respect of persons (προσωπολημψία) requires explanation. Strictly the word would mean mistaking the mask for the actor behind it, and so of distinguishing a man by some accidental property that he possessed, rather than by what is essential to his character. This might merely imply lack of intelligence; but as πρόσωπον (a mask) in its secondary sense acquired an ill meaning, so *respect of persons* came to imply moral obliquity. It means in this place giving full play to a bias for or against a man because of some circumstance which ought not to be considered. S. Peter had learnt in the house of Cornelius that "God is no respecter of persons";[1] S. Paul repeatedly emphasized the fact;[2] and S. James shows in this passage that those who hold the faith of the Lord Jesus must not respect persons either.

Some people have pleaded this doctrine as sanctioning rudeness and disrespect. Nothing, however, could have been farther from the mind of S. James. S. Paul taught, "Let each esteem other better than himself,"[3] and "Render to all their dues: tribute to whom tribute is due, custom to whom custom, fear to whom fear, honour to whom honour."[4] It is S. Peter who tells us to be courteous,[5] and to "honour all men, love the brotherhood, fear God, honour the King."[6] Christians were to be conspicuous for good manners, and so to fulfil the *Royal Law*.

But respect for a man's office or rank may easily

---

[1] Acts x. 34. [2] Gal. ii. 6, Rom ii. 6, Eph vi 9, Col. iii. 25.
[3] Phil. ii. 3. [4] Rom. xiii. 7   [5] 1 Pet. iii. 8.   [6] 1 Pet. ii 17.

blind our eyes and prejudice us in his favour when no office and rank should be considered, while the consciousness that a man has no power or claim to deference may make us forgetful to do him justice or respect his feelings. In these ways we become what S. James calls *respecters of persons* and merit his condemnation.

But S. James's illustration carries us farther than this. He is writing to those who *hold the faith of Our Lord Jesus Christ*, and he would emphasize a new distinction. Church and State are not different aspects of one Body, but two Bodies, although any particular person may belong to both. This being granted, the position held in the world does not confer similar status in the Church. The Church has her own principles, and within her walls those of the world do not apply.

A State, Aristotle taught us, is to be distinguished from a voluntary society or confederation by the fact that it is composed of all sorts of people, having different occupations, and of differing conditions. This, according to S. Paul, is also true of the Church, which is likened to a body with many members and a variety of organs.[1] Church and State also both aim at unity, both are organized for social ends, and social life necessitates orders and subordination. But rank is not accorded in these two bodies for the same reasons. In the State a rich man holds an honoured position as the master of forces necessary for the State's existence; but in the Church no one has a right to influence on the score of riches, because the Church exists for

[1] 1 Cor. xii. 14-27; Eph. i. 23; iv. 16; Rom. xii. 4-6.

spiritual ends which money cannot purchase. The rich man is of importance to the State just in so far as he accumulates and saves: the rich man is only important in the Church just in so far as he gives his wealth away.

But S. James would probably go farther than this. Whether in Church or State, he was alive to the corruption which must ensue if wealth becomes the one criterion of position. Classes and distinctions there must be, and the more we have the better, for no two men are alike, so no two men are equal, no two men are intended for the same work or fitted for the same place. Among primitive men, muscle decides all questions, and might is right. Progress begins when other qualifications for superiority are recognized. First, Age acquires prerogatives, then special families attain pre-eminence, and Birth becomes a matter of importance. As the State grows more complex honours are reserved for certain offices and employments—Rank emerges. As arts and letters are cultivated, education, talent and genius, raise men above the common herd, and manners have a distinction of their own. Lastly, there is Wealth, and in so far as Wealth represents energy, enterprise, foresight and thrift, it merits the influence it enjoys. But when birth, rank and intellect are deprived of all privilege, and manners are neglected, Wealth tends to become the only distinction, and Society being materialized is soon corrupt. It is obvious that if all men are equal, we can only differentiate them in accordance with what they possess; but assuming that all men are unequal, we can strive to assign each his place according to what he is, what he can do, and for what he is responsible. The worship of the wealthy as such, apart from any other quality, ends in a return to the purely savage State where might is right—with this difference, that for the rule of the strong arm there is a better justification than for the rule of the Almighty Dollar.

Now, the Jew of the Dispersion was a cosmopolite suffering from a double social disadvantage. An intense pride of race separated him from the people among whom he dwelt, but this distinction was unrecognized by those whom he despised. Secondly, among his own people there were no longer any recognized ranks. They were all wanderers belonging to no polity, and in consequence wealth became for them the one distinction, and the worship of wealth almost an idolatry.

In Judæa, where there was still an hierarchy and an organized community, the poor but learned Pharisee might attain to the uppermost seat in the Synagogue near to the ark which contained the Sacred Law,[1] but in the synagogues of the Dispersion gay clothes and gold rings were better passports to a cushioned seat and a comfortable footstool. Had S. James been writing to Christians in Palestine, he would no doubt have echoed Our Lord's condemnation of those who struggled for seats on the score of assumed merit. Writing to the Jews of the Dispersion, he condemns the homage paid to a more contemptible ostentation. For the Christian Church has its own polity, and it is based on other principles than those of the world. Birth is of great importance, but makes no distinction where all are brethren, where all belong to one family,

[1] Matt xxiii 6, Mark xii 39; Luke xi 43

and are by Baptism the sons of God. Rank does count for something, for from the beginning there have been Orders, but they are Orders of Ministry, and so imply responsibilities rather than rights, service rather than dominion. Talents and graces have their place, but it is "the Spirit who divides to every man severally as He will."[1] No man dare boast of such distinctions or take credit to himself because of them. They are gifts for which each must thank the Giver, which each must use for the common good. Wealth is rather condemned than extolled. Its dangers are insisted on. Poverty has been consecrated by Christ, and the Gospel is for the poor.[2] Conduct and character are paramount, for they represent the end for which the Church exists, as truly as the State exists for the maintenance of order, prosperity and power.

III.—THE FAITH AND THE GLORY.

We who have inherited the traditions of many Christian generations know how imperfectly we have learnt the lesson which S. James teaches. We ought, in consequence, to sympathize with those Jews of the first age. S. James sympathizes. He begins affectionately, *My brethren*. He is going to hurt, he is going to demonstrate ruthlessly the inconsistency of their conduct, but he reproves as a brother, and appeals to the highest example for his justification: *Hold not the faith of the Lord Jesus Christ, the Glory, in respect of persons.*

In this sentence, first, we note that the faith is objective. There is already a sacred deposit to be held and

[1] 1 Cor. xii 11.   [2] Luke iv. 18; vi. 20, Matt. xi 5

that can be appealed to. S. James is no mere Rabbi or disciple of a Rabbi persuading men by argument. He relies on authority, and the force of his moral exhortations proceeds from a definite creed recognized by himself and his brethren. It is just this common knowledge that he for the most part takes for granted. The argument once fashionable that what a man does not state he does not know is singularly inapplicable to correspondence between friends.

Secondly, the full name of Our Lord is given as in the first verse, with the singular addition of the title, *The Glory*, which S. James adds for a reason of his own. τῆς δόξης is best taken in apposition to the preceding words, and we shall do well to regard it as a translation of the Hebrew Shekinah—the glory of the Lord that appeared in the tabernacle. So S. John writes: "The Word was made flesh and *tabernacled* among us, and we beheld His Glory."[1] That Glory was not merely "of His people Israel,"[2] but Our Lord was also the "Glory of the Father."[3] He had prayed, "And now, O Father, glorify Thou Me with Thine own Self, with the Glory that I had with Thee before the world was,"[4] and the Church has ever believed that He, as man, entered into this glory at His Ascension.[5] S. Paul speaks of the Lord of Glory[6] and of "the Glory of God in the face of Jesus Christ."[7] The idea was common, but the usage is unique, unless we except Ephes. i. 17, and translate "The Father of the Glory."[8] Why, then, does S James use the title here? Did he not know the

---

[1] John i. 14 [2] Luke ii 32. [3] Heb 1. 3.
[4] John xvii. 5 [5] Luke xxiv 26, Acts iii. 13.
[6] 1 Cor ii 8. [7] 2 Cor. iv. 6. [8] Eph 1 17.

words afterwards to be recorded by S. John? "The Glory that Thou gavest Me, I have given them, that they may be one as We are One."[1] If these words were common knowledge, we may interpret his appeal as asking, Would his converts forfeit this glory by truckling to the glory of riches? Would they forfeit this unity by making unreal distinctions between persons? It was theirs to *hold the faith of Our Lord Jesus Christ*, in order that they might receive His glory. It was theirs, then, to ponder on Our Lord's solemn warning, " How can ye believe which receive honour one of another, and seek not the honour which cometh of God only?"[2]

IV.—THE GOLD-RINGED MAN AND THE MAN IN RAGS.

How honour was actually bestowed is vividly brought home to us. *For if there come into your synagogue a man with a gold ring, in goodly apparel, and there come in also a poor man in vile raiment; and ye have regard to him that weareth the gay clothing, and say, Sit thou here in this good place, and ye say to the poor man, Stand thou there, or sit under my footstool: are ye not then partial and become judges with evil thoughts?*

The Revisers were justified in rendering *synagogue* instead of *assembly*, for the word is no doubt used in its historical sense. The definite separation between Church and Synagogue had not yet taken place. S. Paul was for years afterwards to start each mission in the Synagogue of the Jews;[3] and yet from the first Christians had places of assembly for mutual prayer,

[1] John xvii. 22.　　　　　　[2] John v 44
[3] Acts ix. 20, xiii. 14; xiv. 1, xvii. 1, 2, 10, xviii. 4, 19, xix. 8

preaching, counsel, and the Breaking of Bread.[1] Such places they naturally enough called their synagogues, and Epiphanius[2] tells us that in Palestine churches were called synagogues as late as the fourth century. So it is not a Jewish synagogue that is here intended. The possessive pronoun *your*, and the preceding words as to *the faith of Our Lord*, seem decisive on this point.

At the early date S. James was writing there was no secrecy as to Christian worship,[3] so we have no right to assume that either the rich or the poor man was a Christian. The whole point of the incident lies in the fact that neither was known, but both were judged by their clothes

We may easily imagine the entrance of the rich sightseer. He is clad in splendid garments, probably white, and his fingers are adorned with rings. He is emphatically χρυσοδακτύλιος, the gold-ringed man. All eyes are turned; *ye have regard to him*, says S. James: he is ushered to the seat of honour. But if deference be shown to the clothes, it is also insinuated that there is a seat worthy of such magnificence. *Sit thou here in this good place.* We almost suspect an outstretched palm—a suggestion that *the good place* is not for nothing.

Very different is the reception of the poor man following on his heels. He is in the way. He is to stand, or, with amazing condescension, he may *sit under my footstool*. Superiority is at once asserted and delighted in. Many a man would like to make the poor comfortable *under his footstool*. There is no sense of wrong-doing

---

[1] Acts i. 14, ii. 42-47, iv. 23, xii. 12; xiii. 1, xv. 1, xx 7.
[2] Hœr xxx 18.   [3] 1 Cor. xiv 24.

in the rudeness or the patronage. S. James feels it is a case for expostulation, for pleading, and for scorn.

Expostulation comes first. *Are ye not partial?* or *Are ye not divided in your minds?* The verb has been used before in Chapter I., and is there translated *wavering* and *doubting*. The wavering in this case is between the standards of the Church and the world, and the partiality for the world's standard is evident. The consequence is, they have become *judges with evil thoughts*, or *evil-thinking judges*. The moral indecision with regard to themselves is contrasted with the assumption of judgment as regards others. To judge by appearances, without applying any other test is always dangerous, and has been found so by everyone from Eve downwards.[1] To condemn a man simply because he is in rags, is to impute evil without cause. There are people who are always willing to think badly of those not so well off as themselves.

V.—THE RELATION OF THE POOR TO THE CHURCH.

It is with such that S. James would plead. He is more of a preacher than a literary man, and as a preacher he arouses attention: *Hearken, my beloved brethren.* As he proceeds his feelings become warmer, both as regards his subject and those to whom he is writing. He has put a hypothetical case, but he has put it so vividly, that it is now for him a fact about which he must speak out to his imaginary audience. Very affectionate he is, but also quite uncompromising. No one could point out the glaring inconsistency with

[1] Gen iii. 6

sharper emphasis, or show more clearly the cleavage between the ways of God and man. *Did not God choose them that are poor as to this world, to be rich in faith, and heirs of the Kingdom, which He hath promised to them that love Him? But ye have dishonoured the poor man.*

It is to be noted that, unlike S. Paul, our author is not at all concerned with the speculative difficulty as to God's election. He appeals to a fact. God has chosen poor men. As S. Paul found at Corinth, "Not many wise men after the flesh, not many mighty, not many noble are called."[1] This was through no merit in the poor men. It was God who chose them.[2] S. Paul finds a reason for His doing so: S. James is contented with the fact. He is asking, Ought not men in consequence to respect God's ways and pursue His method of selection when dealing with strangers?

To S. James the riches of this world were of little consequence; but he knew the value of spiritual riches. Faith in this passage is "the substance of things hoped for."[3] It is a reality, a present possession, something to be used and enjoyed. It is not merely certitude and trust in God, nor even the vision of reality, but an active power that lifts a man into a higher sphere where the life of God is communicated to him. Faith in this sense is a supernatural gift for which God chooses men. It is not something which their own thought, will, or desire could originate.

But faith in this sense becomes a purely personal possession, and therefore cannot confer rank or social importance. It may entitle a man to respect among the faithful, just as the possession of gold entitles a

[1] 1 Cor. 1. 26. [2] 1 Cor 1 27-29. [3] Heb xi 1.

Respect for Persons

man to respect among the money-makers. It cannot do more. But God has not only chosen the poor to be *rich in faith*, but also to be *heirs of the Kingdom*. Now, inheritance in the Kingdom confers status, and one whom God has chosen to reign in Heaven may not be despised by His representatives on earth.

For long years the Jews expected the Messianic Kingdom. Their literature is full of anticipations. Our Lord had appropriated the language of His contemporaries, corrected their misconceptions, and interpreted the idea in His parabolic teaching.[1] He had come to be a King, He spoke with authority, He demonstrated His power. He called on men—" Follow Me,"[2] " Learn of Me,"[3] " Come unto Me,"[4] " Take My yoke upon you"; His claim was absolute—" He that loveth father or mother more than Me is not worthy of Me: and he that loveth son or daughter more than Me is not worthy of Me."[5]

But a King implies a Kingdom, and it was a Kingdom that Our Lord came to establish. A King is the fount of honour, and it was the King who made poor men His heirs. "Theirs is the Kingdom of Heaven."[6] They were to be gathered "from streets and lanes of the city." They were to be "compelled" to come in "from the highways and hedges."[7] Such was the King's command to His servants, and those who came were heirs of the Kingdom.

The quotation from the parable in S. Luke really answers an objection which might otherwise be made. The converted Jew might say that the poor man thrust

---

[1] John xviii 37   [2] John i. 43, Luke ix. 59.   [3] Matt. xi. 28, 29
[4] *Ibid.*   [5] Matt. x. 37.   [6] Luke vi. 20.   [7] Luke xiv. 21-23

aside was not a Christian, therefore neither rich in faith nor an heir of the Kingdom, and in consequence without status in the Church, or without any claims to special consideration. But S. James's argument is equally valid in the face of such an objection. God has chosen the poor: He cares for them. He sees beneath the vile raiment of a man a candidate for Heaven; those who are His servants must be equally discriminating.

It is true that S. James is under no delusion as to there being any merit in poverty of itself. It is quite as possible to sin by respecting the person of the poor. This was not so for those to whom S. James was writing, but it is so in our day when political power is in the hands of the people. To flatter the poor by abuse of the rich is an easy way to preferment and power, but it is also an admirable instance of that *respect of persons* condemned by S. James. So the matter is summed up in Leviticus: "In judgment thou shalt not respect the person of the poor, nor honour the person of the mighty, but in righteousness shalt thou judge thy neighbour."[1]

To guard against misconceptions on this point, S. James, after saying that poor men have been chosen as *heirs of the Kingdom*, immediately adds, *which God hath promised to them that love Him*. In the previous chapter the same condition is made for those who shall receive the *crown of life*. In God's Kingdom all are sons, all are to be crowned, all are to share in the regality, because Love is the power that is dominant. If this love is real there can be no despising of the poor, for those who love God must love their brothers also.

[1] Lev xix 15.

And where are we to find God's promise? Recent commentators have enlarged on parallel passages from Judaic literature, but the promise seems patent in the Gospel. Our Lord not only commends those who have cared for the poor and afflicted, not only states that work done for them is done for Himself, but He also says, "Come, ye blessed of My Father, and inherit the Kingdom prepared for you from the foundation of the world."[1]

VI.—THE RELATION OF THE RICH TO THE CHURCH.

From this high appeal to first principles, S. James suddenly descends to an *argumentum ad homines*. It is the action of a speaker sensitive to his audience. The ways of God may be too mysterious for them, but they will respond to common sense. At least they are alive to self-interest. So he asks them to consider what harvest they reap from their servile cultivation of the wealthy. Let experience convict them of folly. *Do not rich men oppress you, and themselves drag you before the judgment-seats? Do not they blaspheme the honourable Name by which ye are called?*

The oppression of the rich is elsewhere alluded to in the Epistle. It was from the wealthy Sadducean priests that the first persecution came.[2] It was they who commissioned Saul to go to Damascus and bring any "of this way, whether they were men or women . . . bound to Jerusalem."[3] Until A.D. 70 the Jews were permitted to administer their own law among themselves, even in the Roman cities of the Eastern

---

[1] Matt. xxv. 34.   [2] Acts v. 17
[3] Acts ix. 1, 2.

Provinces.¹ They could not, indeed, pronounce the death sentence, but otherwise they could harass the lives of Jewish converts to the Faith. The spread of Christianity was particularly obnoxious to wealthy Jews, because it appeared to be revolutionary and subversive. They were concerned to maintain the existing régime, and were fearful of arousing Roman suspicion. They were also worshippers of wealth, and therefore contemptuous of the Poor Man of Nazareth, and of His brethren chosen from among the outcasts. Their contempt found expression in what S. James calls *blasphemies*, and his use of the word is significant. A Jew kept it for profane speaking about the Divine; and so, in speaking of *blasphemy against the honourable Name by which ye are called*, he quite incidentally bears witness to his belief in Our Lord's divinity. For *the Name* here must be either the Name of Jesus, or the new Name of God revealed by Jesus. It cannot refer to the word "Christian," because "Christian" at this time was only a term of ridicule in the streets of Antioch,² and therefore not an *honourable name*.

Perhaps we shall understand S. James best by adopting the marginal translation in the Revised Version and reading, *the honourable Name which has been called over you*. Men were baptized into the Lord Jesus, that is, into the new Name of God revealed by Him into the Name of the Father, the Son, and the Holy Ghost.³

It was against Our Lord and His revelation that the rich Jews uttered their blasphemies, and how could Christians, jealous of His honour, cringe to such? Why should they prefer them to the poor, who were

[1] John xviii. 31.   [2] Acts xi. 26.   [3] Matt. xxviii. 19.

notoriously more ready to hearken to the Word? Did the converts of S. James, who were so discouraged by temptation and trials, really welcome oppression or glory in fines and imprisonment when dragged before the judgment-seat?

VII.—THE ROYAL LAW.

S. James seems to pause for a reply. Then there is a swift change of tone. He has passed from expostulation to argument. His argument has taken a personal note. He has pelted his hearers with rhetorical questions. Now, almost as an aside, comes the pitiless sarcasm: *Howbeit, if ye fulfil the royal law according to the Scriptures, Thou shalt love thy neighbour as thyself, ye do well.* Then his voice rises once more as he delivers judgment: *But if ye have respect of persons, ye commit sin, being convicted by the Law as transgressors.*

It is easy to imagine the scene, the letter being read, and the guilty glances of the hearers. Some are uncomfortable, some smile, but the sarcasm is a thrust home. There very likely sits the gold-ringed man in the seat of honour, and no one has the impudence to plead that he placed him there in compliance with any law, royal or otherwise. S. James offers them a complete justification, of which they dare not avail themselves.

But, besides the sarcasm and beneath it, a great truth is expressed. *Respect of persons* in allotting seats or conferring favours is, after all, right or wrong according to the motive. The act has to be viewed in relation to the *royal law, Thou shalt love thy neighbour as thyself.*

The Rabbis before S. James had termed this text of

Leviticus the *supreme* Law.[1] Hillel, for instance, had taught, "What is hateful to thyself do not to thy fellow-man; this is the whole Torah, the rest is only commentary."[2] Perhaps by the term *royal* S. James had only in view the supreme importance attaching to the personal decree of an Oriental despot; but it is more natural to think that as he had just spoken of the Kingdom, so he bears in mind the sovereignty of Jesus, and how He said: "All things whatsoever ye would that men should do unto you, do ye also unto them: for this is the Law and the Prophets."[3]

Here, then, was the law of the King. In the courts of Kings we expect courtesy, and courtesy is one of the choicest blossoms in the garland of love. But if we expect courtesy in an earthly palace, it cannot be absent in the courts of Heaven, and the King's representatives on earth may not despise His law.

It is true that all Christians are equally God's children, and so in the family of God it is intolerable that there should be distinctions which negative this truth; but it might be argued that the *gold-ringed man* was a stranger, and therefore courtesy might suggest that he should be shown the same deference which he had a right to receive in the world outside, which he would naturally suppose to be his due. He, at least, was no member of the family, and therefore he could not be called on to enter into the family life where Roman citizen and slave were brethren. But, alas! that no such courtesy was in the mind of the Synagogue is evident from their conduct towards the poor man. True courtesy would render all at home. The man in vile raiment had

[1] Lev. xix. 18   [2] Shabbeth, 30 B   [3] Matt vii 12.

Respect for Persons

probably no wish to be rendered conspicuous in his rags, neither did he wish to be thrust aside.

The conclusion, then, on the whole subject, can only be reached when we know the motive; but if it be true that we are not to judge by appearances, it is also true that we are "to avoid all appearance of evil."[1] God sees men nakedly, whether adorned in goodly apparel or covered with the poor apology of rags. He sees also into the hearts of those who deal with them. He knows whether they are inspired by motives of courtesy or by a base and slavish adulation of money. There is no exception to His judgment. *If ye have respect of persons, ye commit sin, being convicted by the Law as transgressors.*

Sin ($ἁμαρτία$) here cannot mean merely failure to hit the mark, for it is joined with $ἐργάζεσθε$, and must have an active force; *ye work sin;* you are doing something that will have evil consequences for yourselves, for inquirers in your synagogues, and for the Church at large. You cannot, argues S. James, plead ignorance as your excuse. You deliberately pass over to the world and trespass in her purlieus, though the Law, like a notice-board, is there to forbid you. Long before, Jesus, the son of Sirach, had issued a similar warning: "Accept no person against thy soul, and let not the reverence of any man cause thee to fall."[2]

[1] 1 Thess v. 22.   [2] Ecclus. iv 22.

LECTURE VII

THE ROYAL LAW

"For whosoever shall keep the whole Law, and yet stumble in one point, he is become guilty of all. For He that said, Do not commit adultery, said also, Do not kill Now if thou dost not commit adultery but killest, thou art become a transgressor of the Law. So speak ye, and so do, as men that are to be judged by a law of liberty. For judgment is without mercy to him that hath shewed no mercy Mercy glorieth against judgment."—JAS. ii. 10-13.

I.—CONNEXION OF THOUGHT.

S. JAMES has been speaking of *the Royal Law*. In accordance with it he has condemned men who truckle to the rich and are insolent to the poor, who, in his own phrase, *respect persons*. He goes on to anticipate the excuse: "After all, it is a little sin." Not at all, answers S. James, for *whosoever shall keep the whole Law, and yet stumble in one point, is guilty of all.*

II.—RITUAL AND MORAL LAW.

Here, indeed, is a hard saying, which, apart from its context, is liable to endless misapplication. The Jews, accepting it, were ready to argue that circumcision was commanded by the Law, and that therefore they could say to Gentile converts, "Except ye be circumcised after the manner of Moses, ye cannot be saved."[1]

---
[1] Acts xv 1, *cf* 5

They quoted S. James as their authority both at Antioch and in Galatia,[1] and S. James, in his circular letter from Jerusalem, repudiated the inference that they had drawn.[2] Circumcision[3] was the sign of covenant ordained for Abraham and his seed, but it was not in consequence of obligation on Gentiles converted to Christianity. S. Peter might well ask, "Why tempt ye God, that ye should put a yoke upon the neck of the disciples, which neither our fathers nor we were able to bear?"[4] S. James, at any rate, was doing no such thing. From the context it is clear that his words have reference to *the Royal Law* which he had just quoted, and not to "the Law which gendereth to bondage"[5]—the yoke of Jewish ritual.

But supposing the Jews convinced as to the case just referred to, they might still argue that the first table of the Commandments is as important as the second, and in consequence disobedience to the ritual Law is as sinful as disobedience to the moral Law. There is a sense in which this may be true; but, considering S. James's teaching as to *the implanted word* and *law of liberty*, it is perfectly clear what he would have answered. The moral Law is within a man's heart, and is applicable to all men under all conditions; the ritual Law is imposed from without, and is applicable to those only who have received it. Sin only enters in when a man wilfully disobeys what he knows to be right, or when he puts a stumbling-block in the way of a brother by offending his prejudices in a matter that is indifferent.[6] Had S. James, then,

[1] Gal. ii 4. [2] Acts xv 24. [3] Gen xvii 10-14.
[4] Acts xv 10 [5] Gal. iv 24. [6] 1 Cor viii. 9-11.

been thinking of the ritual Law, he would have been obliged to expand his argument, as S. Paul afterwards did in Rom. xiv. and 1 Cor. viii.[1]

III.—PHARISEES, STOICS, AND ST. PAUL.

No one to-day desires to make Mosaic ritual of obligation for Christians, but modern commentators, anxious to establish the indebtedness of S. James to the thought of his age, quote parallel passages from Rabbinical casuists or Stoic philosophers, according to their belief in the early or late date of the Epistle. In consequence it has become necessary to insist with S. Augustine[2] that the true interpretation of this text must be found within the sphere of Christian thought.

The parallels from Rabbi Jochaman, a contemporary of S. James, are indeed startling. "If a man," he says, "does all things and omits one, he is guilty of each and all." And, again, "Every one who says, I will take upon myself the whole Law and omits one word, he has despised the word of the Lord, and made all His commandments vain." But both these sentences have reference to a complicated code, and not to the Royal Law. The Rabbis, accepting this principle, went on to argue that all acts of disobedience are equally sinful, with the necessary corollary that all commandments, whether moral or ritual, whether in Scripture or received by tradition, were of equal importance. But when once this was established it seemed to follow that all acts of obedience were of equal value, so a conclusion was finally reached by this circular reasoning, that in the keeping of one

[1] Rom. xiv., 1 Cor viii 7-13. [2] Ep clxvii.

The Royal Law

commandment the whole Law was fulfilled. Several Rabbis taught this in reference to the Sabbath, and we find in Rashi, a Rabbinical commentator of the Middle Ages, the same doctrine applied to the Law of Fringes.[1] No wonder, then, that Our Lord condemned those who "took tithes of mint, anise, and cummin, and omitted the weightier matters of the Law,"[2] and those who by pleading it was "Corban," made "void the Word of God by their traditions."[3]

How far S. James was removed from the schools of Jewish legalism may be seen from his declaration: *If a man thinks himself to be religious, while he bridleth not his tongue, but deceiveth his own heart, this man's religion is vain.* Even when condemning *respect for persons* he guards against a merely legalist view by adding: *Howbeit if ye fulfil the Royal Law, according to the Scripture, Thou shalt love thy neighbour as thyself, ye do well.* He is not a lawyer enforcing a code, but a Christian teacher calling on men to examine their motives and see themselves with the eyes of God.

The Pharisees had elaborated an immoral casuistry out of the letter of the Law, and had no conception of the *Law of Liberty*. The Stoics, on the other hand, had no conception of the *Royal Law*, because they had no belief in a Personal God. Life in accordance with Nature was their aim; and, rejecting all external authority, they relied on a *Law of Liberty* by which they should judge themselves, but by which they should not be judged. "Nothing for opinion: all for conscience," is an axiom with Seneca.

Arguing, therefore, from an individual standpoint,

[1] Num. xv 38, 39   [2] Matt xxiii. 23   [3] Mark vii 11-13.

many Stoics taught that all virtues are the same, and all vices are equal, for there is no good and no evil apart from knowledge. Virtue, they maintained, lay in the wise choice, and vice was really ignorance. They taught, indeed, that the ignorance was voluntary, and arose through ignoring the light of reason and preferring the dictates of the passions.

Such teaching, it will be seen at once, however admirable for philosophic discussion, does not provide a morality suitable for social life. So in actual life, Stoics condemned, approved, and discriminated much as the rest of the world. But the doctrine of the schools slowly but surely filters down to the man in the street, to be interpreted by common-sense, with surprising results. "Are all vices equal?" said the man in the street, "then as well be hanged for a sheep as a lamb." S. Jerome in the fourth century found such pseudo-Stoics, who quoted S. James as an authority on their side. S. Jerome answers: "The passage is its own interpreter. James did not say, as a starting-point of the discussion, he who prefers a rich to a poor man in honour is guilty of adultery and murder. That is a delusion of the Stoics, who maintain the equality of sins. But he proceeds thus: *He who said, Thou shalt not commit adultery, said also, Thou shalt not kill: but although thou dost not kill, yet if thou commit adultery, thou art become a transgressor of the Law.* Light offences are compared with light ones, and heavy offences with heavy ones. A fault that deserves the rod must not be avenged with the sword; nor must a crime worthy of the sword be checked with the rod."

While we admire the sound common-sense of

S. Jerome, it is necessary to admit that he has not fully answered his opponent. After all S. James does regard *Respect for persons* as a point in which man offends, and he goes on to say that such a man *has become guilty of all*. The real answer seems to be that S. James is concerned not with the quality of offences, but with the imputation of guilt.

Clearing our minds, then, of Rabbinical casuistry and Stoic commonplaces, we shall find a better guide to the interpretation of this passage in S. Paul. "Owe no man anything, save to love one another: for he that loveth his neighbour hath fulfilled the Law. For this, Thou shalt not commit adultery, Thou shalt not kill, Thou shalt not steal, Thou shalt not covet, and if there be any other commandment, it is summed up in this word, namely, Thou shalt love thy neighbour as thyself. Love worketh no ill to his neighbour: love therefore is the fulfilment of the Law."[1]

IV.—THE LAW AND THE COMMANDMENTS.

S. James, unlike the Stoic, believed in the Personal God, the *Father of Lights*, who was in real and intimate relationship with His people, begetting them by the *Word of Truth*, and sustaining them with His *implanted Word*. To those who receive it, this *Word*, accepted on authority, becomes a *Law of Liberty*. The Christian, then, is called to offer a free response to the *Royal Law* of His Father, and that Royal Law can be summed up in the one word, *Love*.

S. James, unlike so many Jewish contemporaries, did not regard the Law as a series of unrelated command-

[1] Rom. xiii 8-10.

ments. It was for him the expression of God's Mind, and with God is *no variableness nor shadow cast in turning*. This he brings out quite clearly when he goes on. *For He that said, Do not commit adultery, said also, Do not kill*—adultery and murder being two instances in which the Law of Love is set at naught.

S. James, it will be noted, does not say that a man who commits adultery is guilty of murder, but if thou dost not *commit adultery but killest, thou art become a transgressor of the Law*. Like other writers of the New Testament, he is careful to distinguish between commandments (ἐντολαί) and the Law (ὁ νόμος), which is their body and sum.[1]

V.—CRIME, SIN AND GUILT.

But it may be asked what proof can be offered that the Law may be regarded metaphorically as an organic body with the commandments as related members. In Pagan ethics wrong-doing was regarded as vice so far as it injured the wrong-doer, and as crime if it resulted in damage to society. In Christian ethics these distinctions are swallowed up in the one idea of sin—that is, of disobedience to an all-wise and an all-loving God. As God made man, and God wills man's good, it is obvious that all sin must be detrimental to man's true interest, but S. James does not consider this. For him, as for S. John, sin is not a mistake, but sin is lawlessness and therefore involves guilt.[2] It involves guilt all the more as the Law is the Will of a God who is Love.[3]

The pagans made a great distinction between

---

[1] Matt xxii. 36, Rom vii 12, Heb ix 19. [2] 1 John iii 4.
[3] 1 John iv 8

"pietas" and "justitia"—the duty owed to the gods and the duty owed to men. This distinction no longer exists for an author who maintains that *pure religion and undefiled is to visit the fatherless in their affliction*. From the Gospels we may infer that God will resent an injury done to one of His little ones more than an injury done to Himself.[1] Now if sin be rebellion against a Person, and that Person is the One on whom all depend, we can justly argue from the unity of God to the solidarity of His Law.

If, then, we cease to consider the nature of the wrong, and come to judge the person who did it and the person he did it to, we get away from the sphere of the Law Courts; for, in order to determine guilt, we have not to weigh the gravity of the offence, but the degree of disobedience shown by the offender. The child who steals sugar and the man who commits a burglary, obviously do not perpetrate a crime of like magnitude, and probably are not equally sinful in the eyes of God, because they are not equally responsible, or equally informed as to the nature of their acts. But it is possible that a child who deliberately and defiantly disobeys in a matter of little moment, may be more culpable than a man driven into committing a great crime. For an act of grievous wrong-doing may not involve much guilt. It may be done involuntarily, under compulsion, ignorantly, through carelessness, through fear, or without deliberation. So a man or a child may be morally more guilty than a criminal, through persisting in a course of evil, which he knows to be evil, but which Society does not punish.

[1] Matt xviii. 6-14; Mark ix. 42; Luke xvii. 2.

Again, note that S. James does not state that all offences render a man equally guilty in respect of the whole law. A murderer, an adulterer, and a respecter of persons may severally be guilty in a variety of degrees. The Judge, for S. James, is not imperfectly informed: "He is the God of knowledge, and by Him actions are weighed."[1]

VI.—The Importance of Little Sins and Carelessness.

Having attempted to account for S. James's saying, it is necessary to go on and note the practical object that he had for introducing it. When he says, *Whosoever shall keep the whole law and yet stumble in one point, he is become guilty of all*, he makes a crushing reply to man's two favourite excuses—"It is a little sin," and "I could not help it."

There may be petty crimes and trifling frailties which are none the less grievous sins in the eyes of God, who knows how we are made, what our circumstances are, and the nature of our temptations. We are not all tempted alike or in the same way, and the man who sins lightheartedly in little things may never be tried in great matters, and yet be finally condemned. We are all apt to minimize the importance of the sin to which we are inclined.

Every known sin is important that is not repented of, if it be only a lack of consideration for a poor man in the synagogue. If we defy God's Will in a small thing which gives but little trouble, how much more should we defy Him in a great matter wherein all our desires

[1] 1 Sam. ii. 3.

The Royal Law

were engaged? He therefore who consoles himself with the thought that this is only a little sin, may in the final judgment discover that he is *guilty of all*.

Secondly, it is well to mark the word *stumble* (πταίσῃ). Men are too apt to account for serious falls by pleading they could not help it, or that they were not responsible for stumbling over an unexpected obstacle. They say, they could not help it; when at most they should say, they did not intend it. So many acts of unpremeditated wrong-doing might have been avoided by a little foresight, a little care, by watchfulness and prayer. So many would have been overcome had not the offenders been lacking in self-discipline. They were not alert with "their loins girded about and lights burning."[1] The Stoics were right when they asserted that there was a voluntary ignorance; they were only wrong when they maintained that all ignorance was voluntary, and therefore culpable. When we consider the awful results that follow on men's *stumbles*, when we consider how Our Lord condemned the careless and self-confident, when we mark the awful condemnation on want of foresight implied in the Parable of the Ten Virgins,[2] we are bound to confess that S. James was justified in robbing us of all excuse by saying: "*If a man stumble in one point, he is guilty of all.*

This severity is characteristic of the New Testament. It strikes at the very root of Pharisaic self-satisfaction. It prevents anyone from comparing himself favourably with his neighbour. *In many points we all stumble*, says S. James, and he that *stumbles in one point is guilty of all*.

[1] Luke xii. 35.   [2] Matt. xxv 1-13

VII.—SELF-EXAMINATION IN THE LIGHT OF THE JUDGMENT.

He goes on to argue that on the one hand men need to be very careful. *So speak ye and so do, as men that are to be judged by the Law of Liberty;* and, on the other hand, men need to be very charitable as to the faults of others, *for judgment is without mercy to them that have no mercy*. In God's prerogative of mercy he finds the hope of sinners. *Mercy triumpheth over judgment*.

The thought of judgment to come filled the minds of all the writers of the New Testament. This was natural to those suffering from continual injustice, and falling into *divers temptations*. There was some consolation in the thought of a Tribunal where all wrongs would be righted, but S. James would rather have men consider their own ways in the light of that judgment. *So speak ye, and so do as men that are to be judged by the Law of Liberty*.

Speech as well as action is important. S. James has already insisted that men should be *slow to speak, slow to wrath*, and has told them that their *religion is vain* unless they *bridle their tongues*. He is going to dilate on the perils of speech at length, but here he is thinking of Our Lord's declaration, " By thy words thou shalt be justified, and by thy words thou shalt be condemned,"[1] and of that other tremendous saying, " For every idle word that man shall speak, he shall give an account thereof in the day of judgment."[2]

He has also counselled men to be *doers of the word*. He has shown them what they should do and refrain

[1] Matt xii. 37   [2] Matt. xii. 36.

The Royal Law

from doing. He is about to deal with the opposition some maintained between Faith and Works; but here he would insist on the truth, "that God will bring every work into judgment,"[1] and he reminds his converts that they will be judged by the *Law of Liberty*.

The Law of Liberty was treated of in the Fifth Lecture. Here we have only to note that it is in accordance with the law by which men live that they will be judged. The heathen were not altogether in darkness, they could find and care for "the image of God,"[2] which is in every man, however distorted, blurred or defaced. So Our Lord will judge the races which never knew Him, by their conduct to their neighbours.[3] Our Lord when on earth convicted the Jews out of the Mosaic Law, and by that Law He will judge them hereafter. For "as many as have sinned in the law shall be judged in the law . . . in the day when God shall judge the secrets of men by Jesus Christ."[4] The Jews, as indeed all others, will have to give an account of the talents entrusted to them. But God will judge those who have attained "unto the glorious liberty of the Sons of God"[5] by the *Law of Liberty* implanted in their hearts. They have been brought into God's family. They have not been coerced as slaves. God asks from them the free response of sons. *The Law of Liberty*, then, is not a code that can be evaded; and we cannot escape by adhering formally to its letter. To obey it our spirits must be in harmony with the Spirit of God.

Our Lord is the Judge: He is also the Standard of

---

[1] Eccles xii. 14.   [2] Gen. i 27   [3] Matt. xxv. 31-46
[4] Rom ii. 12, 16.   [5] Rom viii. 21

judgment. In Him all humanity is summed up, so that He can say to the heathen, "Inasmuch as ye did it unto one of the least of these My brethren, ye did it unto Me."[1] Again, to the Jews, He came to fulfil the Law, and is He "of whom Moses in the Law and the Prophets did write."[2] So, to Christians, He is the perfect *mirror* for their contemplation. He is also the Saviour who enables with His power. To Christians He says: "Ye therefore shall be perfect as your heavenly Father is perfect."[3]

The Law of Liberty then makes infinite demands on men. It goes deeper than any other; its claim is more pressing, for a slave who rebels against a master's whip is not so culpable as a son who outrages a father's love. Its appeal comes from within, so S. James would drive men to examine themselves and their motives; he would convince them that of this law none could say, "I have kept it from my youth up until now."[4] It is concerned not merely with murder and adultery; it takes cognizance of unbridled language and of rudeness to poor strangers in a synagogue. It takes in everything. As S. Paul commands: "Whether ye eat or drink or whatsoever ye do, do it heartily as unto the Lord."[5] Men examining themselves on these lines can only come to one conclusion—"there is none righteous, no, not one."[6] "God be merciful to me a sinner."[7]

But to obtain mercy there is one condition, men must be merciful. This is an inevitable inference from *the Royal Law, Thou shalt love thy neighbour as thyself.*

[1] Matt xxv. 40 [2] John i. 45. [3] Matt v 48. [4] Mark x. 20
[5] Cor x. 31 [6] Ps. liii. 3. [7] Luke xviii. 13

The Royal Law

If we love our neighbours as ourselves, we shall treat them as we should like to be treated; if we desire mercy, we must show it. Let men be as hard upon themselves as possible, but very charitable to the faults of others, *For judgment is without mercy to him that showed no mercy*. We think at once of the Lord's Beatitude and the Lord's Prayer.[1] We remember His warning, "With what measure ye mete withal, it shall be measured to you again."[2] We remember the Parable of the Two Debtors, and may learn from it not only the perils of the unforgiving temper, but also the operation of God's righteous mercy.[3]

VIII.—JUDGMENT AND THE TRIUMPH OF MERCY.

Mercy, says S. James, *triumpheth over judgment*. There is no connecting particle in the Greek. The words are the conclusion of the whole matter, and they come as an unexpected climax. S. James has been striving to deepen in his converts the conviction of sin, and he suddenly provides them with an antidote against despair.

There was no need for him to dilate on the quality of mercy, for he was writing to Jews who knew the Prophets. Had he been writing for Stoics he would have been obliged to develop his argument. There were teachers then as now who regarded mercy as an undesirable weakness, who acclaimed the strong man as he proceeded on his remorseless way, feeling no need of mercy. But such an ideal is anarchic, and, in consequence, inadmissible to anyone who believes

---
[1] Matt. v. 7, vi. 12. [2] Matt vii 2. [3] Matt xviii 23-35

either in the Unity of Nature or the Unity of God. If all things are related, if all things form one whole, if all things and people are dependent on a single Person, selfishness and isolation are equally opposed to Nature and to God. That love is the dominant force in the world is the only satisfactory explanation; and, under present conditions of rebellion and disorder, Love is inconceivable unless it can manifest itself in mercy.

Still, it may be argued, the Stoics did believe in the Unity of Nature, and reached to some conception that the world spirit was good; but, as they did not believe in a Personal God, they could find no place for mercy in the operation of an impersonal Law. To-day many have been so enthralled with the scientific conception of Law, that they are inclined to say—Nature knows no forgiveness, and we only find that disobedience to her dictates are terribly avenged. But they forget that Physicists only arrive at their laws by abstracting Will and Personality from their consideration. The formula should run, a particular consequence is certain, granting the antecedent and providing that nobody does anything to avert it. But assume the somebody with sufficient knowledge and power to bring some counteracting force into play, and the consequence, naturally inevitable, does not ensue. If, then, there be a God of boundless knowledge and boundless power, there is no reason why He should exact every penalty; there is room for His Mercy and forgiveness.

But it may be asked, again, How can we reconcile God's Justice with His Mercy? *Mercy triumphs over judgment*, says S. James, but he is using words metaphorically. In speaking of the judgment, the analogy

in his mind as a Jew was legal and not philosophical.
In the courts the judge has to decide on the evidence
whether or no the Law has been broken, and to calculate
the damage done. He is bound by the Law which he
administers, and he has to see that personal interest in
the prisoner or his circumstances does not bias his
mind. But behind the judge is the King, with the
prerogative of mercy, who, when his laws have been
vindicated, and the debt calculated to the uttermost
farthing, may remit even the thousand talents on
account of facts which the law did not contemplate, and
for which perhaps it was impossible to provide. *Mercy*,
then, in S. James's phrase, *triumphs over judgment*—a
legal judgment; but does not necessarily triumph over
justice. The judgment may be in accordance with the
law, while justice clamours for mercy.

But we have still to ask, How can the all-righteous
God who "hateth iniquity"[1] ever pardon the sinner
who has planned his evil and rejoiced in it? God
cannot condone sin without participating in it. That
is true; but God only promises to have mercy on the
penitent. Then it may be urged, but there is the
wrong, it is done, and nothing can undo the past.
That also is true, but out of evil God can bring forth
good; in fact, if He is God, and God is good, the end
of all things must be good, in the sense that His Will
must ultimately prevail. Therefore we can abstract
from our consideration the deed done, and view the
question as a personal one between God and the sinner.
Now, when the sinner repents, he deserts his sin, he
hates it, and ranges himself on the side of God. The

[1] Heb 1. 9.

consequences of his sin, and the weakness resulting from his sin, may still follow him, he may have to acknowledge "what I hate, that do I."[1] Yet all the time "he delights in the law of God after the inward man"; and surely the just God must treat him as he is, as he will be, and not as he was when his evil deeds were done. In the Book of the Revelation we read of God's judgment on the liar and adulterer,[2] but it is only applicable while the man remains a liar and an adulterer. The moment he turns from lying and adultery to view them with the eyes of God, he ceases to be a liar and adulterer, and justice demands that he should no longer be treated as such. There is a judgment proper to a lie or to adultery, but *mercy triumphs over judgment* in the moment of repentance, and there is joy among the angels of God.

[1] Rom. vii. 15.   [2] Rev. xxi 8; xxii 15.

LECTURE VIII

FAITH AND WORKS

" What doth it profit, my brethren, if a man say he hath faith, but have not works? Can that faith save him? If a brother or sister be naked, and in lack of daily food, and one of you say unto them, Go in peace, be ye warmed and filled, and yet ye give them not the things needful to the body, what doth it profit? Even so faith, if it have not works, is dead in itself. Yea, a man will say, Thou hast faith, and I have works shew me thy faith apart from thy works, and I by my works will shew thee my faith. Thou believest that God is one; thou doest well. the devils also believe, and shudder. But wilt thou know, O vain man, that faith apart from works is barren! Was not Abraham our father justified by works, in that he offered up Isaac his son upon the altar? Thou seest that faith wrought with his works, and by works was faith made perfect · and the Scripture was fulfilled which saith, And Abraham believed God, and it was reckoned unto him for righteousness, and he was called the friend of God Ye see that by works a man is justified, and not only by faith. And in like manner was not also Rahab the harlot justified by works, in that she received the messengers, and sent them out another way? For as the body apart from the spirit is dead, even so faith apart from works is dead "—JAS ii. 14-26

I.—INTRODUCTION.

S. JAMES is writing a letter, but it is to people whom he has taught. He is writing from living experience as a teacher accustomed to be questioned and contradicted in the contentious atmosphere of the synagogue. He has striven to inspire a dread of doomsday, he has maintained for all the need of mercy, he has concluded *mercy triumphs over judgment*. He hears at once those muttering—'Faith excuses from judgment, else, how are we in better case than Samaritans or idolaters?' He answers at once. 'Faith does not excuse from judgment, for faith can only be proved by works; and therefore your works must be brought to judgment in order that your faith may be established. Much that is called Faith, and has no other name, may be of such a nature that it does not justify—does not do anything—for it is dead.'

He has already told his disciples, *Be ye doers of the word, and not hearers only;* but he has carefully explained the importance of the spirit in which they work. He has condemned the mere formalist who thought that he might be saved by correct ritual, and the mere philanthropist whose works were not done for God. He has shown that good works cannot save a man, and he has called on all to seek for mercy. Now he turns sharply to deal with errors in an opposite direction. Instead of the mere formalist, he sees the man of formulæ proclaiming, "I believe in One God," and doing nothing to justify that belief. Instead of the mere philanthropist, he sees the emotional person full of fine feelings and unctuous sayings, who helps his neighbours only with words. Instead of the careful accumulator of merit, boasting of his righteousness as if he had earned salvation for himself, he sees the man who boasts of his faith and contemns good works as if it were more for the glory of God that he should be saved in his sins. These men, too, need to be warned that Faith does not abrogate *the Royal Law*, and S. James sets out to undermine their position by establishing the intimate relationship between *Faith and Works*.

II.—Various Ways of Regarding Faith and their Relation to the Argument.

Faith is a force that cannot be defined. It is like Love and Reason: we know when we have it, we recognize its results in others, but we cannot account for it. Now all words that cannot be defined are capable of indefinite sense development, and this often leads to confusion of thought. In consequence it will be well to take a general description of Faith, and then consider its meaning according to different categories.

Faith may be described as the Power by which we believe something that we cannot prove on the authority of somebody who merits our trust; and so Christian Faith is the power by which we believe in the revelation of God on the authority of Jesus Christ. Now it is obvious that those accepting this description will interpret it in a somewhat different way according to the importance which they attach to one or other of the terms.

(*a*) For some men the important factor in faith will be the assent which is given to the revelation received on authority. But this assent may be the result of inherited prejudice, may be given from apathy, may be purely notional or may express conviction. The conviction in turn may be intellectual, moral, or both. It may be the effect of a moment's inspiration, it may be the mere memory of such an inspiration in the past, or it may be a habit of the soul. The word Faith will be used in all these cases, but the faith will have very different values. Now the Faith by which " we stand,"[1] and the Faith which "removes mountains,"[2] comes from habitual

---

[1] 2 Cor. 1. 24.   [2] 1 Cor xiii. 2

conviction, and so for many faith and conviction are synonymous. Now, it is obvious that such faith must be the source of action, for what a man really believes determines his doings in more cases than he is aware of. Our Lord told us what Faith as a grain of mustard seed could do.[1] He nowhere tells us of a Faith that can do nothing.

(b) Secondly, many will speculate on the power to believe, which S. Paul reckons as one of "the greater gifts"[2] supernaturally vouchsafed by God. It must be carefully distinguished from "the will to believe" if we would be true to recorded cases of many conversions. This power is given in many ways. It may be received in an instant, seizing on one who had before no will to believe, and transforming his life. Such was the experience of S. Paul. It may be imparted as a grain of mustard seed,[3] and grow by prayer and effort: so it was with the Apostles who prayed, "Lord, increase our faith."[4] It may be the reward of those contemplative souls who *peer into the law of liberty and continue therein,* and the result in an ever increasing insight into spiritual facts and principles. Was not this the interior history of S. John the Divine? But, however given, we may trace its action in the "assurance" which results, the assurance which says, "Let God be true, and every man a liar."[5] This assurance is neither quiescent nor merely acquiescent, it is a Power that must express itself, and therefore we are right to conclude that *Faith without works is dead.*

(c) Again, it is quite possible to think first of the

---

[1] Matt xvii. 20; Luke xvii. 6.
[2] 1 Cor. xii. 31
[3] Mark iv. 31.
[4] Luke xvii. 5.
[5] Rom iii. 4

Revelation to which the assent is given. A man says "my faith," meaning the body of his beliefs, or "the Faith," meaning the things to be believed. Now, a correct Faith is of the utmost importance: first, because we believe that Our Lord and His Apostles did not teach without a purpose; secondly, because conscious heresy indicates self-will; and thirdly, because error in belief must lead ultimately to erroneous conduct. But considering Faith from this point of view, it is very apt to degenerate into being an equivalent for mere belief, and as S. James says, *Devils believe and tremble.* Before such belief can really become Faith in the religious sense, the emotions have to be called into play. "It is with the heart man believeth unto righteousness."[1] When the heart as well as the head has received the creed, Faith comes to be looked upon as an instrument for action. So the eleventh chapter of Hebrews, on the power of Faith,[2] resolves itself into a catalogue of good works; and so S. James compares Faith to the body and its activities to the soul, for action is a condition of life, and the best of all truths without action is as dead as the book in which it is written

(*d*) Fourthly, many pass on from the Revelation received to the Authority from whom it is received, and who summed it up in His own Person. For them the essence of faith lies in the act of self-surrender to Our Lord: they have "Faith in Christ." For them the act is rather of the Will than of the head or the heart, though the whole man co-operates. The power to make this act comes from without, it expresses itself in convictions, and finds its justification in the revelation.

[1] Rom. x 10.   [2] Heb. xi.

In this sense Faith is the basal act of religion, for by self-surrender alone is it conceivable that man should enter into the life of God. So faith in Christ comes to imply trust and loyalty. But you do not trust a person unless you believe him, nor can you be loyal unless you obey his commandments. So once more *the Royal Law* becomes operative, and works become the final test of the Faith being real.

(*e*) Lastly, for many the really distinguishing factor in Faith is that it consists in belief of what cannot be proved. Considering that we all begin to act before we can understand, and all accept the greater part of our knowledge on the authority of others, that none of us can account for half the things that we use, or prove satisfactorily why we act as we do, it is manifest that Faith in this sense is a necessity. And what is true of our connexion with a world too big for our comprehension, must be *a fortiori* more true of the God by whom the world was created. "Man cannot by searching find out God,"[1] and can only know about Him what He has chosen to reveal, and that revelation can in consequence only be received on authority. Faith in this sense may range from blind credulity up to a conclusion drawn from premises in themselves highly probable. There is a great distance, but no gulf, between the faith of the charcoal-burner and the faith of a Pascal. But for people who approach religion with an ever-present sense that it lacks proof, Faith must ever be of the nature of an experiment. They make what they call "ventures of Faith," and explain their growth in certitude by the fact that experience has verified their ven-

[1] Job xi 7

tures. As they proceed, Faith for them becomes synonymous with knowledge, and few men willingly waste their time in proving what they know. Our Lord has promised, "They that do the works shall know of the doctrine";[1] and so approaching the subject from this standpoint, we reach the same conclusion that Faith and Works in life cannot be separated—they act and react on one another.

III.—S. James's Use of the Word Faith.

These various mental attitudes towards the phenomenon of faith are not inconsistent one with another, and the same writer will approach the subject now from one side and now from another. When S. James wrote, the word had been already used in Rabbinic controversies in a variety of senses. S. James, in consequence, like a practical man, uninterested in speculation, writing before the controversy on justification had arisen, naturally uses the word when he wants it in any sense which his readers would understand. He could not anticipate a time when scholars with a passion for labels would wish to distinguish his conception of faith from that of S. Paul, S. Peter or S. John. Considering the amount of misunderstanding which has arisen from an attempt to credit each New Testament writer with an independent theology, it is interesting to note that S. James, apart from the passage before us, only uses the word *Faith* five times, and every time with a different connotation.

(*a*) He tells *how the prayer of faith shall save the sick*,[2]

---

[1] John vii 17 [2] Jas v 15

and illustrates the power of such a prayer by the unshaken conviction of Elijah. (*b*) He asks, *Hath not God chosen the poor in this world rich in faith?*[1] and here faith is the supernatural power bestowed by God. (*c*) He warns, *Hold not the Faith of our Lord Jesus Christ, the Glory, in respect of persons;*[2] and though the Faith here appealed to is objective, it is clear that he must have recognized Faith as meaning the apprehension of a Creed. (*d*) He calls on his disciples to *ask in faith;*[3] and we saw in Lecture II. how the word is used in the sense of moral submission. (*e*) Lastly, he argues that *the proof (i e., trying) of your faith worketh patience;* and here Faith is certainly regarded as opposed to demonstration and as growing by experiment and trial

Hence it seems clear that the word meant for S. James what it meant for other New Testament writers, and it also seems clear that from whichever standpoint the subject is approached, S. James is justified in maintaining that Faith, if genuine, must result in works.

S. James, however, is also ready, as in this passage, to use the word when the Faith in question was not genuine, but spurious. How could he help himself? There was no other word to use. He was face to face with many who boasted of their faith, and he does not waste his time by arguing with them as to the nature of that faith. Like a practical man, he proposes a practical test, and asks, *What doth it profit?* To show that what they call Faith was not Faith as he regarded it, he uses the article and writes $\dot{\eta}\ \pi\iota\sigma\tau\iota\varsigma$. The

[1] Jas ii. 5. [2] Jas. ii 1. [3] Jas i. 6

Revisers translate *that faith*, while the Corbey manuscript and the Speculum read "fides sola."[1]

Out of many kinds of spurious Faith five may be selected as having some bearing on the passage under discussion, and it will be seen that when brought to S. James's test they are found to be wanting, being unfruitful. (*a*) Thinking of Faith as conviction, a man may claim to have faith, because, having accepted the Creed with indifference, he has never been tempted to doubt. (*b*) Thinking of Faith as grace from God, men may delude themselves into thinking that they have it, when they are merely under the influence of somebody else's emotional excitement. (*c*) Thinking of Faith as the genuine apprehension of a Creed, a controversial dogmatist may imagine himself to have apprehended, because he can defend his position with dialectical skill. (*d*) Remembering Faith necessitates self-surrender, we have to beware of the mysticism that ends in self-pleasing and laziness, in dreams and hazy thoughts about being in tune with the infinite. (*e*) Lastly, whereas true Faith is ever a belief in what cannot be proved, there is also a purely superstitious faith possessed by those who, while they cannot conquer their sense that religion is true, are far from desiring to be labourers with God and only wish to escape from Him. This is a fear of the Lord that is not the beginning of wisdom, but only leads to destruction.

[1] Jas. ii 14.

IV.—S. James and the Controversialists.

Let us now try to imagine S. James as he seems to imagine himself, facing a crowd of disputants, all zealous for what Philo, a typical Jew of the Dispersion, calls "the Queen of virtues"—Faith. They are his brethren. He does not doubt their sincerity, or argue as to the meaning of the word. He probably knows that many are merely repeating like parrots the lessons of the synagogues, and have never thought out whither those lessons might lead. He at least is a practical man. He knows no doctrine that is not the source of action. He has all a practical man's impatience for abstract discussion. For him there is but one question, *What doth it profit?*

What does it profit, my brethren, if a man say that he hath faith and hath not works? Can that faith save him? Our Lord had taught S. James, "By their fruits ye shall know them."[1] He had also taught that the branch which did not bear fruit should be cut out of the vine and cast into the fire.[2] So he inquires of each, Is your faith fruitful? A man confesses he has faith without works. S. James asks again: Can the faith that is not profitable to others be profitable to you? can it save you? He expects the answer, No; but it was not likely to be the answer he would receive. The Fourth Book of Esdras teaches that "the seal of eternal life is set on those who have treasured up the faith," and Justin, in his dialogue with Trypho the Jew, argues: "You and others like you deceive yourselves with words, saying that, though you should

[1] Matt. vii. 16.   [2] John xv. 6

Faith and Works 143

be sinners, yet, because you know God, the Lord will not impute sin to you."[1] The opinion was general and remained so. Maimonides, no doubt, reports the tradition of orthodox Judaism when he maintains: "So soon as a man has mastered the thirteen heads of the faith, firmly believing therein, he is to be loved and forgiven and treated in all respects as a brother, and though he may have sinned in every possible way, he is indeed an erring Israelite, and is punished accordingly, but still he inherits eternal life."

S. Paul was, later on, to understand quite clearly that his own doctrine as to Faith might be distorted so as to countenance antinomianism. He faces the question, "Shall we continue in sin that grace may abound?"[2] and answers, "God forbid!" But many since S. Paul have rested in their faith, in their assurance of salvation, in their election or predestination, and argued that *the Law of Liberty* not only excused them from good works, but constituted them chartered libertines. S. Paul and S. James were then at one on the general question. The former writes: "Though I have all faith so that I could remove mountains, and have not charity, I am nothing."[3]

S. James, however, was not working out a system of theology; he was dealing with individuals in danger of the judgment. He knows that none of them think of faith in the same way, and that no two of them really agree together, although they are united in maintaining that faith saves irrespective of works. So he turns first to one and then to another with words

[1] Trypho, 370 D   [2] Rom vi 1.
[3] 1 Cor. xiii 2.

adapted to his individual case. He meets each on his own ground and treats him in a new way. Here is a man to be convicted by an illustration, here a second to be defeated in debate, here a third to be crushed by irony. With a fourth and fifth he will take the Scriptures, and prove them wrong out of their chosen texts. His own conclusion he repeats again and again. That alone does not vary.

(*a*) First, then, there are those who confuse faith with belief. They know all the correct phrases of their religion, and are satisfied with repeating them unctuously on appropriate occasions. They may not be conscious hypocrites, but the trite words have for them no real meaning; they suggest actions which are not performed. To them S. James puts an hypothetical case, and he chooses one appropriate to a time of famine, or when the famine time was only just passed. *If a brother or sister be naked and in lack of daily food, and one of you say unto them, Go in peace, be ye warmed and filled, and yet ye give them not the things which be needful, what doth it profit?* Imagine how hope leapt in the heart of those suppliants as they listened to the pleasant-speaking philanthropist conducting them to the door! Imagine, too, their rage and mortification when they found themselves still naked, still starving, with the door locked against them! They at any rate knew how far the words profited, and for the sake of their Christianity the pious wishes had better not have been uttered. The philanthropist, however, has expressed his faith. It comes to this—God cares, and God will provide for the poor, but not through me. He believes in God, but not that he is a "labourer together with

Faith and Works

God."[1] He is a pious man and wishes all men well, while they die for lack of his assistance. S. James has put his case. Profession without practice is useless; *even so Faith, if it hath not works, is dead*. In saying this, S. James says more than that Faith without works is non-existent. The Faith may have been alive once. It has died for lack of exercise. A mere form survives, like a body without breath; and a dead thing soon becomes corrupt—a thing for loathing and a source of danger.

(*b*) S. James turns to another member of the group. Here is a man who restricts Faith to the Grace infused by God. He can quite well remember his conversion: the earnestness of some Apostle, the tense excitement of the audience, and the glad shout with which he proclaimed himself a changed man. Remembering the event, he is now assured of his salvation, and feels both comfortable and superior. God has looked upon him, saved him according to His own good pleasure, and there is nothing for him to do. He despises good works, and sneers at those who do them. He asks, ' Do they think that they are meriting salvation ?' Far from faith and works being inseparable, he regards them as opposed, as two ways of salvation ; the way of works is a blind alley, while the way of faith is straight to the doors of Heaven. To answer him, S. James introduces a third person into the debate who can speak with a freedom beneath the dignity of an Apostle—one who does not mind appealing to his own works, which S. James himself would shrink from doing. *Yea, a man will say, Thou hast faith and I have works: show me thy*

[1] 1 Cor. iii. 9

faith apart from thy works, and I by my works will show thee my faith. Faith as a power can only be known by its results, and in consequence the challenge is one that cannot be accepted.

(c) The man is reduced to silence, but one standing by appears to support him. He says: " Your argument shows confusion of thought. Acts of faith are not deeds of mercy; the true work of Faith is the confession of a Creed. He looks at the phylactery he is wearing. It contains the verse from Deuteronomy,[1] the Shema, which was recited morning and evening by every Jew. He has been taught that " He who reads the Shema with scrupulous precision as regards its several letters cools Gehinnon ";[2] and also that " whosoever (in saying the Shema) prolongs the utterance of the word *one* shall have his days and years prolonged to him."[3] He is self-confident and contemptuous; but the supporter of S. James crushes him with the retort, *Thou believest that God is one, thou doest well: the Devils also believe and shudder.*

When S. James put these words into the mouth of his fictitious debater, he was no doubt remembering that Sabbath day at Capernaum years before when the Devils spoke through the man possessed, saying: "I know Thee who Thou art, the Holy One of God."[4] Again and again Devils confessed Our Lord before the disciples, and long before S. James had learned to believe in Him. He remembered, too, how he had heard: "Not everyone that saith unto Me, Lord,

---
[1] Deut. vi 4
[2] Berakhoth, p. 156, quoted in Taylor, *Jewish Fathers*, p. 52.
[3] *Ibid*, p 13, B quoted in Knowling
[4] Mark 1 24; *cf.* iii. 24, Luke iv 34

Lord, shall enter into the Kingdom of Heaven: but he that doeth the will of My Father which is in Heaven."[1]

So S. James concludes, *Wilt thou know, O vain man, that faith apart from works is barren?* The *vain man* is Raca, the futile person empty within, and making a brave show without. He is like the barren fig-tree with nothing but leaves; and the barren fig-tree received a curse and not a blessing.[2]

(d) The sharp-witted debater is withdrawn, as a more serious-minded inquirer arises to quote the text: *Abraham believed the Lord, and it was counted to him for righteousness.* Here is a problem for the Schools, and it is fitting that the answer should be authoritative.

The words occur in the fifteenth chapter of Genesis. There Abraham, the old man, complained to God that he was childless,[3] and was shown the multitude of stars, with the assurance, "so shall thy seed be."[4] He trusted in God's promise when fulfilment seemed impossible, and *it was counted to him for righteousness.*[5] Here faith is only concerned with trust, and there is no hint of any work to be performed.

When the dying Mattathias quoted the text to his sons,[6] there was no controversy on the subject. Abraham is one good man among many, and the burden of the speech is zeal for the Law. But as time went on the verse became a touchstone of controversy. Lightfoot[7] notes that in the works of Philo this text is commented on no less than ten times; while the view of orthodox Jews is no doubt preserved for us in the

---

[1] Matt. vii. 21 [2] Mark xi 13, 14. [3] Gen. xv. 3.
[4] Gen. xv. 5. [5] Gen. xv 6. [6] 1 Macc ii. 52
[7] *Galatians*, p 152.

Talmudic treatise "Mechilta." There it is said: "Abraham our Father inherited this world and the world to come, solely by the merit of faith, whereby he believed in the Lord; for it is said, *And he believed in the Lord, and He counted it to him for righteousness.*"

S. James, however, is not disputing as to how or why a man is accounted righteous, but as to how a righteous man will behave. So he turns to his questioner, and asks him to look on to another primary passage for Jewish theology—*Was not Abraham our Father justified by works, in that he offered up Isaac his son upon the altar?*[1] He seems to argue: Granting the point you wish to make, note that the real evidence for Abraham's faith lies in his subsequent conduct. His faith did not end with trusting that God would do everything for him without requiring anything from him. He was ready to comply with a demand for an awful sacrifice. *Thou seest that Faith wrought with his works, and by works was Faith made perfect.* Faith was the necessary antecedent, and the offering its consequence; but, further, when a true faith is acted on, faith itself is confirmed. Abraham's faith had been imperfect when he first received the promise, for he asked a sign.[2] So S. James is justified in saying, *You see how the Scripture was fulfilled, which saith, And Abraham believed God, and it was counted to him for righteousness.* God treats us beforehand, as He the Omniscient sees that we are becoming.

Then S. James, still speaking of Abraham, says: *And he was called the friend of God.* In our English Bibles Abraham is twice called *God's Friend*,[3] but the Hebrew barely countenances the translation, and the LXX.,

[1] Gen. xxii. 1-19 [2] Gen. xv. 8. [3] 2 Chron xx. 7, Isa. xli 8.

with which S. James was no doubt familiar, reads:
" Abraham My beloved," and " Abraham whom I have
loved." There are, however, copies of the LXX. which
have " friend " in the first passage, and Symmachus has
it in the second.

S. James does not profess to be quoting Scripture, and
the title was no doubt current, for it slips into Philo's
citation of Genesis xviii. 17; while the Arabs of to-day
always speak of Abraham as El Khalil, the friend of
God, without any indebtedness to S. James. But why
is the title used here? Does it not add a point to S.
James's argument? A son may be merely submissive and
receptive: a friend receives, gives, and co-operates. In
calling Abraham *the friend of God*, he emphasizes the
fact that he was not merely a passive receiver, but one
who was willing to act with, and sacrifice his best for,
the God in whom he trusted. S. James, it will be
noted, does not deny that faith justifies; his argument
is directed against a spurious faith, common now as
then, which causes a man to allege his trust in God as
an excuse for his own carelessness and inaction. This
sort of faith, he says, is not covered by the text in
Genesis, for Abraham acted in accordance with his
belief. Therefore *you see that by works a man is justified,
and not only by faith*.

(*e*) But there is still another objector to deal with,
and we may imagine him speaking as follows:

' Whether you are right or wrong in your interpretation of the text, you are certainly correct when you say
that Abraham was a righteous man, the friend of God,
who did many good works. But now let us take the
case of Rahab. She was not righteous, but a harlot.

She was not a friend of God, she had no real knowledge of Him. She was a heathen, a stranger, and outside the covenant of grace; yet she believed in what she could not prove—she had faith, and therefore was saved. We still think of her as one of the four fair women. Tradition says she was the mother of eight prophets, and she appears in the genealogy of Our Lord.[1] How do you apply your doctrine as to works in this case? She was not like Father Abraham: she offered no sacrifice.'

S. James accepts this instance also. He can appeal to the story. Jericho was straitly shut up, the terror of the Lord was upon the people.[2] They had heard of the wondrous things that the Lord had wrought, and their hearts melted because of them. But there was one woman, a harlot, whom this superstitious fear stirred to action. Granted that she knew nothing of the God of Israel except by report, granted that she could give no rational account of the faith that possessed her, she was yet willing to make the experiment of co-operating in the cause of the God of Israel. She did not offer sacrifice like Abraham, she knew nothing of worship or ritual; but she showed kindness to the strangers, she risked her life for them, and she pinned her faith to the scarlet cord.[3] Therefore S. James can write: Not only Abraham, but, *in like manner, was not Rahab the harlot justified by works, in that she received the messengers, and sent them out another way?* She had not only received the Spies as guests,[4] she had refused to give them up, she had thrust them forth from the

---

[1] Matt i. 5
[2] Josh vi 1, *cf* ii 9-11
[3] Josh. ii 18.
[4] Josh. ii. 3.

Faith and Works

window, she had sent them another way in order to avoid pursuit.[1] Here, then, says S. James, were works, the product of faith. The faith was very imperfect, unenlightened, but it saved Rahab because it was real. It was real because it manifested itself in works. The superstitious fear of the unknown did not save the men of Jericho; for, though they shared Rahab's faith, they shut themselves up in the vain hope of escaping from God's wrath.

So S. James moves on to his invariable conclusion, which he expresses this time through a strange figure—*For as the body apart from the spirit is dead, even so faith apart from works is dead also.* We should more naturally think of faith as the spirit, and of works as the body by which the spirit was manifested.

But for S. James faith was the source, the means, the ground of action. It was only through faith that he could conceive of works in accordance with *the Royal Law* being performed. Therefore faith is best compared to the body. But the spirit, the life, is only known by its power to act, and therefore works are best compared with the spirit. It is only by acts of faith that faith is proved to be alive, and where there are no acts, the faith is like a corpse that will breed corruption and disease. A barren orthodoxy has ever been the Devil's best argument against the truth of religion. He, too, asks, *What doth it profit?* and the Church dies if it can only give a reason for her faith in terms of logic, and cannot answer the challenge by acts in the sphere of life.

[1] Josh ii. 16.

V.—S. James and S. Paul.

So far the positive value of S. James's argument has been insisted on. It remains to be seen how it needs to be safeguarded, and in what directions it was capable of being perverted. Believing that S. Paul wrote after S. James, when new problems had arisen, we should look to his epistles for a comment, even if we believe, what is improbable, that he had never read the Epistle of S. James. For the two men, sharing the same faith, were in character, temperament, and experience singularly different, and therefore naturally inclined to see the same facts from a different standpoint, and to say the same creed with a different emphasis.

S. James had known Our Lord from His childhood: He had loved Him, followed Him, and been perplexed by His actions and His words.[1] Belief in Him and His Divine claims had come slowly. S. James had not been convinced until after the Resurrection.[2] For him the humanity of Jesus was an ever-present memory, and the conduct of Jesus was the source of his inspiration. He had come to know Him as Lord and Christ, he had come to know himself as His servant, and he had come to see in Him the fulfilment of those Scriptures which he had pondered from his youth up. But there had been no violent break in his life, and no change in his surroundings. The converts to whom he wrote had accepted Jesus as the Messiah. They, too, had found that the Gospel was implicit in the Scriptures; and, intellectually unperplexed, they

---

[1] Matt. xii. 46, John vii. 5. [2] 1 Cor xv. 7.

Faith and Works

were following with many backslidings in the way of righteousness.

S. Paul, on the other hand, had met with Our Lord in the supernatural sphere.[1] Before, he had only known Him by report. His conversion had been a revolution. It had diverted for ever the current of his thoughts, and given an altogether new direction to his activities. It had meant for him a death and a new life. He had been buried with Christ in Baptism, and risen again with Him to newness of life.[2] Dominated by such an experience, it was natural for him to work, and he says, "I laboured more abundantly than they all";[3] but it was "the Grace of God" which enabled him to labour, and the fact amazed him to the end that he was "in Christ," though he had struggled against Him. To explain that fact was the motive of his life. Living in close contact with the Greek world, conscious of its questioning spirit, he could not, like S. James, assume a Creed and take it for granted. To his converts all was new, and they were urgent with many hard questions; they were easily diverted by any plausible theory. They were not familiar with the Scriptures from their youth, and they had not inherited the results of a national training which had extended over some two thousand years.

In consequence, not only should we be prepared for a difference of treatment, but we should expect that an epistle intended for Jewish converts might contain things liable to be misunderstood by Gentile readers. Secondly, knowing as we do how suspicious Jewish

---

[1] Acts ix 3, 1 Cor. xv 8.   [2] Rom. vi 4, Col. ii. 12.
[3] 1 Cor. xv. 10.

converts were of S. Paul's missionary propaganda, we should not be surprised that a letter of S. James written to themselves should be used for controversial purposes.

So it came to pass that when the Legalist controversy was at its height, Jews made use of the teaching of S. James on works to establish the necessity for "works of the Law," while puzzled Gentiles associated his words with a doctrine of merit, contending for what S. Paul calls "dead works"—that is, works done apart from Faith. So also, as controversies arose as to the Person of Our Lord, the value of His death and the reality of His resurrection, many were led impatiently to contemn Theology and maintain that conduct and not creed was a matter of importance. Those inclined to turn Religion into a moral philosophy no doubt turned on Pauline disciples, reminding them that *Devils also believe and shudder*. These two controversies finally centred in a third when S. Paul promulgated his doctrine of justification by faith, and it was natural that his opponents should quote S. James against him, though S. James had written before the controversy began.

As regards the first controversy, it is only fair to note that S. James speaks of *works* without clearly defining his meaning. It ought, no doubt, to be obvious that he was speaking of acts of faith done in accordance with *the Royal Law*, but by isolating the passage the Judaizers were able to interpret *works* as equivalent to "works of the Law." S. James as a Jew, writing to Jews, probably saw no necessity for the distinction. He was himself obedient to the Jewish

Faith and Works

ritual, and expected his converts to be so also. It was sufficient for him to warn them not *to think themselves religious* in consequence. But for S. Paul, writing to Gentiles, the distinction between "good works" and "works of the Law" was of the first importance. He follows closely on S. James when he writes: "Not the hearers of the Law are just before God, but the doers of the Law shall be justified."[1] He does not contradict S. James's assertion, *we are justified by works, and not by faith only*, when he writes, "We are justified by faith without the works of the law";[2] but he is in conflict with a misunderstanding of S. James. Far from disagreeing with S. James's teaching as to works, his Epistles of all periods show an essential agreement. So he prays that the Thessalonians may be established "in every good word and work,"[3] and "by God's grace," he tells the Corinthians, that they "may abound in every good work."[4] He prays that the Colossians "might walk worthy of the Lord unto all pleasing, being fruitful in every good work";[5] and, finally, to Titus he sends his parting exhortation: "This is a faithful saying, and these things I will that thou affirm constantly, that they which have believed in God may be careful to maintain good works."[6]

Turning to the second controversy, we know that there were many who found in S. Paul's theology words hard to be understood.[7] They could take refuge with S. James, and perhaps came to regard him as a purely ethical teacher, protesting against all theology.

---

[1] Rom ii. 13
[2] Rom iii 28; Gal. ii. 16.
[3] 2 Thess ii 17.
[4] 2 Cor ix. 8
[5] Col i. 10.
[6] Titus iii 8.
[7] 2 Pet iii 16

This view has found many exponents in our own day. But we have to remember that S. James was writing to Christians, and writing at so early a date that theological controversy had scarcely arisen. Yet he does write as *the bond-slave of Jesus Christ* to those who had been *begotten by the word of truth*, with a sure confidence of *the coming of the Lord*, and of the awful judgment that is to be.[1] Both he and his correspondents had thought their faith of sufficient importance to embrace, because of it, a life of persecution and *manifold temptations*. He believes in prayer, repentance, and grace. He is the direct exponent of two Sacraments.[2] For him *the Faith of Our Lord Jesus Christ* decides all questions; and even in this passage Faith is assumed to underlie the Christian Life and to be the ground of every work. In fact, we may conclude that this Epistle would be unintelligible apart from a Christian context, although the immediate object of S. James was not to insist on the Creed but on its practice.

Granting, then, that there is a very real agreement between S. James and S. Paul on the necessity of both faith and works, it only remains to be seen if their disagreement on justification is fundamental or only verbal.

Had S. James been writing after S. Paul, he might have avoided the use of the verb to justify ($\delta\iota\kappa\alpha\iota o\hat{\upsilon}\nu$); and he could not possibly have imagined that he had answered S. Paul's argument by his words relating to Abraham. It is more probable that he used the word before it had acquired its sense in technical

[1] Jas v. 8, 9   [2] Jas v 14-16

Faith and Works

theology; and we can well understand how S. Paul, in establishing his doctrine, was embarrassed by having S. James quoted against him. His antagonists were quoting S. James in a different context, and S. Paul has no difficulty in showing that the argument in this connexion can be rebutted.

It seems clear that S. James is not formulating a doctrine of justification, but uses the word *justify* incidentally and in a popular sense. Here, he argues, are men professing faith, but how do they justify that profession? The only evidence that they can offer is their works. It is true, he goes on, in answer to one objection, that Abraham is accounted righteous the moment that he believes; but it is by the God who knows beforehand the result of that belief, and the Scripture is fulfilled when the work is done. God, he argues, justifies before works, and is justified in doing so by the works. What S. James wants is evidence of justification; he is not thinking of why a man is justified, or how. Thinking, then, of justification as the pronouncement of an Omniscient judge in respect of actions yet to be performed, it matters very little whether we speak of justification by faith or justification by works, so long as we remember that faith without works and works without faith are alike unavailing.

But, on the other hand, there was a sense in which S. James's statement was open to objection, not because it was false, but because it might be misunderstood. By isolating the passage it would be possible to maintain a doctrine of human merit, of man's earning salvation for himself.

S. Paul, therefore, takes the instance of Abraham,[1] and begins by showing that the promise was made to him irrespective of works; and he goes on to show that if Abraham was justified (accounted righteous) by works, he had earned his reward, and it was no longer God's gift, but his right.[2] It is needless to point out that S. James had not said that Abraham's offering merited his justification. He had only maintained that it was the evidence of his being justified, and issued in the confirmation of the faith that justifies. *Faith wrought with his works, and by works was faith made perfect.*

[1] Rom. iv. [2] Rom. iv. 4

LECTURE IX

TEACHERS

" Be not many teachers, my brethren, knowing that we shall receive heavier judgment. For in many things we all stumble "—JAS. iii. 1, 2.

I.—CONNEXION OF THOUGHT.

S. JAMES never quotes the Gospels, because they were not written when he wrote, but he had heard with his own ears many of the discourses they report, and pondered their significance. They underlie his thought, and condition the sequence of his ideas. For instance, if we turn to the twenty-third chapter of S. Matthew, we shall find in the first twelve verses the headings to much in this Epistle. Our Lord bids His disciples to "observe and do" whatsoever those "sitting in Moses' seat"[1] commanded; and S. James counsels his disciples to *be doers of the word, and not hearers only.* Our Lord speaks plainly concerning the tyranny of legal customs and traditions, and accuses the Pharisees of unwillingness to share the burdens which they impose.[2] Instead of caring for the fatherless and widows, they are denounced for "devouring widows' houses,"[3] while "for pretence they make long prayers." So S. James tells the *doers of the word* not to think too highly of them-

---

[1] Matt. xxiii. 2.   [2] Matt. xxiii. 4.
[3] Mark xii. 40.   Matt. xxiii 14 is omitted in R.V.

selves, because of ritual correctness, but *to visit the fatherless and widows in their affliction*. Our Lord condemns those who "love the uppermost rooms at feasts and the chief seats in the synagogues";[1] and S. James, going on to denounce *respect of persons*, takes as his illustration the allotment of seats in the Christian assembly. Our Lord noted those who *say* and do not, while they "make broad their phylacteries and enlarge the borders of their garments";[2] S. James declares that profession without practice is useless, and how the very words of the Shema[3] inscribed on phylacteries might be professed by Devils. Our Lord counsels: "Be not ye called Rabbi, for one is your teacher";[4] so S. James proceeds, *Be not many teachers* In the same speech, although not in the same connexion, Our Lord, as reported by S. Mark and S. Luke, speaks of "the greater condemnation"[5] ($περισσότερον\ κρίμα$), and S. James also speaks of the *greater condemnation* ($μεῖζον\ κρίμα$). Finally, we shall see how S. James passes on to inculcate humility, coming to the same conclusion as Our Lord in His discourse.[6]

The similar succession of thought cannot be wholly accidental, but it is probably altogether undesigned. S. James was not delivering a sermon from a text, but memory accounts for his association of ideas. He had heard Our Lord speak of the sins of the Synagogue, and he finds the same sins in the Infant Church. The same people passing from one to the other showed the same characteristics: there was a persistence of old habits and a tendency to old temptations. A Jew,

---

[1] Matt. xxiii. 6.   [2] Matt xxiii 5   [3] Deut. vi. 4, 5
[4] Matt. xxiii. 8.   [5] Mark xii 40; Luke xx. 47   [6] Matt xxiii 12.

convinced that he must not only profess faith in Christ, but work for Him, naturally turned to teaching, and found a congenial occupation in setting others right. The desire to teach is, however, a snare that besets new converts. They are so full of their new knowledge and new hope, that they never ask themselves whether they are qualified to instruct others. Even S. Paul probably made this mistake when he began preaching in the synagogues of Damascus. He felt his need for preparation and entered into the wilderness, and yet his second attempt in Damascus only stirred up enmity. He then proceeded to Jerusalem, where again he was unsuccessful. He returned to Tarsus, and awaited his call from one having authority—S. Barnabas.[1] So the greatest of all teachers was taught by failure.

II.—The Jewish Teacher, or Rabbi.

But in order fully to understand the temptation to teach, and the need of S. James' warning it is necessary to remember the position of the teacher in the Synagogue and Early Church.

Most honourable careers were closed to the Jew by his religion or his race. Among his own people one career only remained open to every one. It was that of the teacher or Rabbi. No one was so esteemed as the successful teacher. Crowds flocked to hear him instruct or dispute. He went from one synagogue to another, and was loaded with gifts. Sometimes he founded a school, and was followed by troops of devout

[1] Acts ix. 20-25, 29 ; xxii. 18 ; Gal. i 17, 21, 22 , Acts xi 25, 26.

and enthusiastic disciples. The reverence paid him was well-nigh idolatrous, and it was explicitly taught that a man might as well defy the Shekinah as quarrel with his Rabbi. So Jesus, the son of Sirach, says of the true teacher: " Nations shall shew forth his wisdom, and the congregation shall declare his praise. If he die he shall leave a greater name than a thousand, and if he live he shall increase it." [1]

It is not surprising that recognition as a teacher should have been the natural ambition of a Jew; nor is it surprising that the struggle among many competitors should lead to jealousy, contention, and strife. Such strife, though really for personal pre-eminence, was professedly for the Truth of God's Law, and the conflict was demoralizing both for the teacher and the taught. Nowhere would the divorce between preaching and practice be more apparent and more disastrous than in the case of the eloquent Rabbi, seeking not man's welfare but man's applause.

"Love the work, but strive not after the honour of a teacher," [2] was an admirable Jewish maxim not over well observed. Simeon, the son of the first Gamaliel, thus bitterly sums up his own experience· "All my days I have grown up among the wise, and have not found aught good for a man but silence; not learning, but doing, is the groundwork, and whoso multiplies words occasions sin." [3]

It will be noted that the Rabbi took the work upon himself, and was responsible to no one. He was not called to the office, and he did not, like the Prophet,

---

[1] Ecclus. xxxix. 10, 11.   [2] Pirke Aboth, 1. 10, quoted by Plumtre
[3] Quoted by Knowling.

Teachers

lay claim to inspiration. He might be a Priest or a Levite, but in most cases he was not. His migratory habits usually prevented his being an official of a Synagogue, for the officials were chiefly given to legal and administrative work, and often took but little part in the actual services. The Ruler of the Synagogue indeed presided. He acted as chairman, and called on whom he would to offer prayer, or read the Lessons from the Law and Prophets. He could also appoint anyone to expound or preach, and it was apparently customary to ask any stranger who was present if he had anything to say.[1]

III.—THE TEACHER IN THE EARLY CHURCH.

Now the Church went forth from the Synagogue, and not only took over its system of psalmody, lections, and prayers, but also regulated its meetings as far as possible in the old accustomed way. At Corinth, where the Christians had been heathen, meetings on the Synagogue pattern led to considerable disorder.[2] Everyone wanted to talk at once, and those with special gifts were only too eager to manifest them.[3] Women desired to be heard, and excessive attention was paid to outbursts of excitement and phenomena, like "speaking with tongues."[4] But in the Churches to which S. James was writing we hear of no such disturbances. The members had been disciplined from their youth up in the traditions of the Synagogue. Theirs were the faults of the Synagogue. They took

[1] Luke iv 16; Acts xiii 15, Acts xvii 2
[2] 1 Cor xiv 29-31
[3] 1 Cor. xiv 34.
[4] 1 Cor. xiv 2-28.

too much pleasure in disputation and debate. They were emulous of recognition as teachers.

A teacher, then, in the Early Church was not necessarily a member of an order nor the holder of an office. He might be an Apostle, like S. Paul,[1] or one of the rulers of the Church,[2] or, again, he might be a simple member of the congregation. S. Paul denounces those "desiring to be teachers of the Law, understanding neither what they say, nor whereof they affirm."[3] He decrees, however, that those presbyters are "worthy of double honour," who not only "rule well," but "labour in the word and teaching."[4] By the time of the Didache, Bishops did the works of Prophets and Deacons that of Teachers,[5] but the lay ministry continued: and Hermas speaks disparagingly of "self-appointed teachers," who "praise themselves as having understanding," "senseless though they be."[6] By the third century Demetrius of Alexandria denied the lawfulness of lay teaching, but Alexander and Theoctistus alleged precedents against him, and so Origen was allowed to teach, and at Cæsarea even to preach, while still a layman.

S. Paul, then, in writing to the Corinthians and Ephesians,[7] was not dealing with the organization of the Church, but with the qualifications certain Christians might, by the gift of God, possess "for the perfecting of the saints, for the work of ministering, for the edifying of the Body of Christ." Such gifts S. Paul arranges in the order of their importance, and the order is not in every respect the same, for the gifts vary in importance

---

[1] 1 Tim. i 7. [2] Acts xiii 1; Titus i 9 [3] 1 Tim. i 7.
[4] 1 Tim. v. 17. [5] C. XV. [6] Sim LX. 22
[7] 1 Cor. xii. 28; Eph. iv 11, 12.

according to circumstances. They are not exclusive, and he himself at different times exercised them all. His main argument is that "the Spirit divides to everyone severally as He wills."[1] So the Spirit has not given to every man the power to be an Apostle, a Prophet, a teacher, to work miracles, to heal, to distribute charity, to organize, or to speak with tongues. So we might argue to-day, not everyone is called to be a priest, and among priests not everyone is endowed with powers to be a good preacher, a good pastor, a good confessor, a good scholar, a good catechist, and a good man of business. Such gifts are useful to a priest, few have them all, and a man may be a scholar, a teacher, or a man of business, and yet have no call to the priesthood. We must beware of cross divisions. Order is one thing, office another, and talent a third. A Peer has his order, a Prime Minister his office, a public speaker his talent, but it would not be possible to divide the world into Peers, Prime Ministers, and public speakers; and it is just as impossible to divide the Church into Apostles, Prophets, teachers, miracle workers, healers, almoners, organizers and enthusiasts. The Holy Spirit might give a man a talent for teaching, and the man might exercise the talent with or without authority. The Church might appoint a man with or without the talent to the office of a teacher. Again, the Church might have named one of the orders in her hierarchy teachers, but for this there is no evidence. In fact, when S. James writes, *Be not many teachers*, he disproves any such assumption. For if the teachers had constituted an order, or even in his time been holders

---

[1] 1 Cor. xii. 11.

of an office, his exhortation would have had to run, "Do not ordain," or "Do not appoint many teachers." And if the teachers had been appointed, S. James would have been the last man to tell them not to fulfil their obligations.

IV.—The Teacher To-day.

Interpreting the text in this way it is applicable to our own age. It would be well if many self-appointed teachers, who from press, platform, and pulpit are striving after a reputation for originality, would ponder the third chapter of S. James. The temptation is still with us to shock, to startle, to contradict, to gain disciples, and to gain applause. A love of notoriety is our besetting sin to-day as it was for the Jews of that first age. In consequence, men arise "speaking perverse things that they may draw away disciples after them"[1] The presbyters of the Church, as S. Paul prophesied, are not proof against the temptation. Too many regard their pulpits as places whence to air views and start discussions; too few believe in the "Ecclesia Docens" and the awful responsibilities of those who teach. And, of the hearers, few come to learn; they have ceased to expect teaching, and only require matter for criticism. Impatient of the ancient verities, they live "to hear and tell some new thing." They repudiate authority to revel in authorities. They will not "endure sound doctrine," but "after their own lusts . . . heap to themselves teachers, having itching ears."[2]

[1] Acts xx. 30   [2] 2 Tim. iv. 3.

V.—THE TEACHER'S RESPONSIBILITY TO GOD.

S. James, it will be noted, confesses himself a teacher, but he feels the awful responsibility of his position. He does not minimize the importance of words; for him they are terrible because of their consequences. For him what a man teaches is not a matter of indifference; he holds that what a man believes ought to condition his whole life. He notes the danger for the teacher—*we shall receive the greater condemnation*. He notes the danger for those taught—*for in many things we all stumble*. He sees the necessity for maturity, for men who are τέλειοι, able to control themselves, *able to bridle the whole body*.

But it may be asked, To what do the words *the greater condemnation*,[1] or *the heavier judgment*,[2] refer, and which translation is to be preferred?

Translating τὸ μεῖζον κρίμα as *the heavier judgment*, it may be plausibly argued that the words refer to human reputation. It is a well-known fact that everyone expects a higher standard of life from those who teach than from those who are taught. We naturally judge men in accordance with their professions, and what would be thought venial in a man of the world insures reprobation in the person of a priest. We execrate in a Renaissance Pope what we regard as natural in an Italian despot of the same period. Alexander VI. was not the worst man of his day, but he called himself the Vicar of Christ, while the others fought frankly for their own hands. His was the heavier judgment because his was the higher claim.

[1] A.V.   [2] R.V.

But if this were all that S. James intended, he was merely suggesting a worldly maxim of very dubious morality, counselling men not to profess too much or preach too high a Gospel, for fear that they should suffer in the estimation of their fellows. This cannot be the true interpretation, nor does it fit in well with the context. It is with a man's words that he is here concerned, and he is going on to speak at length as to the perils of speech. He is not for the moment concerned with the man's other conduct. Throughout his Epistle S. James views all things in the light of Doomsday, and the supreme Judge is the only Judge he fears.

In consequence it were better to translate τὸ μεῖζον κρίμα as *the greater or heavier condemnation*, because the words refer to the sentence of God, and not to the opinions of men.

How, then, is *the greater condemnation* to be justified? We have just noted the universal instinct of humanity to judge a man in accordance with his profession, and to be particularly hard on those who transgress a law they would impose on others. S. Paul says such men are "without excuse,"[1] and to this extent the human instinct reflects the Divine judgment. We also noted in Lecture VII. that all men will be judged according to their knowledge and opportunities, so that the fuller grace implies a fuller responsibility. But these teachers were taking on themselves responsibilities to which they had not been called, and they were, in consequence, rashly courting a judgment from which they might have been excused.

[1] Rom ii. 1.

VI.—THE TEACHER'S RESPONSIBILITY FOR MEN.

Had we interpreted τὸ μεῖζον κρίμα as the heavier judgment, it would have been easy to explain, *for in many things we all stumble*, by quoting the words of Portia: "I can easier teach twenty what were good to be done, than be one of the twenty to follow mine own teaching." But as we have decided that the words refer to the condemnation of God, we must suppose S. James to be providing a reason for God's condemnation. He is thinking of human fallibility and the far-reaching effects of error.

Now, while every man must be in some sense responsible for himself, a teacher assumes responsibilities for others also. If he err from the way of truth, he will lose himself; but if he gives false directions to others, their loss will be due to him. Granted that we cannot altogether avoid stumbling, we can at least refrain from offering ourselves as guides on dangerous paths which we have not explored. "If the blind lead the blind, both shall fall into the ditch."[1]

S. James is writing to his brethren. He is not thinking of the heresiarch, or proud rebel against authority. He imputes no ill motive consciously entertained. He is thinking rather of the self-confident and incompetent teacher willing to instruct, but not willing to study, ready "to rush in where angels fear to tread," and expound mysteries, when the wisest are most reticent. How much of the infidelity and agnosticism of the present day is due to the careless teaching in our public

---

[1] Matt. xv. 14

and private schools. Anyone, it is thought, can explain the Bible; and many without any preparation attempt to do so. The Sunday-school teacher, with an unprepared lesson, goes with virtuous self-complacence to her class, and when she is posed with an inconvenient question, answers at random rather than confess she does not know. The rash preacher who reads nothing but a religious newspaper, denounces on its authority a book he has not read, and more than one member of his congregation is irritated by his irrelevant answers to an argument he does not understand. Another preacher adopts the very latest theory, which was never seriously intended, and assures his hearers that "all critics are agreed" on its results. Some explain themselves carelessly, and some delight in paradox. Perhaps they are proud that they walk so securely and keep their balance; but the weak brother loses his head as he follows them, and falls. S. James was not unmindful of the awful warning of Our Lord to those who "shall cause one of these little ones who believe on Me to stumble."[1] He counsels us to be self-controlled and keep a bridle on our tongues.

Viewing his words in this light, it is possible that many will say, Who can be a teacher when the perils are so great? Teaching is a vocation to which God calls men. Those who hear His call may not disobey. S. James confesses himself to be one when he says, *We shall receive the greater condemnation.* He sat down none the less, and wrote the letter on which we are commenting. He does not say: No one must be a teacher,

[1] Mark ix. 42.

but *Be not many teachers*. If you are called, think not so much of the honour, but of the awful responsibility. Remember that judgment in which you shall give account. Be humble where things are doubtful, and do not presume to be over-wise.

LECTURE X

PERILS OF SPEECH

"If any stumbleth not in word, the same is a perfect man, able to bridle the whole body also. Now, if we put the horses' bridles into their mouths, that they may obey us, we turn about their whole body also. Behold, the ships also, though they are so great, and are driven by rough winds, are yet turned about by a very small rudder, whither the impulse of the steersman willeth. So the tongue also is a little member, and boasteth great things Behold, how much wood is kindled by how small a fire! And the tongue is a fire the world of iniquity among our members is the tongue, which defileth the whole body, and setteth on fire the wheel of nature, and is set on fire by hell. For every kind of beasts and birds, of creeping things and things in the sea, is tamed, and hath been tamed by mankind: but the tongue can no man tame, it is a restless evil, it is full of deadly poison. Therewith bless we the Lord and Father, and therewith curse we men, which are made after the likeness of God out of the same mouth cometh forth blessing and cursing My brethren, these things ought not so to be Doth the fountain send forth from the same opening sweet water and bitter? Can a fig-tree, my brethren, yield olives, or a vine figs? Neither can salt water yield sweet."—JAS. III. 2-12

I.—THE IMPORTANCE OF SPEECH.

As the trials of his converts led S. James from considering life as a probation to consider how and why men are tempted; as an improper preference in assigning seats led him to consider *the Royal Law*, and the duty of practising it; so, after warning his disciples as to the dangers of teaching, he passes on to consider the perils of speech and the difficulties in the way of self-control.

He starts with a general proposition. *If a man stumble not in word, the same is a perfect man, able to bridle the whole body.* This is a somewhat extreme statement if taken alone, but S. James illustrates his meaning, and, by his illustrations, he develops his own thought.

II.—THE PERILS OF SPEECH DUE TO LACK OF SELF-CONTROL.

He proceeds in his vivid, eager manner, saying, *Lo this*, and *behold that*,[1] to illustrate his statement; and it is chararacteristic of S. James that he finds in each analogy a step to a fresh argument. So he writes: *For lo, we put bits into the horses' mouths that they may obey us, and turn about their whole body also. And behold the ships of the sea, though they are so great and are driven by rough winds, are yet turned about by a very small rudder, whither the impulse of the steersman willeth. So the tongue also is a little member, and boasteth great things. Behold, how a great forest is kindled by how small a fire!*

The illustrations are not new. They may be found in poets and parable makers of all languages; but they must here be considered in their own context, and nothing but confusion of thought would result from citing parallel passages. *We put bits into the horses' mouths that they may obey us, and turn about their whole body also:* just so can a man who bridles his tongue control his whole body. Such is the argument; but it may be urged that the analogy is not exact, for we actually control a horse with a bit, but we do not control our passions with a bridled tongue. S. James, indeed, might argue that laxity of speech usually leads to looseness of action, and that the sinful lusts of the flesh get out of hand when free rein is given to the lascivious

[1] *Vide* Mayor *in loco* for a defence of the reading ἴδε γάρ.

tongue. But S. James is still thinking of the teacher, and it is with the tongue that we command others. Will the teacher stumble in his path? will he curb his temper? will his words run away from him? He must needs be discreet in conduct as in speech, he must say what he means and practise it, he must neither mislead nor mystify, he must not unduly discourage nor unduly praise—in fact, he must never be carried away. Now, argues S. James, the man who can bridle his tongue has achieved something which will make all other forms of self-mastery easy. We may conclude that he who can control his tongue has like control over his other activities. For he who can "keep the door of his lips"[1] has the secret of power. He is τέλειος, the perfect man, self-sufficient and complete.

III.—The Perils of Speech due to Lack of Understanding.

But let us suppose a rider, with his horse under perfect control, who does not know his way. The power he possesses is then of but little value. He is like a ship with an excellent rudder and an incompetent steersman. Self-control is not everything: the teacher needs knowledge, wisdom, and skill. It is this thought which accounts for this illustration. *Behold, the ships also, though they are so great, and are driven by rough winds, are yet turned about by a very small rudder, whither the impulse of the steersman willeth.*

Here we have not merely to think of the ship and the rudder, but also of the sea and the rough winds. These latter images symbolize man's environment—the

[1] Ps. cxli. 3.

Perils of Speech

wicked world. The swelling waves are like its pomp, and the blustering wind like its headlong vanity. Self-control will sustain the steersman in his conflict with the elements, but will not mitigate their force, or bring the ship to port. Granted, says S. James, that the steersman is at his post and the ship answers to her helm, she may yet be driven on the rocks for want of knowledge, or swamped for lack of skill. So also the teacher has need of both knowledge and wisdom if he would steer his course aright. In undertaking to teach others, the ship he directs is not merely his own body but the Ark of Christ's Church. For her safety he is responsible amid the storms and floods of the world.

It is easy to see the importance of the rudder; what is overlooked is the fact that the rudder misapplied may lead to the ship being wrecked. So it is impossible to overrate the importance of the tongue—*a little member boasting great things;* but, wrongly used, the tongue is the cause of ruin, and that is not much to boast of. S. James had no doubt listened to the fiery eloquence of the Zealots; he had seen faces glow, and hot hands clenched, as the result of their burning words. Nothing much had happened when he wrote, but S James had foresight. He feared the sparks from the crackling thorns beneath the pot.[1] Trouble was brewing, and the tongue was the fire. So he turns to the would-be teachers among his converts, and exhorts them to forbear. Men boast of their power, they acclaim the orator. They point to the influence of words to make and unmake worlds; and with quiet irony S. James replies to them: Behold, *how great a forest is kindled by how small a fire!*

[1] Ps. lviii. 9.

IV.—THE AWFUL CONSEQUENCES OF SPEECH.

There is no more splendid sight than a forest fire at a distance, and nothing inspires more terror when seen close at hand. It is irresistible in its might, seemingly capricious in its direction, it licks up "the trees of gladness with the flame of its wicked tongue."[1] None can contend with it, none can repair its ravages, nothing is so complete as the devastation it occasions. It is only exhausted when it has exhausted the material on which it feeds; and it leaves behind waste places—black, charred, ugly—where once had been leafy branches, the song of birds, vistas flickering with green and golden light, where soft moss had tempted the weary to repose in cool sequestered glades.

And what causes the forest fire? As a rule no man knows. Perhaps it was a spark, falling at random into dry herbage, and fanned by a light breeze. Shall we boast of the spark because its power has been proven? or shall we not rather moralize on how contemptible was the cause of such widespread desolation? Had we been there, what should we have done? Jesus, the son of Sirach, says: "If thou blow the spark, it shall burn; if thou spit on it, it shall be quenched; and both these came out of thy mouth."[2] S. James at least can see nothing to boast of in the fool fury caused by fanatics and demagogues. He turns and considers his illustrations, and deduces from them the conclusion that the uncontrolled and misused tongue is largely responsible for the sinful lusts of the flesh, for the discord in the world of men, and is the instrument of the

[1] Pss of Sol. XII. 3.   [2] Ecclus xxviii. 12.

Devil himself. So he proceeds to his great indictment: *The tongue is a fire; the world of iniquity among our members is the tongue, which defileth the whole body, and setteth on fire the wheel of life, and is set on fire by Hell.*

V.—THE PERVASIVE POWER OF SPEECH.

The tongue is a fire, says S. James, and he immediately thinks how does it blacken? what does it consume? whence does it derive its power? These questions are suggested by his last illustration, but in order to develop his thought he needs a new metaphor allied to humanity, and so goes on to describe the tongue as the *world of iniquity among our members*.

This phrase has given rise to many interpretations. The word κόσμος is used five times by S. James—once in its more literal sense when he speaks of *the poor in the world*,[1] and four times in the sense of society as organized apart from God, and it has no doubt the latter meaning here.[2] *The world of iniquity* is, then, the wicked world which we renounce at our Baptism, and what the wicked world is in respect to society that the tongue is in regard to our other members. As the spirit of the world seeks to dominate us, so we tend to become enslaved to the tyrannous power of our own words. Our peculiar shibboleths harden into prejudices, and render us at enmity with those who cannot pronounce them. We know, also, how pervasive the spirit of worldliness is, how subtly it communicates itself, how it endeavours to shape everybody and everything, how hard it is *to keep ourselves unspotted from the*

[1] Jas. ii 5   [2] Jas i 27; iv. 4.

world. So, argues S. James, the tongue is pervasive, words react on the thought that produced them, for we think in words that the tongue has formed, and words apart from utterance could not ultimately be conceived of. So all our members are controlled, directed and brought into association by suggestions that take their form and force from language.

These metaphors, perhaps, may seem to some exaggerated, but just as we can renounce the wicked world with its pomps and vanities, so we may renounce the wicked word with its foul suggestiveness; and just as we may live in the world as not abusing it, so we may employ human language to express both truth and love. In pondering the words of S. James, we must not forget how Our Lord said: "I have overcome the world."[1] If the Word of God tabernacles with us, our tongues may catch His accents and, like the world, be redeemed.[2]

VI.—THE EFFECT ON CHARACTER.

Just as the unreclaimed world spots and defiles; so, says S. James, the uncontrolled tongue *defileth the whole body*. Temptations, so long as they remain vague impulses, are of but little force. It is when we have found words for them that they become dangerous, for then we can relate them to life and action. When the thoughts have passed into utterance and we are not ashamed to speak them, then we have in most cases lost our self-control. This brings us back to the first illustration—we cannot bridle the body when we have lost control of the tongue. The most innocent actions

[1] John xvi. 33. [2] John i. 14

become obscene through suggestions, insinuations, and innuendo. Foul language leads to foul thought, until the whole world becomes impure. Everything is coloured and defined for us by the words and metaphors we habitually use.

Few people recognize the power that lies in continual affirmation. Belief grows by repetition. The man who tells a lie often enough comes to believe that it is true, or at least that there is something in it. Many a man can talk himself into a passion. "He works himself up," so he says; and when he has talked sufficiently he is ready for violence. A man will threaten terrible things without a thought of performance, and is driven finally into act, much to his own surprise. It is true that a man who threatens to commit suicide is pretty certain not to do it then; but a man who constantly threatens to destroy himself is very likely to do it sometime. The idea has become so familiar that the will is hypnotized. This self-affirmation has within us very much the same power as public opinion has on society at large.

VII.—SPEECH AND MAN'S ENVIRONMENT.

But words do not end with ourselves, their results are not confined to ourselves, and so S. James says that the tongue not only *defileth the whole body*, but *setteth on fire the wheel of life*.

The word γένεσις, as in Lecture V., can be applied to what is seen and temporal, to all that is comprised between birth and the grave. *Life*, in consequence, seems a better translation than either *nature* or *birth*.

The wheel of life is, therefore, the sphere in which a man lives, what we should now call his environment. It is like a wheel in motion, for it "never continueth in one stay," and the tongue may be compared to the axle. Just as the ship may be wrecked by a wrong use of the rudder, as the wheel may be destroyed by an axle on fire, so the tongue may embroil an entire neighbourhood. Social life, harmony, happiness, and co-operation are all at the mercy of the tongue. All the violence, brutality, and dishonesty in the world account for far less misery than the fruits of the tongue—suspicions excited, scandal repeated, contempt expressed, unkind criticism, the blazing indiscretion, the spiteful imputation, the angry retort, misunderstanding and deceit. All this was no doubt especially brought home to S. James in those early days of the infant Church. The Christian Jews formed very small communities, and were largely isolated from the rest of the world. The members were inevitably thrown much together, and their love for one another would be sorely tried by tittle-tattle and gossip. Since then, all religious communities have found some rule of silence, more or less strict, necessary for the preservation of the common life.

Discord was probably the first thought in the mind of S. James when he penned this phrase, but it is equally applicable to "the evil communications which corrupt good manners."[1] It is by the tongue that the knowledge of evil grows and one man tempts another, the prurient secret is whispered, and the profligate boasts of his triumph. It is with the tongue that frailties are explained away and sins excused. It is the

[1] 1 Cor. xv. 33

Perils of Speech

tongue that uses euphemisms for things in themselves gross and repulsive. The tongue finds in innuendo the secret of an evil power, and becomes the Procuress of Hell, deriving from Hell her inspiration.

VIII.—THE INSPIRATION OF HELL.

This brings us to the final clause of the indictment. *The tongue is a fire* which sets ablaze *the wheel of life;* but the fire is not kindled by the motion of the wheel, it *is set on fire by Hell.* As in the first chapter we find not only the unruly desires, but the Tempter with his enticements, so here we find no self-originated fire, but an incendiary. The present participle is used both for the setting on fire of *the wheel of life* and the setting *on fire by Hell.* For as the advancing wheel represents the perpetual motion of life, so the fire that cannot be quenched is ever mounting up to ignite and consume.

Gehenna, in the New Testament, is said to be a furnace or lake of fire, and the final portion of the wicked.[1] It is already the abode of the Devil and his angels, and so S. James, piling metaphor upon metaphor, sees in the flames of Gehenna mounting up the activity of evil spirits in the world of men.

As the Angels of God are likened to flames of fire, so are the angels of darkness.[2] For if fire quickens, it also consumes; if it purifies, it also destroys; if it warms, it also burns; if it lights, it also blackens all things with its smoke. It has quickness, intensity, ardour; it typifies equally love and hate; it cannot

---

[1] Matt. xiii. 42, 50, Rev xix. 20; xx. 10.
[2] Heb 1. 7, Ps civ 4.

be satisfied. So the Angels of God and the angels of darkness are creatures of like substance, but they are inspired with a contrary purpose.

So S. James sees behind the world's outward show the enemies of mankind at work. They are like flames rising from a real Gehenna to tempt and fire men's tongues.

Every man knows the strange and foreign thought of evil that intrudes on his astonished mind. He regards it as a temptation and puts it by. He is no more responsible for it than for the suggestion made by a neighbour, for spirit communes with spirit, and there is no need of sound. Every man also has at times been puzzled with his own impulsive sayings. He never meant them, never meant to say them. He is conscious that it was not his real self that spoke. For a moment he was possessed and became the instrument of evil; but in this case he is in some degree responsible, for he cannot have been watchful or in a state of grace.

S. James, however, means even more than this. He knows that the infection of evil is worse than the act, though the act implies that the infection has been caught. He knows also how much mischief and how many misunderstandings are the result of words spoken with no evil intention by the man who uttered them. Such a man denies quite rightly all responsibility for evil results it was impossible to foresee. He may have been the instrument of evil, he cannot be its cause. Behind him S. James sees the imps of Hell blowing sparks into a blaze. A belief in causation almost necessitates some such explanation. In so many misunderstandings no one appears to blame. The world was only seen by firelight; there were strange shifting shadows, and something was transfigured by the fitful glow. The flame went out suddenly, and an accident happened in the dark. So innocent words are misinterpreted and explanations are prevented, and in gloom we ask one another why it all happened. S. James has his answer. If the Spirit of God descends in tongues of fire to fill men with wisdom, truth, and love, the spirits of evil ascend in tongues of fire to torture men's minds and sear their souls, to inflame discord and quicken hate.

IX.—THE IMPOSSIBILITY OF LIMITING FREEDOM OF SPEECH.

The next verse beginning πᾶσα γάρ at first sight looks as if it must be the proof and justification of the preceding words, but S. James is as careless of grammatical connexion as he is about being consecutive in thought. With him one thought suggests another, which may or may not be dependent upon it. He is not systematic in his treatment, and he changes his position without a note of warning. So he has striven to restrain the would-be teachers, and has set before them the awful perils of speech, and he now turns back to look at the question as it affects himself. He is a Ruler of the Church, and how is he to keep unruly tongues in order? He can teach the Faith, enforce discipline, appoint presbyters, decide disputes; but in all the plentitude of his Apostolic power he knows that he can neither silence nor control the tongues of men. Every ruler has found this true. Even under Louis XIV., "despotism was tempered with epigrams," and Frederick the Great boasted of his compromise with his people—"they were to say what they liked and he was to do what he liked." This may satisfy a War Lord concerned with material power, but it cannot satisfy one who would unite men together for their own spiritual improvement. S. James felt his failure acutely and writes: *For every kind of beasts and birds, of serpents, and things in the sea is tamed, and hath been tamed, by mankind; but the tongue can no man tame; it is a restless evil, it is full of deadly poison.*

Man has "been crowned with glory and honour,"[1] as far as the creatures are concerned. S. Augustine says, "the image of God tames the wild beast."[2] Man's dominion starts from the very beginning, but S. James was probably thinking of how it was ratified to Noah: "The fear of you and the dread of you shall be upon every beast of the field, and upon every fowl of the air, and upon all that moveth on the earth, and upon all the fishes of the sea; into your hands are they delivered."[3]

All that walk, fly, creep, or swim—the inhabitants of earth, air, and water—*are tame and have been tamed by mankind*. The dominion was given and is being exercised. *But the tongue can no man tame.* You can command men's bodies and prescribe their actions, you cannot control their speech. S. Augustine, however, notes, "he does not say no one can tame the tongue, but no man: so that when the tongue is tamed we confess that it has become so by the pity of God, by the help of God, by the Grace of God."[4]

[1] Ps viii 5-8   [2] Gen. i. 28.   [3] Gen ix 2
[4] *De Nat. et Grat* c. xv

X.—THE ABUSE OF FREEDOM OF SPEECH.

Perhaps exception will be taken to the rhetorical manner of S. James, but the wild beast and the venomous serpent are compared with the restlessness and malice of the tongue, *it is a restless evil, it is full of deadly poison.*

There have been men burning with the sense of some awful wrong, who have given their lives and sacrificed everything to set the wrong right. They are inscribed in the roll of heroes. But there is also a much larger class, there are men full of discontent, who make a livelihood out of the discontent of others. No career is in most respects so easy as that of the professional agitator. He needs no training, no skill, no knowledge, no particular abilities, and no great excellence of character. The work is not hard, and it is wellnigh impossible to make him responsible. He only needs to be thoroughly reckless and brazen in order to find the way open to notoriety, to a comfortable living, and perhaps to power. All rulers have found the professional agitator a nuisance, if not a danger. If he be endured, then as "a ramping and roaring lion "[1] he excites the evil passions of men; but if he be suppressed, he creeps from one secret society to another, and "the poison of asps is under his lips."[2] He is perhaps most dangerous when he is half in earnest, and cannot distinguish between his convictions and his self-seeking. Ever restless, ever ready to destroy someone or something, he poisons the wells of life lest men should live together in peace. The evil had already arisen in the infant Church. There were

[1] Ps xxii. 13   [2] Rom iii 13, Ps. cxl. 3

those who were puffed up and fomented discord at Corinth.[1] Even S. John had to deal with Diotrephes "who loveth to have the pre-eminence."[2]

XI.—BLESSING AND CURSING.

The venomous tongue is often double-edged. There are men of whom it can be said: "Their words are softer than butter, yet be they very swords."[3] The reckless tongue, on the other hand, may be possessed by one who is simply heedless and irresponsible. "The beginning of the words of his mouth are foolishness, and the end of his talk is mischievous madness."[4] But both the venomous and the restless tongues suggest the inconsistency revealed by speech. So S. James goes on to say of the tongue, *Therewith bless we the Lord and Father, and therewith curse we men who are made after the similitude of God: out of the same mouth cometh forth blessing and cursing*. S. James has already condemned the double-minded man, he goes on to deal with the double-tongued. But he identifies himself with his disciples here, for the best men know they are not free from inconsistency in speech. So he ends with a note of pleading: *My brethren, these things ought not so to be. Doth the fountain send forth from the same opening sweet water and bitter? Can a fig tree, my brethren, yield olives, or a vine figs? Neither can salt water yield sweet.*

Every Jew, when he mentioned the name of God, added, "Blessed be He." The phrase had become conventional, but in the mouth of an angry man the

[1] 1 Cor. i. 11, iii. 3
[2] 3 John 9, 10.
[3] Ps. lv. 21.
[4] Eccles x 13

Perils of Speech

inconsistency amounted to profanity. S. James, however, was here probably thinking of the Eighteen Benedictions which all the Jews were bound to repeat three times a day, and no doubt continued to repeat after they had become Christians. In three of these Benedictions the words *Lord and Father* occur, and it is natural for S. James as a Christian to emphasize the title *Father*, especially when he is about to speak of the *similitude* (ὁμοίωσις) belonging to God's sons. So the Rabbis had taught that murder was wrong as diminishing *the likeness*, and the fact that man was "made in the image of God"[1] was much insisted on by New Testament writers preaching the Incarnation. In studying S. James, we are so often, as here, made conscious of the theology underlying his thought. His immediate object is to illustrate the inconsistency of man's speech, but he does so by reminding us that those who bless God the Father must beware how they curse any of his sons. As S. John was subsequently to write, "If a man say, I love God, and hateth his brother, he is a liar. For he that loveth not his brother whom he hath seen, how can he love God whom he hath not seen?"[2] It is, after all, because of *the likeness* that we are able to know God, and the likeness is "express"[3] in the Person of Our Lord. But in every man the likeness exists for those who seek for it, however blurred, obliterated, or distorted it may have been. The Jews were too apt to say, "This people that knoweth not the law is cursed";[4] but the Father from Heaven answers for every prodigal, "He is My son."

[1] Gen 1 26, 27
[2] 1 John iv 20
[3] Heb. 1 3.
[4] John vii 49

XII.—THE LAST APPEAL.

S. James starting from the thought of the Prophet, "Have we not all one Father, hath not one God created us?"[1] turns to pleading with his brethren. Moral indignation ends when he is no longer denouncing sin in its hatefulness, but is dealing with the sinner in his shame. There is once more the note of affection: *My brethren, these things ought not so to be.*

The little parables that follow are all quite natural to a dweller in Palestine. There is the fountain from the limestone hills, the fig-tree, the vine and the olive, while some commentators find also a reference to the Dead Sea in the South, in the *salt water that cannot yield sweet*. All the parables teach that Nature is consistent and harmonious, whereas discord and inconsistency are found among men. They all illustrate the folly of sin, but each also has its own lesson besides. There is something spontaneous about the gushing forth of the fountain, though it be ever true to its nature. So S. James would like speech to be free and spontaneous, but it should flow from a pure source. The fig, the grape, and the olive are all alike good, but each is to be gathered from its proper tree. The mistake of so many talkers, whether teachers or not, is to pretend to thoughts which are not really their own, but are borrowed from others and used before they are understood. Lastly, *the salt sea cannot yield sweet water*, and neither can the bitter heart yield kind words. This last little parable once more directs our thoughts inwards, and reminds us that the change must come from

[1] Mal ii. 10.

within. The whole passage is no doubt reminiscent of Our Lord's teaching. "A good tree bringeth not forth corrupt fruit, neither doth a corrupt tree bring forth good fruit. For every tree is known by its fruit. For of thorns men do not gather figs, nor of a bramble bush gather they grapes. A good man out of the good treasure of his heart bringeth forth that which is good; and an evil man out of the evil treasure of his heart bringeth forth that which is evil; for out of the abundance of the heart his mouth speaketh."[1]

[1] Luke vi. 43-45.

LECTURE XI

WISDOM

"Who is wise and understanding among you? Let him shew by his good life works in meekness of wisdom. But if ye have bitter jealousy and faction in your heart, glory not, and lie not against the truth. This wisdom is not a wisdom that cometh down from above, but is earthly, sensual, devilish. For where jealousy and faction are, there is confusion and every vile deed. But the wisdom that is from above is first pure, then peaceable, gentle, easy to be intreated, full of mercy and good fruits, without variance, without hypocrisy. And the fruit of righteousness is sown in peace for them that make peace."—JAS. III. 13-18

I.—CONNEXION OF THOUGHT.

S. JAMES is still dealing with the teacher, though his words, as in the previous Lecture, are capable of a wider application. We have seen how the last of his little parables revealed his consciousness that speech was only a manifestation of the spirit within. So now he turns abruptly and asks: *Who is wise and understanding among you?* Then, with practical common-sense, he goes on to declare that if anyone professes to be wise and understanding, *let him show out of a good conversation his works in meekness of wisdom*. He knows that among those who boast and exult in their wisdom are many envious persons full of party spirit. He admonishes them, saying, *If ye have bitter jealousy and faction in your hearts, glory not, and lie not against the Truth.* He does not deny that they have wisdom of a sort, but *it is*

Wisdom

earthly, sensual, and devilish. It results in *confusion and every vile deed.* It is altogether unlike the wisdom coming from above which he proceeds to describe. That wisdom is *the fruit of righteousness, and is sown in peace for them that make peace.* Such seems to be his line of argument, but, in order fully to understand it, we have to consider carefully his use of terms.

II.—WISDOM AND UNDERSTANDING.

The teacher was to be both *wise and understanding.* The first is a moral quality, the second an intellectual. *Understanding* meant for the Jew very much what "scholarship" means in academic circles. The man of understanding is the man who has not only acquired his facts, but mastered them, who can handle and apply them, who knows how they are related one to another. Now the necessity for the teacher having *understanding* in this sense has only to be stated in order to be taken for granted; but S. James has to amplify and explain his conception of wisdom, for wisdom to different Jews meant very different things.

For S. James, at any rate, *wisdom* has nothing necessarily to do with great intellectual powers, or with mental grip, penetration or discernment. It has to do with the temper rather than with the mind, it provides an atmosphere in which we see things, it is shown by the spirit in which we act. It implies a sympathy within a man to what is external to him. The sympathy may be with nature, society, God, or with all three. It is in consequence quite possible to talk of a worldly wisdom as well as of a wisdom that defies the world's standards. Granted a society organized without reference to God, worldly maxims may be valid and true, but once admit "the fear of the Lord"[1] as the starting-point " of wisdom," and " the wisdom of this world" is seen to be "foolishness with God."[2]

S. James does not trouble to deny the claim made by the man of the world to wisdom, any more than he cared to dispute on the definition of faith; but he upholds the higher wisdom as alone worth having, and brings out its superiority by vivid contrasts. It is for him not natural, but supernatural in origin. Men are to *pray for the wisdom that they lack*.[3] It comes, like all other good gifts, *down from the Father of Lights*.[4] It is, in fact, the bestowal of God's own Spirit—the Holy Ghost.

Every practical person knows how foolish the merely clever man can be, because, notwithstanding his abilities, he is often altogether out of touch with his surroundings: he understands his principles, but not the world in which they have to be applied. S. James not only knows this, but he knows also that sagacity has much more to do with our moral attitude than with our mental aptitude. He is by nature practical, and not at all given to speculation. The God whom he worships is the God who works,[5] who " by wisdom founded the earth,"[6] who calls on men to be "labourers together with Himself."[7] For S. James the spirit of wisdom is best typified as " brooding over the face of the waters "[8] and bringing harmony, order,

---

[1] Job xxviii 28; *cf*. Ps cxi 10, Prov. i 7 *et seq*
[2] 1 Cor. iii 19
[3] Jas. i. 5
[4] Jas. i. 17.
[5] John v 17, ix. 4
[6] Prov. iii. 19
[7] 1 Cor. iii 9.
[8] Gen. i 2

beauty, light, and form out of chaos and out of the void. So he turns on the pretender to wisdom and proposes a practical test. *Let him show out of a good conversation his works in meekness of wisdom.*

III.—THE CHARACTERISTIC OF HEAVENLY WISDOM IS MEEKNESS. IT SEEKS THE GOOD OF OTHERS.

In 1611 the word *conversation* was an exact equivalent for ἀναστροφή, but the word in this sense has long been obsolete. The Revisers adopted the word *life* which barely suggests the meaning, and perhaps the nearest translation would be *social intercourse*. In social intercourse it is best seen whether men act in *meekness of wisdom*. *Works* here, as in Chapter II., are those "good works" dear to the heart of S. James; and when he speaks of the *meekness of wisdom* he would emphasize the fact that for him, at any rate, *meekness* is a necessary attribute of the true wisdom, for such wisdom is not only conscious of its source in "the fear of the Lord," but seeks its satisfaction in the peaceable persuasion of men.

No doubt S. James remembered how the son of Sirach taught: "The fear of the Lord is all wisdom; and in all wisdom is the performance of the Law, and the knowledge of His Omnipotency:"[1] of how the Book of Proverbs declares that "with the lowly is wisdom:"[2] while in Ecclesiasticus we read again, "My son, go on with thy business (ἔργα, works) in meekness; so shalt thou be loved of him that is approved."[3] And he knows that it is just this *meekness*

---
[1] Ecclus. xix. 20. [2] Prov. xi. 2. [3] Ecclus. iii. 17

of wisdom that is so necessary for the teachers to whom he is writing. As S. Peter says, "Be ready to give an answer to every man that asketh you a reason concerning the hope that is in you, yet with *meekness* and fear."[1]

IV.—THE CHARACTERISTIC OF WORLDLY WISDOM IS BOASTFULNESS. ITS OBJECT IS SELF-ADVANCEMENT.

Then S. James turns on the boasters who glory over one another on the score of their superior attainments. He can see in their conduct very little of *the meekness of wisdom*, and he warns them accordingly: *but if ye have bitter envy and faction in your heart, glory not, and lie not against the Truth*. So S. Paul wrote to the Corinthians, "For ye are yet carnal: for as there is among you envying and strife and divisions, are ye not yet carnal and walk as men?"[2] For both writers true wisdom was of heavenly origin. It caused men to walk together; and "can two walk together except they be agreed?"[3]

It is perhaps worth noticing as a mark of the pastoral character of the Epistle, that S. James asks his converts to recognize true wisdom in the intercourse of men—that is, he proposes an external test for their observation of other men's wisdom. But he also asks them to examine their own hearts to see if there be jealousy and factiousness there—that is, he drives his readers to self-examination, in order that they may be convinced how little wisdom there is in themselves. He is striving to prove to them that envy and party spirit are inconsistent with wisdom.

[1] 1 Pet. iii 15.   [2] 1 Cor. iii. 3.   [3] Amos iii 3.

Wisdom

The word for envy (ζῆλος) might have the good sense of zeal, that is the jealousy of the devout for the cause of truth; but with the adjective *bitter* (πικρός) it has the bad sense of envy, a jealousy of others because they are preferred. And with the *bitter envy* went the spirit of *faction* which made men at Corinth say, " I am of Paul, and I of Apollos, and I of Cephas, and I of Christ;" [1] which at Antioch and elsewhere made those that came from James, with this Epistle probably in their hands, attempt to undermine the work of S. Paul.[2]

The word for faction (ἐριθεία) is derived from ἔριθος, a hireling or day labourer, the idea being that the factious men were often paid to make a disturbance. But it is also true that the thorough partisan ceases to be free; he does not exercise his own judgment; he sells himself and his reason to insure the triumph of his party. He invents arguments to prove his party right; he no longer follows the truth whither it leads. He is proud of his loyalty and glories in it; he has ceased to blush when he lies against the Truth. In fact, he ceases to believe that his party can be wrong; he will acknowledge no fact that makes against its interest. And yet how much craft, cleverness, adroitness, diplomacy, and skill go to insure a party triumph! Men boast of their wisdom in these respects; their finger is on the pulse of public opinion; they exult in the way they can divert attention from awkward facts by confusing the issues; they chuckle over the way they set class against class, or bring about a combination of cliques to further an end wanted by none of them. How great is their glory when an opponent is worsted

[1] 1 Cor 1 12.   [2] Gal ii 12.

or his misdemeanours exposed! There is no such truculence as that shown in a party triumph; but, asks S. James, is all this cleverness and scheming really the fruit of wisdom? For him to identify such qualities with wisdom is to *lie against the Truth*.

What exactly does S. James mean by *lying against the Truth*? At first the phrase looks as if it were pleonastic; but we have to remember that the author has already spoken of being *begotten by the word of Truth*, and we found in that place that the Truth stood for the Gospel, *the faith of Our Lord Jesus Christ*, as he calls it later on. In the last Lecture we shall find him writing, *if any of you do err from the Truth*. So, as in other places, the Truth is objective, something that is acknowledged and can be appealed to: it is "the Truth as it is in Jesus,"[1] as it is revealed by the Holy Spirit, who is at once the Spirit of wisdom and the Spirit of Truth, who comes forth to guide the Church into all Truth. Thinking of the Truth in this way, what shall we say of faction in the Church which is the One Body, endued with the One Spirit? Faction inflamed with envy produces fruit so far from wisdom that it may be spoken of as "blasphemy against the Holy Ghost,"[2] the sin which "shall not be forgiven." No one can read the history of the Church without coming to the conclusion that party spirit has been largely responsible for shattering the unity of the Church, now stands in the way of reunion, and has at all times dimmed the lustre of that Truth which the Church exists to propagate.

[1] Eph. iv. 21. [2] Matt. xii 31

V.—Worldly Wisdom: its Nature.

Party leaders may glory in their astuteness, and call it wisdom if they please. S. James grants that it is wisdom, but it is the wisdom of the world. *This wisdom is not a wisdom that cometh from above, but is earthly, sensual, devilish.*

The three words, *earthly, sensual, devilish,* are in relation to man's body, soul, and spirit,[1] and the wisdom proper to each, unless in union with the heavenly spirit, can only result in *confusion and every vile deed.*

The first word, *earthly,* is in direct antithesis to the wisdom from above. It is the wisdom of the body; the animal instinct that urges men to self-preservation and the satisfaction of their lusts; it is the low brute-cunning that is so often found in the most debased, and is most highly developed in the otherwise mentally defective. There are men "whose God is their belly, who glory in their shame, who mind earthly things."[2] There are men not so base, who look on professional success chiefly as a means for procuring loaves and fishes, and there were no doubt among the would-be teachers, thought of by S. James, some whose envy and party spirit arose from a confusion between gain and godliness.[3]

The second word, *sensual* ($\psi\upsilon\chi\iota\kappa\acute{\eta}$), must here be understood of the soul. By nature the mind can only feed on what it can see and hear, and selects what is pleasing to itself. It needs the assistance of a spiritual wisdom if it is to rise above what is palpable and attain to principles. To receive this wisdom the mind needs

[1] 1 Thess. v. 23.   [2] Phil. iii. 19.   [3] 1 Tim. vi. 5

to be converted, just as much as the heart, and to start again humbly in "the fear of the Lord." Otherwise its wisdom will never have more than an æsthetic value. "Beauty is truth, truth beauty," would be an admirable maxim if only we had a fixed standard for either; but tastes differ, and so do opinions; and in consequence the sensual wisdom degenerates into the jargon of a coterie or the patter of a school. It leads to separation rather than to unity. "There be they," says S. Jude,[1] "who separate themselves; sensual, not having the spirit." For men to unite, an authority must be acknowledged which is higher than an individual's conceit. So in the Book of Proverbs we read: "He that separateth himself seeketh his own desire, and rageth against all sound wisdom."[2] The men of unconverted minds claim to eat at will of the Tree of Knowledge of Good and Evil, and to decide for themselves what good and evil are. They differ according to their appetite, and *confusion* is the inevitable result. They claim to teach what they think at the moment, without regard to authority, without respect for their disciples, and without foresight as to the consequences. Truth for them is a matter of debate; they unsettle weak minds and undermine the principles of morality, and their intellectual vanity is the parent of many a *vile deed*.

The third word, *devilish* ($\delta\alpha\iota\mu\text{o}\nu\iota\omega\delta\eta\varsigma$), should be translated, as the American Revisers suggested, *demoniacal*. S. James not only believed in Satan, but in those rebel angels "who kept not their own principality, but left their proper habitation."[3] He knew the Jewish tradition that these rebels were to be identified with

[1] Jude 19. [2] Prov. xviii. 1. [3] Jude 6.

Wisdom

"the Sons of God who saw the daughters of men that they were fair,"[1] and that spiritual wickedness resulted from their marriage.[2] Whether he believed this or not, he undoubtedly accepted the fact that a lying spirit was in the mouth of the Prophets who persuaded Ahab to go up to Ramoth Gilead;[3] and he probably shared with S. Paul in the belief, that "the Wicked One"[4] would come "after the working of Satan with all power, signs and lying wonders," to make those " believe a lie " who had not with love received the Truth. Anyhow, he had seen men possessed; and when he notes how bitter is the wrangling in the Church, it reminds him rather of a company of demoniacs than of men inspired with the Holy Spirit of Love.

It is through the Spirit that we have communion with God, but it is also because we are spiritual that we can be influenced by the rebel angels and imbibe their *wisdom*. They call on us to be independent, "to be as Gods";[5] they incite our curiosity to explore their ways; they offer to open our eyes to the hideous facts of their hidden evil. They would divorce thought from life, that thought and life may be alike irrational. With subtle malignity they tempt us to seek truth for ourselves, until we find ourselves befogged, doubtful as to whether Truth exists or any principles are sound. They can prove evil good, and good evil; they would justify every *vile fact*, and call it natural. They fascinate us with such facts, and insinuate that they have special claims on our attention. So they infect healthy souls and minister to minds diseased. They urge tolerance

---

[1] Gen. vi. 2. [2] Enoch xvi. 3 [3] 1 Kings xxii. 22.
[4] 2 Thess ii 8-11 [5] Gen. iii. 5

of the *earthly wisdom*, its cunning lust and greed. They flatter the *sensual wisdom*, its vanity and self-sufficiency. They prove to man's proud spirit that there is no authority to which he ought to defer, and no Superior with claims upon his homage. Their wisdom never admits of one thing—a confession of error. They exist to *lie against the Truth*. Envy offers them a habitation, and faction is the means whereby they work. Their object is to murder Love.

VI.—Its Results in War and Confusion.

S. James finds bitter *envy and faction* among teachers boasting of their wisdom. He shows them that such wisdom as they have is *earthly, sensual, devilish*, in its origin, and he proceeds to note its results. Where *envy and faction are, there is confusion and every vile deed*.

The word πρᾶγμα should be translated *fact*, and not *deed*, for it refers to something in existence without reference to the agent. S. James knew how hopeless it would be to convince any of his wrangling teachers that they were responsible for the ugly blots on Church life. An argument of that sort could only end in recriminations. On the contrary, he asks them to note that where envy and strife exists, there also is confusion and hateful facts. They are unable to deny it. So he says, we will not argue as to who is to blame or attempt to apportion the blame, but let everyone try to expel envy and party spirit out of his heart, and then we shall see if there be not a growing sense of order, more co-operation, and fewer scandals.

Now, it is quite clear that confusion and scandals

Wisdom

cannot be the result of a wisdom proceeding from above, for "God is not the Author of confusion, but of peace."[1] Neither do *the vile facts* call for continual comment: order and reunion are not promoted by one side reminding the other of its past misdeeds.

It is necessary sometimes to expose abuses and discover their source. It is to the interest of the world that there should be plenty of light and air. But there are men of nasty minds, full of suspicion, who concentrate their attention on all that is base, and find vile reasons for everything. They pride themselves on their wisdom, but it is a wisdom that causes more evil than it cures. "The knowledge of wickedness is not wisdom," says the Book of Proverbs; and S. Paul was right when he wished: "I would have you wise unto that which is good, and simple to all evil."[2]

The *vile fact* is obvious: it is something to be taken in hand, and altered or removed. But to hunt for vile facts reveals an interest in them, and they are created by the search. "Dirt" has been defined as "matter misplaced," and what is in its wrong place should at once be removed. But if we disturb too many things in our search for dirt, we create what we are looking for. It is children who make a mess, and say that they are tidying. We do not call them wise; and, when we find their elders doing the same, we are justified in accusing them of folly.

[1] 1 Cor. xiv. 33   [2] Rom. xvi 19.

VII.—HEAVENLY WISDOM.

S. James, having exposed the nature and result of worldly wisdom, goes on to describe the wisdom that he desires. *But the wisdom that is from above is first pure, then peaceable, gentle, easy to be intreated, full of mercy and good fruits, without variance, and without hypocrisy.* These words at once suggest a comparison with another famous description. " For Wisdom, which is the worker of all things, taught me: for in her is an understanding spirit, holy, one only, manifold, subtle, lively, clear, undefiled, plain, not subject to hurt, loving the thing that is good, quick, which cannot be letted, ready to do good, kind to man, steadfast, sure, free from care, having all power, overseeing all things, and going through all things, pure and most subtle spirits."[1] But when we compare the two descriptions, we are struck with a great difference and a great advance of thought. Out of the Book of Wisdom we are unable to obtain any very definite conception. We approve each epithet, but they are hardly in order, and there is but little relation between them; they are strung together like pearls of different sizes and colours on one thread. In S. James, on the other hand, it will be shown that each epithet is in its place. He has built himself a palace for Wisdom to inhabit. It is four-square, and adorned within and without. We would, in consequence, compare the regularity of his mental architecture rather with the Beatitudes than with the Book of Wisdom. It shows the discipline of Our Lord's training, and we feel the inspiration of the Holy Spirit. It is noteworthy

[1] Wisd. vii. 22, 23.

that the first four epithets suggest the qualities which are symbolized by the Dove; and it is probably as a dove that S. James himself saw the Holy Spirit descend on Our Lord at His Baptism.

I said that S. James has himself built a palace for Wisdom. We may approach it from four sides, or, standing within, look out of it from four windows. He couples together the inner and outer aspects. What is purity within is peaceableness when seen from outside. What is sweet reasonableness within, shows itself as docility in the outer world. Mercy within manifests itself outwardly in good works. Steadfastness and consistency within is known by an absence of pretence and hypocrisy without. And the wisdom that cometh from above is like the sun shining on a dome of many-coloured glass, shedding radiance within; while from without the dome crowns the whole building, giving it a unity—a meaning of its own. The various parts are connected together for a common purpose in a way that satisfies the eye. It is one building with four aspects, each different, but each in relation to the others. Architecture alone seems to provide metaphors by which to understand the conception of S. James. As in many other places in his Epistle he is not content to describe from a single point of view, but surveys his subject from all sides, and makes us understand through single words the perfect balance of his judgment, and the sense of due proportion which characterizes his thought.

VIII.—ITS DESCRIPTION.

S. James describes his conception of wisdom according to the order of his thought; he is not concerned with the order of time. He begins from within, and says: *The wisdom that cometh from above is first pure and then peaceable.* Such wisdom must needs be *pure.* It is not confused by passion, obscured by prejudice, or soiled by self-conceit, self-seeking, or pride. It is inconsistent with mixed motives and muddled methods. Wisdom lies in the gift of clear vision. It is "the pure in heart who see God,"[1] *the Father of lights* and source of all truth. Such wisdom will manifest itself by being peaceable. It has naturally the harmlessness of the dove. Worldly wisdom may counsel "*divide et impera*"; heavenly wisdom with a nobler method commands, "*pacifica et impera.*" Worldly wisdom starts with duplicity and aims at tyranny; the heavenly wisdom is *first pure and then peaceable.* And here we note this wisdom not only seeks for peace but is itself peaceable. It does not get excited and brawl. It is confident in its cause, for it is linked with the Eternal and in harmony with Nature. It knows "Truth is great, and it prevails."[2]

S. James turns from the emotional aspect of wisdom to contemplate the mental. This is not clear from our translation, which proceeds, *gentle, and easy to be intreated;* but gentle ($\epsilon\pi\iota\epsilon\iota\kappa\eta$s) might perhaps be rendered *modest,* while *easy to be intreated* would be better understood if translated *docile* or *tractable.* In the Epistle to the Philippians,[3] the old translators render τὸ ἐπιεικές,

---

[1] Matt. v 8.   [2] 1 Esdras iv. 41.   [3] Phil. iv 5.

"moderation," and the Revisers have changed it into "forbearance." Matthew Arnold prefers "sweet reasonableness," Thayer suggests "modesty," and we must remember that ἐπιείκεια has a long history as an equivalent for "equity." When we think of the word in connexion with wisdom, we think of that delicate veneration for Truth, which forbids a man to assert too much in her name. The wise man, we may say, is more anxious to arrive at the truth than to prove himself right. He is not puffed up, and does not clamour for recognition. He is fully conscious of the limitations of his knowledge, and does not claim to have fully comprehended when he has only heard one side of a question. He is patient under contradiction, and will be ready to examine the views of an opponent. Within he is modest, and so he is ever learning. He is docile, tractable, *easy to be intreated*. The modest man has the windows of his mind wide open to receive the light. Those who cannot be taught never become wise, for they have a mistaken notion that wisdom is already theirs.

After considering the emotional and mental aspects of wisdom, S. James views it on the practical side. For S. James a wisdom that was not active would not be wisdom at all. So he goes on, if within the wise man be pure and modest, he will also be *full of mercy ;* if he be peaceable and docile in his relations with the outer world, he will also be *full of good fruits*. The pure in heart and modest in mind must be merciful to their neighbours, for the pure in heart can have no ill desires as regards others, and the modest in mind will not be censorious and hard upon others' failings; they will know when and how to make allowances, their judgment will err on the side of mercy if at all. And is not such mercy rightly an attribute of wisdom, for it arises out of sympathy with others which we have seen is the necessary condition of all wise action? It is true that the merciful are not always wise, but the truly wise are always merciful; and their mercy results in *good fruits*. Note S. James says *good fruits*, for there are many good intentions and good endeavours inspired by anything but wisdom; but for *good fruits* there must be wisdom, though it be the simple wisdom of the pure of heart.

S. James turns lastly to see how wisdom concerns itself with the spirit in which a man approaches life. He says it is *without variance and without hypocrisy*. He does not mean that the wise man never changes his opinion. The wise man always does so on receiving new and better information. Circumstances alter cases, and there is a consistency which is far from wise. We have already seen that docility is an attribute of wisdom. In saying that wisdom is *without variance*, S. James is thinking how *the Wisdom that cometh from above* is one of the gifts that proceeds from *the Father of Lights with whom is no variableness nor shadow cast in turning*. We remember how he has already condemned the man of wavering mind, and the man who shows partiality for unworthy reasons. A worldly wisdom may acclaim the Opportunist who always follows the line of least resistance and professes what seems immediately convenient. The heavenly wisdom shows itself to be *without variance*. It is the result of single-mindedness, it is steadfast. Such being the character within, it manifests itself outwardly in transparent sincerity. It is, says S. James, *without hypocrisy*. Wisdom need not pretend: it needs no drapery, no disguise. It does not call attention to itself in flamboyant advertisements. It can win its way on its own merits. It does not *vaunt itself or lie against the Truth*.

IX.—Its Results in Peace and Harmony.

S. James, having described the nature of the heavenly wisdom, concludes, *The fruit of righteousness is sown in peace for them that make peace*. For him the heavenly wisdom is manifested in righteousness, just as certainly as the earthly wisdom in confusion. He has already told us *that the wrath of man worketh not the righteousness of God*,[1] so he tells us how *the wisdom that cometh from above* results in a *righteousness* that makes for *peace*.[2]

By speaking of *the fruit of righteousness* he carries the thought still further. All actions have their consequences, and righteousness has its own fruit. We sow a seed that it may be multiplied in harvest. We enjoy the fruit, but there is enough left over that we may sow again. So one good deed leads to another, and "Wisdom is justified of her children."[3]

That *the fruit of righteousness is sown in peace* is a reminder that the works of the highest wisdom do not clamour for recognition. "The words of the wise are heard in quiet more than the cry of him who ruleth among fools."[4] On earth we know who causes wars,

---

[1] Jas i 20   [2] Jas iii. 18   [3] Matt. xi. 19, Luke vii. 35
[4] Eccles ix. 17

tumults, strikes—the authors of confusion fill many pages of history; but oftentimes we cannot trace the forces that make for peace—to know the power of the saints, we must wait for Heaven. In the Book of Ecclesiastes we read of "the poor wise man," who "by his wisdom delivered the city; yet no man remembered that same poor man."[1] The wisdom that is without hypocrisy is never ostentatious. Even in the simple duty of almsgiving a very little reflection will enable us to approve Our Lord's command, "Let not thy left hand know what thy right hand doeth."[2] The well-advertised bounty is almost certain to fall into the wrong hands. This text also reminds us of Our Lord's parable of the seed growing secretly.[3] The wise man acts rightly in accordance with his conscience, and the consequences follow, he knows not how or why, in the certainty and silence of Nature. Wisdom is not the same as knowledge. God's spirit enlightens us sufficiently to see the next stage. He does not always vouchsafe the knowledge by which we may scheme and plan the end.

And who is ultimately to benefit by this wisdom that cometh from above? The fruits of righteousness are *for them that make peace*. They are the sons of God, and for them is the Kingdom of Heaven. The children of this world with the wisdom of this world sow the seeds of envy and reap the harvest of confusion: "There is no peace, saith my God, for the wicked."[4] The children of God, full of His Spirit, sow to themselves the peace-

---

[1] Eccles ix 14, 15
[2] Matt. vi. 3.
[3] Mark iv. 26, 29.
[4] Isa. lvii 21.

able fruit of righteousness and reap in due season an abundant harvest. After all, the highest wisdom lies in identification with the Will of God. We confess with Dante:

> "E la sua voluntade è nostra pace."[1]

---

[1] *Par.* iii 85.

LECTURE XII

THE WORLD

" Whence come wars and whence come fightings among you ? Come they not hence, even of your pleasures that war in your members ? Ye lust, and have not · ye kill, and covet, and cannot obtain ye fight and war, ye have not, because ye ask not Ye ask, and receive not, because ye ask amiss, that ye may spend it in your pleasures Ye adulteresses, know ye not that friendship with the world is enmity with God ? Whosoever therefore would be a friend of the world maketh himself an enemy of God Or think ye that the Scripture speaketh in vain ? Doth the spirit that He made to dwell in us long unto envying ? But he giveth more grace Wherefore the Scripture saith, God resisteth the proud, but giveth grace to the humble "—JAS. IV. 1-6

I.—CONNEXION OF THOUGHT.

S. JAMES is no longer concerned merely with the teachers. His remarks henceforth are addressed to all who read his letter. He has dealt with the question, *Who is wise and understanding among you?* He has shown that the Heavenly *wisdom* issues in peace, but when he looks on the world, as he knows it, he finds no peace there. He has shown that the *wisdom* which is *earthly, sensual, and devilish,* results in jealousy, strife, confusion, and actions that are vile. He now asks the question as to why this is so, and finds his answer in the fact that worldly wisdom is concerned with the pursuit of pleasure. The search for pleasure, he teaches, leads to discord, whether we seek to satisfy the lusts of the flesh or are consumed by a covetousness " which is

The World

idolatry."[1] The life lived for pleasure, moreover, is a manifest failure, and that his converts are living for pleasure is shown not only by their prayers, but also by their discontent. This leads him to convict them of a *friendship with the world which is enmity with God*. In vain they plead that God is responsible for their nature and its desires. S. James refers them to the gift of grace. It is not indeed always effective, but that is due to human pride. The only hope of satisfaction is held out to the humble. God will exalt those only who are willing to abase themselves.

II.—THE WORLD AS KNOWN TO S. JAMES.

S. James has perfect faith in his own gospel, but he is under no illusion as to the actual condition of his converts. He recognizes failure; it is patent, and he proceeds to analyze its cause.

Yet the opening words of this section startle and surprise us. They seem more appropriate to the Wars of Religion in the sixteenth and seventeenth centuries than to the days of the Primitive Church. Some commentators have proposed to minimize their meaning, and maintain that *wars and fightings* are rhetorical equivalents for " sustained resentment " and " outbursts of passion." But as we pause on the word *kill*, we are driven to believe that if our author did not refer to armies and battles, he was at any rate thinking of actual violence and possible murders. He was a rhetorician without doubt, but he was a rhetorician concerned at least with what was possible, if he were

[1] Col. iii. 5.

not referring to something that had occurred. We must remember that he was dwelling in Jerusalem, and that "righteousness had once lodged there, but now murderers."[1] He was old enough to remember the anarchy that had prevailed in the country when Varus was Prefect of Syria. He knew all about the later excesses under Judas the Gaulonite, and had lived through the agony of persecution which followed on the stoning of Stephen. Perhaps he has in mind the war between Philadelphia and Pelea, or is thinking of the insurrection of Theudas. The Sicarii and Zealots were born, and were agitating even if the days of their fury had not come. Jerusalem was a city of tumults, where S. James himself was to be a victim, and the conditions of life about him dominate his thoughts. It is not, then, surprising that he should write of *wars and fighting*.

But, it may be objected, whatever the Jews were as a nation, surely there was a different spirit among those converted to Christianity! There was; but the converts were men of the same race, inheritors of the same traditions, and liable to the same temptations. The mob that tried to murder S. Paul[2] a few years later was probably, in part, composed of Jewish Christians.

While admitting all this, we must not forget that we are dealing with a circular letter sent out far and wide to the Christian Synagogues of the Dispersion, so we have no right to suppose that the author had in view any particular acts of violence. Assuming the very early date of the Epistle, we may remember also that the separation between Jew and Christian was not yet complete, and so we can imagine S. James addressing

[1] Isa. i. 21.   [2] Acts xxi. 28-31

Christian Jews very much as a Quaker in war-time might address Englishmen of his own persuasion. Neither he nor they could help regarding themselves as involved in what they looked upon with horror.

III.—THE WORLD AND THE FAILURE OF THE LIFE LIVED FOR PLEASURE.

S. James, the Christian Jew, may be thought of as appealing to all Jews, whether Christian or not. He asks them the question: *Whence come wars, and whence come fightings among you?* He suggests the answer in the form of another question: *Come they not hence, even of your pleasures that war in your members?* He wishes his readers to think the matter out for themselves. For once he is not authoritative, although we may conclude from what follows that he had made up his own mind.

Parallel statements are to be found in Plato, Cicero, and Philo, but they occur in a different context, and lead to different conclusions. In the *Testaments of the Twelve Patriarchs*, on the other hand, we find an author with the same point of view as S. James. He writes: "Keep, my children, the commandments of the Lord and obey His Law . . . and ye shall not fall into pleasure and turmoil, but ye shall be in peace, having the God of Peace, and no war shall harm you."[1]

The point of view is the same, but the text just quoted hardly helps us to the understanding of the passage. Why, it may be asked, should the external conflict of the first question be explained by something relating to the internal conflict of the soul. We have,

[1] *Testaments of the Twelve Patriarchs* Dan v.

then, to discover how the warfare in the microcosm leads to warfare in a wider world. We are not here dealing with an analogy: the author assumes a relationship of cause and effect.

S. James is, of course, speaking generally. He is not speaking of this pleasure or that, or of this person or that, but of the struggle that goes on in each who shares the common humanity. He does not condemn all pleasure by implication, for pleasure has its rightful place in life, and therefore is quite rightly one of the motives for action. We may give others pleasure or do ourselves what is pleasurable, offering our thanks to the God who wishes us to be happy, and "gives us richly all things to enjoy."[1] No, it is not pleasure that is condemned, but those *pleasures that war in our members*, that are in conflict with our work, our progress, our development, our duty, or our God.

And here it is to be noted that war is an inadequate translation of στρατευομένων. S. James was thinking of an army encamped in a hostile country. People often excuse themselves for self-indulgence, and plead that their pleasures are natural. As a matter of fact, they are very often the result of acquired tastes. Such pleasures take possession of us, and are all the more dangerous and all the more tyrannous because they are not natural, and nature rebels against them.

But leaving pleasures for a moment out of account, it is true that each man has within him an appetite for pleasure which ought to be kept under control and subordinated to such restrictions as religion and reason, prudence and temperance, suggest; indulged, it becomes

[1] 1 Tim vi 17

utterly reckless, and will produce disorder, provoke conflict, and drive a man to ruin.

Now, while the appetite for pleasure is within, the thing that pleases is generally to be found in the external world. We are not self-contained, and the war within is transferred without when pleasure seeks her fruition. When a man seeks his own and not another's good, he soon finds himself in conflict with all those who are actuated by the same spirit and engaged on the same search. Hence come wars and fightings between nations, classes, or individuals. For, first, in this world there are not enough of those things most desired to satisfy everyone. In fact, when free rein is given to the desires, a man becomes loath to share his pleasures. The last of the pleasures is this, that no one else can have them. So man strives to monopolize, and finds in his monopoly no content. Alexander wept because there were no more worlds to conquer; the conquered wept because Alexander was possessed of all they wanted for themselves. "Hell and destruction are never full: so the eyes of man are never satisfied."[1] Secondly, the pleasure of one is not always a pleasure to another. Tastes differ, and a small boy with a mouth-organ may be a terror to his friends. Not only do tastes differ, but many pleasures can only be obtained at the expense of others. There is the gay cheap dress that is the result of sweated labour, and the gay young man about town, whose sisters in the country are so dowdy that he despises them. Thirdly, in many cases the pleasure lies in the actual pain or disappointment of others. The spectators at gladiatorial shows revelled in blood

[1] Prov. xxvii 20.

and wounds, the winner of a competition finds his pleasure partly in his prize and partly in the number whom he has defeated, while there is the keen delight of the controversialist in the thrust that goes home. When we come to fanaticism and the wars of religion, it is harder to discover how they originate in the unrestrained inclination to pleasure. S. James, however, probably considered that all indulgence in passion was prompted by the desire for pleasure. He probably also guessed that the violence of the fanatic was often merely an echo of a fierce conflict between competing desires going on in the man's own soul. It is also true that reformed rakes make very intolerant saints. They give up one life of excitement and excess to embrace another with equal ardour. For soured natures there is no such pleasure as proving others in the wrong, and the lust for cruelty is the last perversion in the life lived for pleasure. Many men are cruel, and in persecutions or religious wars cruel men may indulge their inclinations and salve their consciences while doing so.

IV.—Pleasure and the Philosophy of the Godless.

S. James was not a philosopher engaged in formulating a system; he was rather a critic of the life which he saw about him. And yet in attributing wars and fightings to the pleasures encamped within our members, he is arguing against the world's morality which assumes pleasure to be motive of all action and its only intelligible end. Now, directly we try to organize or even to explain life without reference to God, we are

bound sooner or later to assume this position. For we
cannot believe in an immutable standard of right and
wrong without some speculation as to its sanction; we
cannot admit a moral consciousness without assuming
that it has a source. To believe in a life in accordance
with Nature, to believe in duty, to believe in an ordered
evolution of morality, means sooner or later a belief in
God. You can only get rid of God by arguing that
pleasure is the motive of all action. You then make
yourself and your own experience the criterion of all
things; you become independent, Gods unto yourselves.
The world, as S. James uses the word, has, then, a
morality of its own—but does S. James mean that it
can only lead to *wars and fighting* ?

First, we may not argue that because all strife is the
result of *pleasures that war in our members*, therefore all
pleasure must end in strife and war. Pleasure must
have a recognized place in life, and all pleasure does
not mean war within. Even among those who acknowledge no higher motive are many who lead lives of
outward peace. The refined æsthetic, who professedly
lives for pleasure, may be a man of quiet disposition,
maintaining himself with fastidious frugality, and faithful to his one canon, μηδὲν ἄγαν. Again, an austere
philanthropist, like John Stuart Mill, may find his highest
pleasure in promoting the welfare of the race, and lead
a useful life which merits respectful admiration. Such
men profess to follow pleasure, but only find it in the
way of reason, if indeed they find it at all. Their lives
do not lead to strife, but the principles they advocate
do, and their lives are the best support of a false philosophy. The truth is, that those who believe pleasure to

be the one motive for action, cannot find any real place in their system for that self-sacrifice on which all society has been based. Pleasure is a purely personal feeling, and therefore the pursuit of pleasure has for its end self-satisfaction. It is true that we experience pleasure in seeing the happiness of others, and that man, being a social creature, finds enjoyment in company. But when pleasure is the dominating motive, the happiness of others is secondary to that of self, and the company is only tolerated so long as it ministers to one's own enjoyment. Hence, as a motive for action, it will only unite men so long as they are conscious of a common need that has to be satisfied by common action. The moment the need is satisfied the bond is broken, and it is probable that they will quarrel over their shares. Again, because pleasure is a purely personal feeling and tastes differ, the best of good reasons for the life of virtue will be inoperative for those who have desires that are not virtuous. John Stuart Mill may preach a splendid sermon on benevolence, and find his highest pleasure in its practice; but few men are like him, and Jones prefers wine and women. He says to the philosopher: "Stop talking! I have but one life to live, and I shall live it for my own pleasure and not yours." Jones is honest, and the philosopher needs some other argument not in his armoury if he would convince Jones that there is a more excellent way.

Pleasure, then, is only one of the motives for action, and not the highest. For man's highest happiness is to attain to God; and oftentimes loyalty, duty, love, and admiration, calls us to that self-sacrifice in which pleasure is forgotten. We find the joy we had not sought when we forget ourselves.

V.—THE RESULTS ON CHARACTER OF LIVING FOR PLEASURE.

S. James is not thinking of philosophers like John Stuart Mill, he is dealing with men of hot blood and violent passions. He sees *wars and fightings*, with all the misery and horror that they entail. For him it is all the result of following in the world's way instead of following God. But he sees not merely the misery which results from men pursuing their own pleasures, he sees also the failure of the pleasure-seekers. He turns on them, and says : *Ye lust, and have not : ye kill, and covet, and cannot obtain : ye fight and war.*

This verse has given rise to much discussion. A sense for style repudiates *ye kill and covet*, and it has been suggested that the text is corrupt.

Nevertheless, I imagine S. James wrote *ye kill and covet* with careful deliberation. He wanted to bring out the illogical sequences in the life devoted to pleasure. Such a life achieves nothing, and ends in an anticlimax. He sees men lusting, discontented, envious. He hears the cry: "I must be satisfied." He sees the reckless act by which they grasp at their desires. He notes their disappointment in possession. They still covet.

We may go on and say he sees something further. He sees how the passions of the body, which provoke the young man to violence, are succeeded by the meaner passions of the mind ; how concupiscence gives place to avarice ; and how avarice, like lust, adds to the disorder of the world.

He sees still further into man's moral nature—the inevitable deterioration caused by sin. In the Bible we note Saul's splendid pride ending in a pitiful jealousy,[1] and Ahab, the masterful tyrant, who had warred and conquered kingdoms, sulking like a child because he could not have his garden of pot-herbs on the site which he had chosen.[2] First comes the splendid sin, and then the mean one. Many a duellist who has killed his man would have scorned the thought that he could possibly cheat him, but great crimes unrepented of lead to crimes that are despicable, and a man who has sinned boldly in his youth may sin like a sneak as he grows old.

But it is the fact of failure that S. James would most certainly impress upon us. In the life lived for pleasure there is always the lack of that peace which cometh from God only. S. Augustine pressed hard after many of the prizes offered by the world, but he learnt the truth at last, came to God and said: " Quia fecisti nos ad Te, et inquietum cor nostrum, donec requiescat in Te."[3]

VI.—THE WORLDLINESS OF CHRISTIANS SHOWN IN THEIR PRAYERS.

But S. James is not merely concerned with the wicked. His converts, he knew, were often actuated by worldliness even in the practice of their religion. They thought that their acceptance of the faith constituted a claim upon God, and still believed that righteousness must be rewarded with mundane pleasures. Hence they were discontented and rebellious against God when they found themselves

[1] 1 Sam xviii 8, 9   [2] 1 Kings xxi. 4   [3] Confessions 1 1.

harassed with trials and temptations. They were not at one with God, and their worldliness was equally shown by the way in which they did not pray, and the way in which they prayed amiss.

Our Blessed Lord had said, "Ask, and ye shall receive, that your joy may be full;"[1] but many who call themselves Christians, and say their prayers, think it more reverent not to ask God for temporal blessings, or to talk to Him about the ordinary affairs of everyday life. For these, there is a sphere in which God works, and another sphere with which, as far as they are concerned, He has no interest. This is not only to deny the sovereignty of God, but to make a little world apart from Him. The great saint, it is true, may be utterly indifferent to the affairs of this life, and therefore not speak of them in his prayers; but let us be quite sure that we share the saint's indifference, before we give up communicating to God our temporal concerns. Do not let us say by rote the prayers of the saints, while our minds are harassed with the difficulty which we find in paying our butcher's bill. Do not let us spend the day in planning some amusement, and refuse at night to speak to God on the subject. Do not let us, at any rate, take up the attitude of those who refuse to ask and then complain that they do not receive. To them S. James says plainly, *ye have not, because ye ask not.*

But there were many who could reply: "We have asked, and have not received." S. James answers: *Ye ask amiss, that ye may spend it on your pleasures.* They, too, are worldly, but more superstitious and more

[1] John xvi. 24.

logical than the others. They practise their religion for what they can get out of it. They fulfil certain duties by which they think to propitiate the Deity, and then demand that He will do what they want. Their conception of prayer is magical, and not religious. They have no desire for communion with God, but think that they can make use of His power to serve their own ends. They are living for pleasure, and intend to utilize all means in order to satisfy their selfish inclinations.

Prayer, however, implies a personal relationship. When we pray we are addressing a God, and not a machine. God is not like a shopman, saying, "What can I do for you?" He is a Father interested in all that concerns His children, and desirous that we should tell Him everything But we must approach Him as sons, and not as customers. We must ask in Christ's name—that is, in the filial spirit. Trusting in God's perfect knowledge and wisdom, we must say, "Thy will be done"; but God's love is such that He wants to do our will, and so encourages us by saying, "Ask, and ye shall receive." If we do not receive the answer we expect, we may be sure that it is through our ignorance in asking. "Every way of a man is right in his own eyes, but the Lord pondereth the hearts."[1] We are so often deluded by appearances into asking what God, who weigheth our hearts, knows that we should not like if we received. "The too indulgent Gods," said Juvenal, "have ere now overthrown whole households by answering their prayers."

[1] Prov xxi 2.

VII.—Friendship with the World is Spiritual Adultery.

After ascribing the disorder of the world to the life lived for pleasure, S. James has shown the failure of the pleasure-seeker both in the material and spiritual sphere. He has convicted his converts of manifesting this worldly spirit even in their prayers, and he now turns to condemn them, saying: *Ye adulteresses, know ye not that friendship with the world is enmity with God? Whosoever, therefore, would be a friend of the world maketh himself an enemy of God. Or think ye that the Scripture speaketh in vain?*

The term *adulteresses* is not, of course, to be taken literally, neither is its feminine form merely due to contempt. S. James was saturated in the Hebrew Scriptures, and he was writing to Jews who could not mistake his allusion. Isaiah had written, "Thy Maker is thy husband";[1] and in Jeremiah we read: "Turn, O backsliding children, saith the Lord, for I am married to you";[2] while both Hosea and Ezekiel stigmatize as adultery any unfaithfulness to the covenant of Jehovah.[3] The simile passed on quite naturally into the New Testament, where Christ is the Bridegroom and the Church His Bride.[4] The desire of a wife is to her husband, and the Church which desires the world as well as Christ is an *adulteress*. The word φιλία, translated *friendship*, carries on the metaphor, for it does not merely imply goodwill, but an inclination derived from sense and emotion. S. James is in another way teaching what Our Lord meant when He

[1] Isa. liv. 5.
[2] Jer. iii. 14
[3] Hos. ii 2, Ezek. xxiii.
[4] Eph. v 25, 27.

said: "No man can serve two masters." We "cannot serve God and Mammon,"[1] for both alike demand an undivided allegiance.

VIII.—THE OPPOSITION OF THE CHURCH AND THE WORLD.

In classical usage the word κόσμος often stands for the external order, for the totality of things seen. We understand therefore how in the New Testament the word came to represent something in opposition to "the things not seen as yet."[2] This opposition is not of Nature, but is due to the wills of men and evil spirits. It cannot always be traced in operation, for if men have sold themselves to sin, redemptive forces are also now at work, so that we can no longer say with precision, this is of the world and this of the Church. But, when S. James wrote, the antagonism between the world and God was obvious and unmistakable. The State was the one supreme sovereign entity, material well-being was the one acknowledged good, pleasure was the only recognized motive for action, right and might were equivalents, and power was vested in the big battalions. Temples were reared to the merely material forces, and men were deified because of their worldly success. The growing cult of the Cæsars was an idolatry of material achievement.

Stoics indeed taught differently, but Stoicism was at the time suspect. It was the philosophy of discontented and disinherited aristocrats at Rome, and the world as known to S. James was the terrible democracy, with its bureaucratic system and its tyrant head.

[1] Matt. vi. 24. [2] Heb. xi. 1-3.

Over against the solidarity of this world was the little Church. She claimed that her Faith alone was true, she demanded a complete surrender and refused all compromise. She taught the sovereignty of God, she proclaimed a Gospel for the poor, she upheld duty as the ruling motive, and insisted that love and truth were the prevailing powers. She despised the material forces, her saints were men "of whom the world was not worthy,"[1] she sought the New Jerusalem and promised eternal life.

A man had then to choose between the Church and the World, for by becoming a Christian he cut himself adrift. He had to bear the accusation of being an atheist, because he acknowledged none of the thousand and one Gods who were worshipped He was called an enemy of mankind, because he could not participate in the social customs of his times without compromising his faith. The days were soon coming when he would be accused of treason, because his religion forbade compliance with what the public service required. The Early Church in the great towns of the Empire started to build up society anew from the very foundations. For three centuries Rome strove in vain to destroy the Church, and was then forced to surrender at discretion.

The Old World was conquered, but its spirit survived, and has ever since been reacting on Christendom. In fact, at the present day, there are indications that the old battle will have to be fought afresh on the same clearly defined issues. Once more men are dreaming of a purely secular state, organized without reference to God, which shall be all powerful and control the whole of life from the cradle to the grave. Once more men

---

[1] Heb. xi. 38.

are being taught that material well-being is alone of importance. Once more it is urged that, though right and wrong may be matters of opinion, though truth and falsehood may be matters for discussion, the will of the majority alone shall count—a majority which may be manipulated and drilled to be more tyrannical than the big battalions of the Roman Imperator.

IX.—WORLDLINESS OF TO-DAY.

Meantime we are ever face to face with what we have learnt to call *worldliness*. It is a pervasive spirit that may be found equally in the counting-house of a banker or in the garret of a bankrupt, in drawing-rooms and in churches, in a nation's Senate or in a hermit's cell. We can neither stamp any particular class or society as worldly, nor any particular business or amusement. We have passed beyond the position of those who thought a theatre wicked, but crowded to a dramatic performance in a hall. But we have not passed beyond the teaching of S. James, and have still to learn how *friendship with the world is enmity with God*.

The text insists on the sovereignty of God. He will accept no divided allegiance, and claims to be concerned in all we do.[1] He is a jealous God, who repudiates a merely lukewarm attachment, and says to each of us: "My son, give Me thy heart."[2] But a man's heart may be given elsewhere. The world is the great seducer, who comes offering gifts—palpable, tangible offerings, and we are led by "the deceitfulness of riches"[3] to embrace her. The gifts may be real in a way, but they are fleeting: moth and rust decay them,

[1] Exod xx 5. [2] Prov. xxiii. 26. [3] Matt. xiii. 22.

thieves break through and steal them.[1] God may give such gifts as well as the world, but He does not offer them as a bribe. He only offers Himself as our perfect satisfaction. It is the harlot who sells herself for a price, and cares not for the person but the money.

But to all this it may be answered, 'It takes two parties to insure a friendship; φιλία not only implies loving but being loved. Now, *the God* you are speaking of is a Person, but your World is merely an abstraction. In what sense can we speak of a friendship with an abstraction?' *The world* is composed of individuals, and it has a collective being, which expresses itself as Public Opinion. Public Opinion in itself may be good or bad, but to court its approval and live for its awards aptly sums up what S. James means by *friendship with the world*.

Public Opinion may be our refuge from the voice of conscience. Human pride rebelling against the sense of its imperfections is consoled by the tolerance of society, and the assurance that others are no better.

Public Opinion makes cowards of men. Few dare to stand alone, to be remarked, to be jeered at, to be despised, as the followers of Christ.

Public Opinion makes men hypocrites. It causes them to fast, to pray, to give alms that they may be seen of others. They seek the friendship of the world, and S. James warns them, *friendship with the world is enmity with God*.

But it may be asked: "Is it wrong to be popular?" No, because popularity may be ours without being sought. The danger lies in living for popularity, and so Our Lord warns us to beware when all men speak

[1] Matt. vi 19.

well of us; but everything depends on the motive which inspires our conduct. S. James saw this quite clearly. Even in the second chapter he admits that a rich man may be placed in the best seat out of consideration for *the Royal Law*. So here he guards against a too absolute application of his dictum by adding, *Whosoever therefore would* (βουληθῇ) *be a friend of the world maketh himself an enemy of God*. Let men examine their motives. Are they living for popularity, or are their pleasant ways prompted by love, by duty, by devotion to Our Lord?

S. James, then, has spoken directly to those whom he brands as *adulteresses*. He has summed up the teaching of the Prophets, and he ends on a satirical note. Am I right, he asks, *or think ye that the Scripture speaketh in vain?* The teaching of Scripture has been faithfully applied, and the converts cannot reject S. James without repudiating the Prophets.

X.—THE NATURAL LUSTS AND GOD-GIVEN GRACE.

It has been customary to take these last words, *Or think ye that the Scripture speaketh in vain?* with what follows, but an alternative argument is implied by the word *or*, and no such argument can be made out of the following verse. Besides, that verse is in no sense a quotation from Scripture, so it is better to take it as a fresh contribution to S. James's theme. The verse is indeed full of difficulty, and the text is not certain. The Revisers give us no less than three translations, so they were agreed in nothing but a desire to alter the Authorized Version. With some hesitation I adopt

The World

the following rendering: *The spirit that He hath made to dwell in us lusteth unto envying, but He giveth more grace.*

The first question to be solved is the connexion of thought. As in so many passages, S. James was writing with his converts in mind. Having condemned that "covetousness which is idolatry,"[1] and in consequence spiritual adultery, he anticipates how someone will reply: "I covet, I am envious, but I did not make myself. I am what I am because God made me so, and God is responsible." He does not deny the fact, but shows that the conclusion does not follow. Let it be granted that *the spirit He hath made to dwell in us lusteth unto envying*, still it must not be forgotten *He giveth grace* more than sufficient to counterbalance the defects of nature. Next he imagines the objector ready with his retort, "Such grace has not been given to me, and why has it not been given?" S. James rejoins by quoting a verse from the Book of Proverbs: *He resisteth the proud, and giveth grace unto the humble.*

This argument is fairly clear, but it is obvious that S. James by writing *lusteth unto envying* ($\pi\rho\grave{o}s$ $\phi\theta\acute{o}\nu o\nu$ $\dot{\epsilon}\pi\iota\pi o\theta\epsilon\hat{\iota}$) hints at a distinction which he does not care to press. We are all born with more desires than can be gratified in a single life on earth; and it is the best men who are most conscious of longings which can never be satisfied in this world. Such longings are not only natural, but they provide the momentum that makes for progress both in the individual life and the life of nations. But with the slothful and inert they lead to discontent. A man ceases to pursue his legitimate aspirations, and cannot bear to see others who are more

[1] Col. iii. 5.

fortunate. He wishes them to be deprived of what he has not got, and cannot obtain. He is envious. It will in consequence be seen that whereas our desires are natural, our lack of satisfaction is due to our circumstances or our indolence, and the attitude we adopt with regard to our failure is due to ourselves alone.

S. James merely indicates this line of defence which might be replied to. He prefers to appeal to fact rather than to reasoning. He says, even granting you are right, there is the fact of *grace* which cannot be left out of account.

In saying, He giveth more grace, he appeals to experience. Theological disputations as to the nature, mode, and effect of grace had not yet arisen. The various charismata were at the time well recognized facts in the Church. Not only did men speak with tongues and perform miracles, but men were changed, transformed, and ennobled as they passed out of darkness into the marvellous light of the Gospel. Let men consider. The Church was being formed out of very unpromising material. From the beginning, publicans and harlots had pressed into it. Unlearned men were holding their own with trained Rabbis, poor men and slaves were rising superior to their degradation, out of the mouths of babes and sucklings God was perfecting praise.[1] Who could have imagined that the little band who gathered on the mountain-side to hear Our Lord's commission were the men to discipline all nations and turn the world upside down?[2] Here was Mary Magdalene, out of whom the Lord cast seven devils; Matthew the Publican; the rash, headstrong Peter guiding the

[1] Ps. viii. 2 , Matt. xxi. 16.   [2] Matt xxviii. 19, 20.

Church with discretion and forbearance; Saul the persecutor become Paul the Apostle. The work of the Spirit was mighty in operation. S. Mark, the man whom S. Paul rejected for his cowardice when starting on his second missionary journey, was to become the man upon whom the same S. Paul was to rely in the hour of his own supreme trial;[1] while the hot-headed Son of Thunder was to be transformed into the Apostle of Love. Out of weakness men were made strong, and waxed valiant in fight.[2] Men surrendered their possessions voluntarily,[3] men broke away from their old lives and dearest ties. They surmounted their defeats, and grew to hate their darling sins. They suffered cheerfully deprivations, persecutions, and pain, and they acknowledged He was faithful who had promised, "My grace is sufficient for you."[4]

XI.—GOD RESISTS THE PROUD.

Such was the evidence to which S. James appealed with confidence, but he recognized how some of his readers would reply, "No such grace has been vouchsafed to me!" This perhaps he might have denied, but had he done so he could not have proved his point. He prefers to state why Grace may not be given, or if given may be inoperative. He says: *God resisteth the proud, and giveth grace unto the humble.*

It may be thought that, being led into quotation,[5] S. James has inverted his real meaning; but had he said, "the proud resist God," he would have uttered a

---

[1] 2 Tim iv. 11. [2] Heb xi 34. [3] Acts iv 34.
[4] 2 Cor xii 9 [5] Prov iii. 34

platitude, whereas by saying, *God resisteth the proud*, he provides matter for thought. To some it seems more consonant with the Divine dignity that God should be indifferent to man's rebellion. For them it is inconceivable that God should accept man's challenge, and "scatter the Proud in the imagination of their hearts."[1] They say: 'A great statesman cares nothing for the reptile Press that assails him, and will God enter into conflict with a man?' A great statesman has only limited energy and a limited time to work in, and he cannot waste either in setting fools right, but God knows no such limitations. The Almighty can care for the great things and the small. But the objector proceeds: 'The statesman shows his superiority by not replying, it is inconsistent with his dignity to do so. He is indifferent to abuse, he does not care. Why is God not equally indifferent?' Because God is Love. It is in amazement that the Psalmist cries: "Who is like unto the Lord our God, that hath His dwelling so high, and yet humbleth Himself to behold the things that are in heaven and earth?"[2] Had God been indifferent, man would have been left to his fate. There would have been no Incarnation, no Cross, no Atonement. God is not indifferent to any individual soul, however corrupt. He pleads with every sinner. "He would have all men to be saved, and come to the knowledge of the truth."[3] So He *resists the proud*, who claim to be independent of Him. It is just because He cares for the proud that He condescends to oppose. It is because He cares for them sufficiently that He does not destroy them, but reverences the wills which He has

[1] Luke i 51.   [2] Ps. cxiii 5   [3] 1 Tim. ii. 4

made. When God would redeem men from servitude to sin and Satan, He did not assert His Power by any tremendous theophany. He became man, and fought the battle as a man. He came to resist the proud, but He did not come proudly. He humbled Himself to meet His foes under equal conditions, and won the victory through pain and death.

But another reason may be given for God's resistance of the proud. "Humiliations," says S. Bernard, "are the road to humility"; and it is only when we have been made to realize our own sinfulness and our complete failure that we become suppliants for God's grace. Humility is not a virtue of our fallen nature. In fact, some of the greatest moralists have regarded it with contempt. And yet it is the necessary condition of progress, and the secret of peace. S. Peter, when commenting like S. James on this text, regards humility itself as a supernatural gift. He tells his converts to be "clothed with it,"[1] and what we are clothed with is not of nature. It is for him like the bridal garment spoken of by Our Lord,[2] something offered by the King that must be accepted and put on before we go in to the heavenly banquet to feast on the gifts of God.

So long as we are not humble, our ultimate conclusion is that of the Miltonic Devil, "Better to reign in Hell than serve in Heaven," and just so long we shall tend to produce the conditions of Hell—discord and confusion. "Give me the hearts of all men humbled," said Richard Hooker, "and what is there to disturb or overthrow the peace of the world? wherein many things are the cause of much evil, but pride of all."[3]

[1] 1 Pet. v. 5. [2] Matt. xxii. 11 [3] Hooker, vol. iii., 606.

LECTURE XIII

HUMILITY

"Be subject therefore unto God, but resist the Devil, and he will flee from you Draw nigh to God, and He will draw nigh to you. Cleanse your hands, ye sinners, and purify your hearts, ye double-minded. Be afflicted, and mourn, and weep let your laughter be turned into mourning, and your joy to heaviness Humble yourselves in the sight of the Lord, and He shall exalt you."—
Jas. iv. 7-10

I.—Connexion of Thought.

S. James has dealt with the distinction between earthly and heavenly wisdom. He has shown the results of worldliness, and proclaimed the value of God's grace. He has found the final obstacle to peace in human pride, and the condition of progress in humility.

He now turns to exhortation. If God sets Himself against the proud, let men set themselves under God. This will involve them in warfare with the Devil, but as they *draw nigh to God, God will draw nigh to them.* He knows, indeed, that men must have "clean hands and pure hearts"[1] if they would appear in God's Presence; but he knows also that purification has become a possibility, and that God will not reject the penitent. So he urges men to mortify themselves and express their humility in action. Salvation is not necessarily for the humbled, but for those who humble themselves. So he concludes: *Humble yourselves therefore in the sight of the Lord, and He will exalt you.*

[1] Ps. xxiv 4

II.—THE VIRTUE OF HUMILITY.

There is, of course, a false humility, and many know the virtue only by a counterfeit presentment. For them it is a euphemism for cowardice, a cloak assumed by the hypocrite, or the last virtue which a scoundrel pretends to when it is quite obvious that he has no other. But there would be no counterfeit claim if there were no attractiveness in the virtue, and humility when genuine insures the love of God and men, though men often love the humble without knowing why.

Everyone acknowledges that it is better to look up than to look down, to be filled with admiration, and not with contempt. They forget that admiration comes naturally from the lowly, but has to be extorted from the proud. Everyone likes those who think of others rather than themselves, and it is just because the humble think but little of themselves that they have time to spend on others. Most men rebel against condescension, and are not very grateful for the most splendid patronage: it is only the humble who can meet all men on their own level, and confer benefits as if they were freewill offerings. Man's noblest aspiration is to serve, and it is our God who comes as the humble Jesus, saying: "Lo, I am among you as one that serveth."[1]

Men in this world cannot be independent and prosper, but they can choose their own masters, and, having chosen a master, there is no disgrace in being a good servant. Humility, then, does not imply the cringing of a whipped spaniel, but the voluntary abasement of the true lover, conscious of his own unworthiness, but

[1] Luke xxii 27

eager to give all that he has for the perfection he adores. Every high-spirited man chafes under an enforced subjection, while every noble-spirited man longs to serve where he loves. The tyrants of this world would make men conscious of their compulsion; it is God alone who refuses to compel, it is only therefore in His service that there is perfect freedom. So S. Peter calls on men to "humble" themselves "under the mighty hand of God,"[1] and S. James commands, *Be subject therefore unto God.* Both writers were recruiting for the noblest of all services, they would have men be like S. Christopher, unwilling to serve any but the strongest of all.

III.—THE CONFLICT OF THE HUMBLE.

Humility may be a purely passive quality—an acquiescence in inferiority. It may betoken a mean-spirited refusal to meet opposition. Such, however, was not the humility preached by S. James. For him submission to God entails conflict with that Devil, who is "as a roaring lion, walking about, seeking whom he may devour."[2] There are people who believe that submission to God will immediately result in outward peace and inward calm. The Apostles knew better. They remembered how our Blessed Lord on the very day after His Baptism was led by the Spirit into the wilderness,[3] to be alone with the wild beasts and to be tempted of the Devil.

The Devil can leave the indifferent to drift, he can lull the proud into a feeling of security, but he girds himself for battle against those who submit to God.

[1] 1 Pet. v 6.   [2] 1 Pet v. 8.   [3] Mark i. 12, 13.

Humility

S. James tells his disciples not to be frightened. He calls on them to take part in God's warfare if they are God's servants. *God resisteth the proud*, and the Devil is their master. Therefore he says, *Resist the Devil*, and adds God's promise, *he shall flee from you*. It is God's promise, and therefore *shall* is better than *will*. S. James is not merely stating a fact, but making an announcement, thus it shall be.

Many commentators have supposed that here we have a saying of Our Lord's, because both S. Peter and S. Paul have similar exhortations.[1] But all three writers were probably thinking of the Temptation, and when S. James adds *he shall flee from you*, he was not unmindful of how Satan was obliged to depart, when the words "Get thee behind Me"[2] were spoken. S. James has just been teaching that *friendship with the world is enmity with God*, which makes his allusion still more clear. On the mountain-top the Devil had claimed this world as his own, and offered his dominion here for an act of homage. Our Lord had rejected the easy and immediate triumph, and S. James commands resistance when any offer of like nature shall be made.

But, it may be asked, does humility really qualify a man to resist? It is a great mistake to suppose that the humble are incapable of fighting. They do not boast and brag, they may not be aggressive or challenge opposition; but they are often endowed with tenacity and powers of endurance, while for many reasons they are more likely than the proud to be valiant in defence. S. Peter tells those who fight the Devil to "be sober and vigilant,"[3] and the humble are

[1] 1 Pet v. 9, Eph vi. 13 [2] Luke iv 8 [3] 1 Pet. v 8.

most likely to be both, whereas the proud are apt to be careless. S. Paul counsels, " put on the whole armour of God."[1] He knew men would need all the protection they could get. He knew that they could not conquer in their own strength He tells them " to use the sword of the Spirit, which is the word of God,"[2] for it was thus Our Lord vanquished the Devil, using the words of Scripture. Here, again, is a reason why the humble rather than the proud should prevail. The proud are too sure of their own strength, too self-confident; they are apt to be surprised, and are tempted to despair when what they deemed impossible has happened. The proud are ever impatient of failure, the humble have hardly hoped to succeed. The proud expect a triumph as their due, while the humble know that they must be prepared to accept "the same sufferings which are accomplished in their brethren."[3]

IV.—THE ASPIRATIONS OF THE HUMBLE.

Humility, then, lies in submission to God, and submission to God entails warfare with the Devil. That warfare in turn should render men more humble, for in the stress of the conflict they will feel more and more their need of God's assistance *Draw nigh to God*, says S. James, and promises, *God will draw nigh to you*. The Adversary may be strong and crafty, but with God, our Helper, no defeat is possible.

But it may be asked, Can we designate men as humble who dare to aspire to God? I think we can, for men are most conscious of their low estate when

[1] Eph. vi. 11 [2] Eph vi. 17 [3] 1 Pet. v. 9

Humility

their eyes are fixed on the everlasting hills. Some humble folk are indeed content with gazing, but they do not cease to be humble when they begin to climb. They only become proud when they stop and look down. So long as they look up, the height seems to grow as they advance, they make mistakes and have to retrace their steps, fresh difficulties are always confronting them worse than those they have just surmounted, they progress painfully on their hands and knees, and acknowledge with gratitude every assistance that is offered. Nothing keeps men so humble as the highest aspirations.

The proud, on the other hand, only wish to dominate the plain. They treat the world as if it belonged to them; or, wrapt in self-contemplation, pretend to be indifferent as to whom the world belongs. They pose upon a pedestal which they have themselves erected, and look down with disdain on those who look up to them. But to pose upon a pedestal is to remain stationary, and the pedestal is after all only just above the level of the crowd. It is well not to be jostled as one of a herd, but there is no happiness in isolation, and no progress for the isolated.

This does not mean that a proud man may not be great. He may. He is sometimes one who has climbed to a certain height and stopped. Again, a man may be progressing in some directions and stationary in others. For instance, a proud Peer may be a very humble politician; and a proud poet may be a very humble citizen. The truth remains that humility is necessary for progress.

Even in the world of men the same truth is brought

home to us. An aristocrat may be proud and yet maintain his position. He can keep others at a distance even though he cannot himself advance. The cynic will tell the man who wishes to rise that he will have to creep and crawl in order to do so. The cynic sneers, and the cynic is to some extent right. But it is not the creeping and crawling that render men contemptible, but the things they creep for and the persons they crawl to. The climber is not ashamed as he crawls along the perilous ridge, the lover is not ashamed as he kneels to his mistress, and the Christian need not be ashamed as he creeps to the Cross. Reverence shows that we recognize something above us. Only fools are blind to that fact, and in consequence contented with their own altitude.

But it may be questioned, granting that we acknowledge a God above us, have we any power to *draw nigh?* Did not Our Lord say, "Ye have not chosen Me, but I have chosen you"?[1] Has not S. James taught us that *of His own will begat He us with the word of Truth?* Must we not in consequence wait for Him to *draw nigh,* and is it consistent with humility that we should *draw nigh* to Him? These questions are due to forgetfulness of the context. S. James is addressing Christians who have wandered from the way, and he is urging them to return. The Prodigal Son was born of the Father's will, but went into a "far country" following his own.[2] It was also of his own will that he returned, and when he was yet a long way off the father ran to meet him.[3] Our birth, our family, our country, our talents, opportunities, and election, are all due to God; but we can

[1] John xv. 16 [2] Luke xv 13 [3] Luke xv. 20.

err and stray and desert Our Father's home. We can keep out of His way, or can *draw nigh* to Him. As Azariah, the son of Oded, told Asa : " The Lord is with you, while you be with Him ; and if ye seek Him, He will be found of you ; but if you forsake Him, He will forsake you."[1] God refuses to keep us in leading strings, but He is ever ready to hasten to our call. The conflict with the Devil may be severe, the path of progress will be certainly uphill, but the promise standeth sure, *Draw nigh to God, and He will draw nigh to you.*

V.—Penitence: the Characteristic of the Humble.

It is, then, in resisting the Devil that the humble draw nigh to God; and it is through the flight of the Devil that the world is restored to God. As the Devil is cast out, "the meek inherit the earth";[2] they are God's children, and He is among them. But before men can draw nigh to God there must be some proof of their humility. It is not sufficient to recognize a power above us. To be really humble we must be convinced of our own unworthiness and feel the conviction of our past sins. There is no better test of our humility than a willingness to confess ourselves wrong. It is joyous no doubt "to go up to the house of the Lord with those who keep holy day,"[3] but the humble are bound to ask, " Who shall ascend into the Hill of the Lord, and who shall stand in His Holy Place?"[4] The answer comes, " Even he that hath clean hands and a pure heart."[5]

[1] 2 Chron xv. 2. [2] Matt v. 5 [3] Ps. xlii 4
[4] Ps. xxiv. 3 [5] Ps. xxiv. 4

Now, S. James has just convicted his converts of *fighting and wars*. He has said to them, *Ye kill and covet*. He has also called them *adulteresses*, because they have not been faithful, but have wavered in their loyalty through friendship with the world. In consequence, while encouraging them to *draw nigh* to God, he sternly reminds them of the conditions. *Cleanse your hands, ye sinners; and purify your hearts, ye double-minded.*

The verb ἐγγίζειν (to draw near) has in the Septuagint a technical meaning, and is used for the ascent of the Priests to the Altar. In the ritual law we read that before the Priests draw near, "they shall wash their hands and feet that they die not."[1] The Psalmist sings, "I will wash my hands in innocency, and so will I go to Thy altar";[2] and the Psalmist prays, "Give me a clean heart, O God; and renew a right spirit within me."[3] The Prophets knew that something more was necessary than ceremonial purification. Jeremiah pleads, "O Jerusalem, wash thine heart from wickedness that thou mayest be saved."[4]

It was natural for S. James to adopt the symbolical language of the Old Testament. The *hands* are mentioned as the instruments of action. It is with them men *fight and war*; and it is only when "lifting up holy hands"[5] men dare to pray. The *heart* in Hebrew symbolism stands not merely for the emotions, but for the entire character. It is with the heart men cleave unto God. The double-minded men, however, only express an entire devotion, while thinking of their own advantage and advancement. To them the Psalmist

[1] Exod xxx. 20 [2] Ps xxvi. 6. [3] Ps li. 10.
[4] Jer. iv. 14. [5] 1 Tim. ii. 8.

Humility

says, "The Lord shall cut off all flattering lips, and the tongue that speaketh proud things."[1] With such a threat in mind, S. James cries to his converts, *Purify your hearts, ye double-minded.*

The converts might indeed answer, How can we cleanse our hands and purify our hearts? It is impossible to undo the past, and we cannot change our natures We have ceased to hope that the blood of bulls and goats can wash away sin,[2] and sin is a bondage from which we cannot escape.

S. James, however, has already said, *mercy triumphs over judgment*, and though you may have become evil, yet *He giveth more grace*. He might now go on, and show that the way of forgiveness has been opened up through the cleansing blood of Jesus. He might show them that with the Great High Priest they might "draw near with boldness unto the throne of grace."[3] But S. James is here more concerned with man's approach to God than with God's approach to man, and so he develops his sense of what true repentance requires; it is, after all, only to the penitent that pardon is offered. Those who "turn to God" must "do works meet for repentance."[4] The cleansing is God's act. Men cannot merit forgiveness, but they must seek it in the appointed way They have to acknowledge that their hands are not clean nor their hearts pure; but there are many, conscious of this, who will not face humiliation. S. James, in consequence, exhorts them: *Be afflicted, and mourn, and weep; let your laughter be turned into mourning, and your joy into heaviness.*

[1] Ps. xii 3
[2] Heb x. 4.
[3] Heb. iv. 16.
[4] Acts xxvi. 20.

VI.—Mortification: The Way of the Humble.

There is indeed a false humility which causes men to submit from fear. Such men recognize God's power, and would escape God's punishment. But the truly humble are in pain because of the Love against which they have so grievously offended. They not only want to be at one again with God, but they want also to make clear to themselves, to God, and their neighbours, that they are sorry. They feel that they not only deserve, but need correction. They are eager to accept any penance, to repent, if need be, in sackcloth and ashes.

S. James, himself an ascetic, sympathizes with this feeling. He would have the sinners he is dealing with feel it also, and calls on them to *be afflicted*. The word suggests fasting and corporal austerities. S. Paul wrote later, "I buffet my body to bring it into subjection."[1] He tells how he was "in fastings often."[2] He exhorts S. Timothy "to endure hardness as a good soldier of Jesus Christ."[3] Self-discipline must include the discipline of the body, and humility to be perfect must include the subjection of the proud flesh. The modern world has revolted from such teaching and would explain it away. Men pet and pamper the body, they regard its health and comfort as of the very first importance; but when they come to discuss religion, they pretend that the body is of no account. They have invented a religion which they call spiritual, and it is such that neither the Incarnation nor the Cross can have any meaning for them. Christ's sacrifice for us

[1] 1 Cor. ix. 27 (R.V.).   [2] 2 Cor. xi. 27   [3] 2 Tim. ii. 3

is our only hope of salvation, but His true disciples would identify themselves as far as possible with His offering. They know that He commands them to take up their cross and follow after Him.[1] They would, in S. Paul's startling phrase, "fill up that which is behind of the sufferings of Christ."[2]

By afflicting themselves Christians would show their sorrow. They have no idea of propitiating God. Men cannot atone for sin. If they could there would be no need for mourning. We do not mourn over what we can put right. So S. James goes on, *mourn and weep*. The two words are often found together in Scripture, and relate to the inward emotion and the outward expression. Both have their place, for there is no relief until we have found a vent for pent up feelings.

Men may bewail their sins, and go to sin again. They may seek absolution, and desire to be cleansed from the past, and yet not be steadfastly purposed to lead a new life. What they want is a new nature. So S. James goes on, *Let your laughter be turned into mourning, and your joy into heaviness*. In this sentence the word *your* is important. Joy and laughter are alike good, but it is the laughter and joy of those whom he is addressing which must be renounced. It is the scornful laughter of the proud whom God resisteth which is to be turned into mourning. It is the joy of the worldling which is to be turned into heaviness. This joy proceeds from satisfying the lust of the eyes. Those, therefore, who have lifted up their eyes that they may behold vanity,[3] must cast them down in shame. The word for heaviness ($κατήφεια$) literally means a casting down of the eyes.

[1] Mark viii. 34 [2] Col. i. 24. [3] Ps. xxiv 4.

So we are reminded of the Publican, who, "standing afar off, would not lift up so much as his eyes unto Heaven, but smote upon his breast, saying, God be merciful to me a sinner."[1]

VII.—THE EXALTATION OF THE HUMBLE.

S. James is careful that men should not be misled. As he reminded them in the first chapter that their deeds of mercy were to be done *before God and the Father*, so here he says, *Humble yourselves therefore in the sight of the Lord*, for there is an asceticism which is only practised to be seen of men. It is true that the Church recognizes public penance, and has authority to impose it; but such penance is not self-chosen, and is imposed because the sin against God is also a scandal to the community. But public penance is not here in the mind of S. James He is concerned only with the way in which the humble penitent should approach God.

Christianity has sometimes been called the religion of sorrow, which is false, but it is the only religion for the sorrowful. And here it is to be noted that S. James does not advocate a life spent in affliction and weeping. His words are addressed to the sinner and the double-minded. They must humble themselves, and, when they have done so, they will find nothing of bitterness in the glad tears of reconciliation.

Then we come to the conclusion of the whole matter. S. James says, if you humble yourselves in the sight of the Lord, *He shall exalt you*. He repeats a promise of Jesus, "He that humbleth himself shall be exalted."[2]

[1] Luke xviii 13   [2] Luke xiv. 11.

He has shown in part what that exaltation means. It means a victory over the Devil and renewed intercourse with God, it means progress in the future and a blotting out of the past, it means a new nature and a new outlook. We cannot also help thinking of the lowliness of that handmaiden with whom God was well pleased.[1] We know that she is called blessed throughout all generations. God has highly exalted her, the pattern of humility; and God says to us, " Humble yourselves likewise, and I will exalt you."

[1] Luke i. 48.

LECTURE XIV

CRITICISM

"Speak not one against another, brethren He that speaketh against a brother, or judgeth his brother, speaketh against the law, and judgeth the law but if thou judgest the law, thou art not a doer of the law, but a judge. One only is the lawgiver and judge, even He who is able to save and to destroy but who art thou that judgest thy neighbour?"—JAS IV. 11, 12

I.—CONNEXION OF THOUGHT.

IN reading this passage we are at first surprised by what seems to be the abrupt inconsequence of its introduction. As we weigh the words, however, we are compelled to acknowledge that they are especially characteristic of S. James, and, as we master their significance, we are led to see the association of ideas in the author's mind.

S. James is far from being systematic in his treatment. He assumes to the full the licence of a letter-writer. But he is ever consistent in his point of view, and in the emphasis he lays on certain fundamental ideas. Here he adopts once more his attitude towards *the Law*, and towards those who are *Judges with evil thoughts*. He once more insists on *doing* rather than *talking*, and he reinforces what he has written on the perils of speech by bringing his readers face to face with their *Judge*. He has already spoken of the judgment to come, and he is about to develop his teaching as to the sovereign Lawgiver.

His argument may seem to proceed at random, but that is largely due to the fact that he is writing with definite correspondents in view. He pauses as a phrase is completed, and thinks of someone or some class to whom it may be applied. The result is something unexpected, but there is a true sequence of thought. In this passage he has just finished speaking of humility, and he turns to condemn the arrogance with which men judge one another, and the presumption which they show in usurping the functions of God.

It is the abruptness of the style that startles us, and it is quite possible that S. James calculated on its effect. We can imagine a man who had heard with complacence the exhortation to humility, suddenly convicted of presumption and pride by the ensuing verses now under consideration. In the thirtieth chapter of S. Clement's Epistle, we can follow the same sequence of thought without receiving any shock. He begins with a list of sins to be forsaken, ending with "hateful pride." He then quotes the same text as S. James, *God resisteth the proud, and giveth grace to the humble*. He goes on to urge the virtue of humility and a consequent avoidance of evil speaking (καταλαλία). His method is more clear, but is it so effective?

II.—RUDENESS AND GOSSIP.

S. James starts with a very simple exhortation, *Speak not one against another, brethren;* and first we would note that καταλαλέω always implies detraction, but not always backbiting. This point is worth making, for there are many who, although they condemn backbiting, at any rate in theory, are rather proud of their rudeness, which they call "plainness of speech." Backbiting is, of course, detestable in a friend; but when the backbiter is detected, it is not so much what he has said, but his duplicity and insincerity, that merits opprobrium. On the other hand, everyone is aware that his own conduct and manners are matters for comment, but he would much prefer that the comment should be delayed until he has departed. What would be comparatively harmless if said in our absence, might be very offensive if spoken to our face. S. James exhorts men generally not to speak one against another. He condemns not only secret defamation but the open rudeness that provokes resentment.

We can easily imagine how necessary this exhortation was when Christians lived together in small communities, and everyone knew everyone else. In such communities it is tempting to talk of others, because the person you are talking to is also interested in them. In such communities stories are certain to be repeated, because the society is too self-contained and its interests are too personal for the current of gossip to be cut off. In a big society A tells B a story about C, but B talks to a dozen people before he meets one who would be interested in the repetition of the story, by which time he has probably forgotten it. In a small society the story is repeated within a few minutes, and it circulates with rapidity, gathering volume as it goes. If the story to start with was an ill-natured one, C is certain to suffer in reputation, and is almost as certain to hear it himself in its most exaggerated form. He then, as likely as not, does not quarrel with A, but with

Criticism

Z, who heard it last of all as a matter of common knowledge, and is in no way responsible for its inception, growth, or embellishments. Speaking against neighbours without any sense of responsibility is always wrong, but it is most dangerous in small places and among little communities.

But it may be asked, Is all gossip wrong? There are certain people, indeed, who pretend to be superior to it. They are often prigs, and nearly always dull. There are dear, delightful, good people who indulge in it moderately, but do so with an uneasy conscience. The evils attending gossip are patent, but do they flow from an abuse, or is gossip in itself wrong? Now, though "the noblest study of mankind is" not "man" but God, man ranks higher than the weather, than any science or any art. Man, in consequence, is the natural subject of most conversation, and man refuses to be treated as an abstraction: he is only real when he is a personality. Social creatures, though not given to study, cannot fail to be interested in one another, and also in one another's concerns. This interest finds its natural vent in talk, and as we are more interested in our neighbours than in politicians or royalties, we talk more about them. A middle-aged man probably knows no greater pleasure than to meet someone whom he has not seen for some years, and talk over old times and old friends. But it is impossible to do so except from a certain standpoint. It is the standpoint that matters. Kindly gossip is quite innocent. S. James does not say, "Do not speak about one another," but *Do not speak against one another* κατα in this case has a strictly adversative force.

No one is so charming as the man who talks well of his neighbours, and is appreciative of their good qualities. We soon grow tired of the biting tongue. All men have their shortcomings, their failures, and their sins; do not let us dwell on them; and, if we must write of them, let us write as our Saviour did in the dust.[1] Some men feel that they exalt themselves by casting others down; our Saviour bent Himself to the ground that He should not see a woman's shame. Pride finds its justification in proving the faults of superiors; humility finds a reason for hopefulness in the virtues of the worst. Malice delights in retailing what will lead to another's abasement, while " charity covers a multitude of sins."[2] *Speak not one against another, brethren*, cries S. James, and he did not add that word *brethren* without a reason. Christians were then known as *the brethren*. They formed the Church, which is the family of God. Brothers must be careful in speech when the reputation of the family is at stake. They should naturally wish to hide one another's faults, for to blazon the faults of a brother is to blacken one's own escutcheon.

III.—Speaking against our Neighbour a Sin against God.

Although S. James begins by considering the ideal relations that should subsist among brethren, he immediately remembers that those relations only obtain through the common dependence on One Father. Therefore he bases his argument against scandal and criticism on the fact that they contravene the law of

[1] John viii 6.   [2] 1 Pet. iv. 8.

that Father who is our God. It is of God he would have us think rather than of man. If man is in a right relation with God, he must be in a right relation with his fellows; but an attempt to preserve union among brethren on grounds of common interest or mere expediency might end in alienation from God and the consequent dissolution of the brotherhood. S. James for this reason refuses to dwell on the social inconveniency which arises from scandal, and passes on to the sin and presumption of the ill-natured critic. He is not a philosopher commending a scheme of ethics to students, but a preacher commissioned to convict men of sin. So he proceeds: *He that speaketh against a brother, or judgeth a brother, speaketh against the law, and judgeth the law; but if thou judgeth the law, thou art not a doer of the law, but a judge. One only is the Lawgiver and the Judge, even He that is able to save and destroy; but who art thou that judgest another?*

IV.—EVIL SPEAKING A CRITICISM OF THE LAW.

The first thing here to decide is the sense in which S. James uses the word law, νόμος without the article. The Jews, it is true, often made no distinction between the moral, legal, and ritual codes. All were to them of like importance. They did not recognize the very necessary distinction between things that are forbidden because they are wrong, and things that are wrong because they are forbidden. Certain critics, in consequence, assuming that S. James is here referring to the Torah, have found in this passage an attack on S. Paul. He criticized the law, and so made himself a judge, and placed himself in opposition to the supreme Lawgiver. S. Paul, of course, did nothing of the kind, and if S. James imagined that he did, he surely had a very inept way of introducing his argument. If the critics were right, they would have to go on and confess that the passage is an obvious interpolation, for it would be absolutely irreconcilable with the context. Thus, having found the passage an interpolation, they would cease to have any additional evidence for an opposition between S. Paul and S. James. Personally, I believe this letter was written before the Pauline controversy began; I am ready to admit that Judaizers, tearing the words out of their context, may have used them against S. Paul—controversialists are capable of anything, but critics boasting of a scientific method should know better. If S. James were referring to the Torah at all, we should have in this case to seek for some definite commandment, such as "Thou shalt not go up and down as a talebearer among the people";[1] but had S. James the Torah in view? He has already spoken of *the Law of Liberty* implanted in the heart, he has already quoted *the Royal Law, Thou shalt love thy neighbour as thyself*, and here he has the same conception in view. He has, as we saw in Lecture VII., Rabbinic authority for this usage, and is entirely at one with S. Paul, who says, "Love is the fulfilling of the Law."[2]

Our Lord had said: "A new commandment give I unto you, that ye love one another."[3] Here is the Law by which Christians are to be tried, and S. James would have men review the scandal they talk and the judgment they pronounce in the light of that law. He would

[1] Lev. xix 16. [2] Rom xiii. 10 [3] John xiii. 34.

have them also remember that behind the Law is the Lawgiver speaking with a voice of warning: "Judge not, and ye shall not be judged."[1]

V.—THE LIMITS OF CRITICISM.

These words of Our Lord no doubt account for the new term introduced into the argument. It is now concerned not only with the man who *speaketh against his brother*, but with the man *who judgeth his brother*. We pause here to ask if it is possible to live without forming judgments on others, and if it be not our duty sometimes to publish them ? The *Didache*, which is quite as definite as S. James on the subject of slander, says: " Thou shalt hate no man, but some thou shalt reprove, and for some thou shalt pray, and some thou shalt love more than thy soul."[2] Here is a call to discrimination that involves judgment, but it is not the sort of judgment deprecated by S. James.

In one sense it is quite true that man is a creature who forms judgments. He cannot help himself, for he was made in the image of that God who is *the Judge*. Neither can he restrict this faculty to things in general or to abstractions. He must apply it to persons. He forms an opinion as to a man's conduct which passes inevitably into a judgment on a man's character, and is he in consequence to be condemned ? S. James would answer: " No, not necessarily." He would go on to explain that he did not use the word judge for one who deliberates, but in a narrower sense for one who pronounces sentence. Yet this would not prevent him from

[1] Luke vi 37.   [2] *Didache*, ii. 7

maintaining that, in coming to the most private and personal conclusions, we needed to be informed by the spirit of Love, and that we were bound by the Law of Love in making those decisions known. If we love our neighbours, we shall incline to the more favourable interpretation; and if that be too improbable, we shall be ready to give them the benefit of the doubt. Hard judgments should be condemned—we dare not press the letter of the Law; but hasty judgments should be impossible—we should hear the other side. We need to beware of partiality and prejudice, and not to be too certain that we are right. All our judgments are provisional, for we can never know all the facts. The whole sphere of motive, for instance, must ever be dark to us. We may have our suspicions, but they are only more or less probable, and in consequence men are well advised to keep their judgments on others as far as possible to themselves.

Secondly, it is strictly true that men demand judgment from their fellows "No man liveth to himself alone."[1] No poet publishes his verse, no artist exhibits his picture, no statesman proposes a new law, and no schoolboy shows off his latest accomplishment, but asks a verdict from his fellows. And the verdict on his work must be a verdict on himself. In fact, the more sincere his work, the more personal will be the verdict. The artist at least knows that he has put himself into it. He tells you that he willingly runs the risk of condemnation. Anything he prefers to chill indifference: and surely S. James does not prohibit the verdict being given? Certainly not. For S. James *the judge* was not

[1] Rom xiv 7

Criticism

the true critic, but the person who has, or arrogates to himself, the right to censure. S. James, however, would remind the critic that he, too, is bound by the law of love; he, too, has to remember that "with what measure he metes, it will be measured to him again."[1] The busy fault-finder may be always right, and yet not be the most useful critic. The power to appreciate the right things is more valuable in criticism than the power to detect what is wrong. The merely negative or destructive critic is certainly *not a doer of the work, but a judge*. He is not always even competent, but hazards a sounding judgment for which he does not know enough to give the reasons.

So when S. James speaks of a *judge*, he does not primarily refer to the man who makes up his mind as to his neighbours, or to a man who accepts an invitation to express his opinion. He intends one who claims a right to settle a question by pronouncing sentence or presumes to publish his censures.

Thirdly, it must not be forgotten that the supreme Lawgiver has, under certain conditions, entrusted His law to the administration of men. The magistrate is God's minister, and "beareth not the sword in vain."[2] The priest is God's minister; he is a "steward of the Mysteries";[3] to him has been entrusted the awful power of the keys.[4] The parent is the minister of God, with authority to discipline and chastise. Schoolmasters, employers, officers in the Army and Navy, civil servants, and others, are all bound to issue decisions and enforce them. These judges are not, however, irresponsible;

---

[1] Matt vii 2, Luke vi 38.
[2] Rom xiii. 4
[3] 1 Cor iv 1.
[4] Matt. xvi 19.

they exercise a delegated commission. The King has
his unction, he rules by the grace of God. The priest
has his orders, he has been consecrated for his work.
The parent's position is in accordance with nature, and
nature is the Will of God. Employers are told to
remember that they, too, "have a Master in Heaven."[1]
All are responsible to God for their acts; all are, or
ought to be, bound by His Law; and to God, in all cases,
is the ultimate appeal. Those, therefore, who judge
others have to remember that they are not tyrants, but
administrators. When duty necessitates it, a judgment
must be given; but when it is not our duty to decide,
we do well to be silent.

Now, S. James, by his wording, carefully precludes
such judgments from his view. He is only dealing with
him who judges his brother. There is equality among
brethren; and when men meet as brethren, to none of
them has been entrusted authority as judge.

In conclusion, to S. James the word "Judge" did not
mean an administrator of the Law. He distinguishes
between a *doer of the Law* and *a Judge*. He does not
use the word in a strictly forensic sense, for we note that
for him the *Judge* and the *Lawgiver* are one. He is a
Jew writing to Jews, and in Hebrew there is one word
for Judge and Ruler.

VI.—THE TRUE JUDGE.

When S. James writes, *He that speaketh against his
brother or judgeth his brother, speaketh against the Law
and judgeth the Law*, he has in view the people who
seem to say, "With our tongues will we prevail; our

[1] Eph vi. 9.

lips are our own: who is lord over us?"[1] Self-appointed judges recognize no responsibility for their decisions, they act as if there were no law, they are a law unto themselves. S. James does not mean that they put their criticism of the Law into words, or make a formal claim to revise God's Commandments. Had they done so, they would have been beyond the reach of his expostulation. His words are written to enlighten *brethren* as to what is involved and implied by the pride and arrogance of their censures. They are pretending to exercise a power for which they have received no authority, and are exercising it in a way which is contrary to the known law of their brotherhood. What, then, could they plead in justification of themselves? They could only justify themselves by speaking against the Law, or by maintaining that they were the judges as to when that Law was applicable. Such people would not be *doers of the Law*, that is, administrators, but were presuming to *be judges*, that is, rulers with power to issue their own decrees. What, then, should be our relation to the Law? We may administer it, we must obey it, we dare not criticize it, for One only is the *Lawgiver and the Judge*, and He is God.

The unique sovereignty of God was an idea ever present to the mind of the devout Jew. He pondered the awful claim: "I, even I, am He, and there is no God beside Me: I kill, and I make alive; I wound, and I heal: neither is there any who can deliver out of Mine hand."[2] Remembering this, we see the significance of the fact that S. James in the fifth chapter, like S. Paul, attributes the coming judgment to Our Lord.[3] In this

[1] Ps. xii 4.   [2] Deut xxxii 39.   [3] Acts xvii 31.

passage, when condemning evil-speaking and presumptuous judgments, he no doubt remembers Him who said: "By thy words thou shalt be justified, and by thy words thou shalt be condemned."[1] And "with what measure ye mete withal, it shall be measured to you again."[2]

S. James, then, was thinking of Our Lord when he characterizes the Lawgiver and Judge as *even He who is able to save and destroy*. The words preclude the idea of an administrator of the Law, for an administrator can only condemn, but cannot really destroy; he has no authority to save the guilty. It is, however, inherent in Our Lord's power both to *save and destroy*. He is the Saviour who can pardon the guilty, He is the Lord who can destroy the impenitent. He represents a higher justice than human thought can formulate, and a higher power than human thought can conceive. Perfectly just, there is a finality about His judgments, and from them there is no appeal.

Such being the case, we need not be surprised at S. James's scornful inquiry, *Who art thou that judgest thy neighbour?* Canst thou *save or destroy?*"

When a man cannot enforce his decrees, he renders himself ridiculous by publishing them. When a man presumes to play the master with his fellow-servants, he is liable to receive an unpleasant reminder that his business is to be himself obedient, to be a *doer of the Law*. When a man lives in fear of his own imminent judgment, he will be careful as to the condemnation he passes upon others. So S. Paul teaches, "Who art thou that judgest another man's servant? To his own

[1] Matt. xii. 37.   [2] Luke vi 38.

master he standeth and falleth. . . . Why dost thou judge thy brother? and why dost thou set at nought thy brother? for we shall all stand before the judgment-seat of Christ. . . . Let us not therefore judge one another: but judge this rather, that no man put a stumbling-block on an occasion to fall in his brother's way."[1]

[1] Rom. xiv. 4, 10, 13.

LECTURE XV

PRESUMPTION AND PLANS

"Go to now, ye that say, To-day or to morrow we will go into this city, and spend a year there, and trade, and get gain whereas ye know not what shall be on the morrow. What is your life? For ye are a vapour, that appeareth for a little time, and then vanisheth away. For that ye ought to say, If the Lord will, we shall both live, and do this or that. But now ye glory in your vauntings all such glorying is evil. To him therefore that knoweth to do good, and doeth it not, to him it is sin."—JAS. IV. 13-17

I.—CONNEXION OF THOUGHT.

S. JAMES has dealt with a man's presumption in judging his fellows; he now turns to deal with his presumption in planning his own future. Once more he brings his readers face to face with the Sovereignty of God.

God is not only the Lawgiver and the Judge, but times and seasons are in His Hands. Men dare not in consequence plan their lives without reference to HIM. They ought to ask humbly, "What wilt Thou have us to do?"[1] They cannot settle on selfish projects for *to-day and to-morrow and the year to come.* God may have other work for them to do, and no one has the right to live unto himself alone.

[1] Acts ix. 6.

II.—THE JEW TRADER.

The passage is primarily addressed to the busy trading class. The Semite was a born trader, and every land and sea was full of Jews. Together with the Phœnicians they controlled the carrying trade of the world. Our Lord made several allusions to commerce, and told the Parables of the merchantman seeking goodly pearls,[1] and of the master who went abroad leaving funds with his servants to be put out at usury.[2] Probably it was no unusual thing for a son to ask for his portion and to seek his fortune in some far country.[3] The Mishna has special regulations for Jews travelling both by land and sea. It definitely allows trade in everything not directly required for heathen sacrifice. Jews might not sell fir cones and myrtles because sacred to Venus, but they might sell slaves and traffic in the souls of men sacred to the Almighty.

At Antioch, Alexandria, Cyrene, and a few other places, Jews as Jews had rights of citizenship, but even then their religion excluded them almost entirely from civic life. In most places they were excluded from citizenship by law, and therefore had no ties with the places where they dwelt and no interest in them, save in so far as they offered opportunities to *get gain*.

Nevertheless, among themselves they were highly organized. Wherever they went they built synagogues, or had places of prayer, and introduced their law and preserved their racial customs. Just because they were a people apart, they were bound more closely together. They had connexions everywhere, and were

[1] Matt. xiii. 45, 46.   [2] Matt. xxv 14-30   [3] Luke xv 12, 13

not anywhere at home. They followed their trade, and were continually on the move. For instance, Aquila, a Jew of Pontus, came from Rome to Corinth, and proceeded very shortly to Ephesus. He was once more at Rome, when S. Paul wrote to that Church, and again at Ephesus when S. Paul was nearing his end.[1] Sometimes, as S. James has already reminded us, *the rich man faded away in his goings*, but the Jew was ever an optimist when business was to be done. He was quite confident in saying, *I will go unto this city, and spend a year there, and trade, and get gain*. S. James replies to him with a scornful, *Go to, ye know not what shall be on the morrow*. He feels contempt for the presumption with which such men map their lives.

It is a pity that the weight of manuscript authority is against reading *to-day and to-morrow*, which would add a note of definiteness to the trader's project and limit the distance he intended to travel. Apart from that, with what a dramatic instinct S. James writes! The man knows that it is *this* city he is bound for. He has decided to stay *one year*. He is not going to look for work, but has considered the openings for *trade*. He has even calculated on his profits: he will *get gain*. He ticks off the items as he piles up the conjunctions. He will go, *and* stay, *and* trade *and* get gain; but he leaves God out of account. S. James reminds him, *Ye know not what will be on the morrow*. All depends on your life, which is like *a mist that appeareth for a little time, and then vanisheth away*.

[1] Acts xviii. 1, 2, 18; Rom. xvi. 3; 2 Tim. iv. 19

III.—The Getting of Gain as an End in Itself.

It will be noted that the man not only shows presumption by making his plans without reference to God, but he shows his presumption likewise in pursuing an end with which God has nothing to do. There are too many with no further object than to *get gain*. They may be honest and respectable, they may have religious beliefs and be punctual in the performance of religious duties, but they are not "seeking first the Kingdom of God and His righteousness."[1] They pursue those things which "their Heavenly Father knows that they have need of,"[2] without a thought of His Providence, and without respect for His Law—in fact, although perhaps unconsciously, they are recognizing two divinities, God and Mammon, and are trying to serve them both. They keep their religion and their working lives quite distinct. They have the world in their heart, and dare not ask God to share in their efforts to *get gain*. They have not mastered S. James's previous lesson on *friendship with the world being enmity with God.*

It is not the getting of gain that is wrong. The laws of Nature suggest increase, while to be fruitful and multiply is the first divine command.[3] It is leaving God out of account that is wrong. It is because God is left out of account in business, that we have a loose commercial morality, exploited classes, sweating, and all its attendant evils. Trade must ultimately improve if conducted with a view to mutual service—that is, in accordance with the *Royal Law ;* but cut-throat competition, tyrannous monopolists, and the extortions of

[1] Matt. vi. 33.   [2] Matt vi. 32   [3] Gen 1. 28.

the covetous, only enrich individuals, and cannot be for the permanent advance of trade. A few become over-rich at the expense of the many becoming poor. In time the number of consumers and their purchasing power becomes less and less. Trade declines and profits disappear, because gain has been sought presumptuously without a thought of God and in direct contravention of His Law.

Long ages ago Aristotle taught the world that wealth could not be regarded as an end in itself, but undoubtedly it is the end proposed by many in the commercial classes. They might not feel inclined to admit it in argument, but the fact remains that they live to amass money with no idea of spending it or enjoying it. They may not even have a child to inherit their accumulations. *To get gain* is for them veritably an end.

An excuse indeed might be found for them in Aristotle, where he teaches that ἐνέργεια is so much important than τό ἔργον which results from it. So it can be argued that men go on working and making money, because they enjoy using the many faculties called into play by business, and not because they are greedy of the gains for which they have no use. This is no doubt true in numberless cases, but it only proves that there is a vast expenditure of energy which ought to be directed into other channels. It is just because money-makers tend to become so engrossed in their pursuit, that they lose sight of the things that are more excellent. They have forgotten God, they have forgotten how to enjoy life, they have sold themselves to be machines, and at last their splendid faculties and glorious energy can only be utilized in the service of Mammon.

No man ever started life with such an end in view. At worst, most men begin with the selfish idea of enjoying the fruits of their labours. As time goes on they cease to be capable of that enjoyment, and it is then that gain for the sake of gain becomes their irrational end. Traders are especially liable to this form of madness, because gain is for them the only result of their labours. The poet has his poem, the painter his picture, the artisan his craft, the professional man his skill. They, too, work for gain, but in estimating their success there are other values not to be reckoned in coin. They know, moreover, that directly they concentrate their minds on money-making they produce pot-boilers and shoddy goods. On the other hand, wealth tends to be the one test of the trader's success.

In saying this there is no intention of decrying trade. The world owes much to its Merchant Princes. Trade has proved to be for the world's welfare. It has had a civilizing effect. It breaks down the barriers between nations. It enables the human race to pool the product of their many labours for the common benefit. What do we not owe to the enterprise of men who have discovered new markets, developed new industries, introduced new arts, and made the resources of the whole earth everywhere available? What, too, do we not owe to the public spirit and munificence of men whose wealth has been the result of trade? But such men were not merely money-grabbers, they did not merely live to *get gain*, they lived to serve God and their fellows, and so the argument of S. James does not apply to them.

IV.—LIFE APART FROM GOD.

It is, however, well to remember that if gain is *the especial* snare of the trader, selfishness in the possession of riches and presumption in attaining them is a temptation to all classes. Philo has a parable about a husbandman who said: "I will cast seeds; I will plant; the seeds will grow and bear fruit. . . . But he who made these calculations did not enjoy them, but died beforehand. It is best to trust in God, and not uncertain calculations." Similarly Our Lord told the Parable of the Rich Fool who pulled down his barns and built greater, until he could say to his soul: "Soul, thou hast much goods laid up for many years; take thine ease, eat, drink, and be merry. But God said unto him, Thou fool, this night thy soul shall be required of thee, then whose shall these things be which thou hast provided? So is he that layeth up treasure for himself, but is not rich before God."[1]

The parables are superficially alike, but the moral is different. Philo is in reality only counselling prudence. We must have God on our side if we would enjoy the fruits of our labours. Our Lord, on the other hand, is insisting on how great is the value of a man's soul, and how little the value of his temporary possessions. He does not insist on the man's disappointment, but on God's. It is God who requires the soul. It comes to Him in poverty-stricken nakedness. It comes to the Judge *with power to save and destroy*.

Now, it is from Our Lord's standpoint that S. James asks the greedy accumulator, *What is your life?* and

[1] Luke xii 20-21.

answers his own question by saying, *Ye are like a mist that appeareth for a little time, and then vanisheth away.*

The simile was not new, but it is here especially appropriate.[1] *The mist* rises from the earth; it is formless, variable in density, and moves. Within it nothing is clear; it is chill, damp, and dreary; but the sun dispels it altogether, and no trace is left behind. So says S. James to the grasping Jew: "You are of the earth, but have no settled home and no certain principles. Your way is dark, dreary and chill; you are without vision and without love, for you have wilfully excluded the light of God. But God is still in His heaven, and when the Sun of righteousness ariseth, His light is spread abroad and you vanish away."

V.—Presumptuous Plans.

What, then, ought men to do? Should they not make plans, and ought they to fold their hands in idleness and wait for God to provide? Certainly not; S. James forbids any such thought when he writes: *Ye ought to say, If the Lord will, we shall both live, and do this or that.* Here by implication we are directed to plan our future, but to do so in co-operation with God. So Our Lord did not say, "Take no thought," but "Be not anxious for the things of to-morrow."[2] Men are to exercise forethought—it is a God-given faculty; they are to plan and to labour—God demands industry in the use of their talents. But a man is a fool who does not allow for the uncertainty of life, or who plans to *do this or that* apart from God's Law. A man is irreligious who

[1] Wisd ii. 4 [2] Matt. vi. 31.

only works for himself without a thought for his Maker. God made man for Himself, and whatever man's vocation, whether it be to rule empires or sweep crossings, the work is of God's election, and must be done in conformity with His Will. *If the Lord will* is not merely a pietistic phrase, but should be an act of submission, a recognition of the fact that we do not belong to ourselves, that we have a vocation, and intend our oft-repeated prayer: "Thy will be done on earth as it is done in Heaven."[1]

There are some people, with great respect for the letter of Scripture, who scatter the initials D.V. throughout their correspondence; but a person who lives in the consciousness that he exists to do God's Will does not need to parade it. Neither is the practice really commendable. The mere fact of the abbreviations shows a lack of that high seriousness with which the name of God should be invoked. It savours too much of the phylacteries of the Pharisees, and it irritates the ungodly. They are, moreover, amused to see it sometimes written above the line, and laugh over the fact that it is sometimes altogether forgotten. They mark how the man who proposes to pay a visit D.V. on a postcard, makes a verbal engagement with them next day without any such formula. The initials, too, may be written through mere superstition as a charm against being disappointed; and some people use them in much the same spirit that others touch wood. S. James wanted men in all things to submit to God's Will; he did not wish to provide them with a magic formula for getting their own way. He did not wish them to

[1] Matt. vi 10.

Presumption and Plans

attract attention to their superior piety. He wanted them to be humble and without presumption. *But now*, he says, *ye glory in your boastings: all such glorying is evil.*

VI.—SELF-CONFIDENCE AND SELF-SUFFICIENCY.

In the Book of Proverbs we read, "Boast not thyself of to-morrow, for thou knowest not what a day may bring forth."[1] This is common-sense. Rabbi Simeon tells how he was returning from a feast where a man had boasted of the old wine he was laying down for his son, when he met an Angel who declared that he was sent forth to slay the boastful, and that the son should not live thirty days. This story is susceptible of no higher teaching than the Greek legend of Niobe. It is consistent with a belief in a tyrant God, jealous of human happiness. S. James has a deeper insight than the author of the Proverbs, and a fuller grasp of moral values than the Rabbi, when he tells us *all such glorying is evil*. There is a glorying that is good S. Paul gloried in the Cross of Christ.[2] Men ought to rejoice and glory also in all the powers God has given them and in all the opportunities God offers. S. James only condemns *such glorying* as that of the man setting out to *get gain* for himself and by himself.

Self-confidence is in many ways to be commended. Unless a man realizes his ability, he will never be able to do much. But the self-confident need especially to beware lest they forget the God who has endowed them with their powers. If they do, their self-confidence passes into self-conceit. They live as if they had made

[1] Prov. xxvii 1. [2] Gal. vi. 14

themselves, and soon go on to live only for themselves.
They plan, they succeed, and take all the credit to
themselves for their success. They grasp the gains
they have achieved as if they were their very own to do
as they like with. They no longer consider others, and
so come to identify what they want with what is right.
They despise the weakling and the failure, and begin to
quarrel with their rivals. They do not perceive how
evil they have become, and are quite unconscious of
the evil that they do. They live presumptuously and
die miserably, no one loving, no one pitying them.
They have boasted of their self-sufficiency, they have
asked no sympathy, they have given none. Social life
depends on our sense of mutual need, and both
individual and social life only finds its explanation in a
humble dependence on the love of God.

VII.—RESPONSIBILITY FOR WEALTH AND SINS OF OMISSION.

For such reasons *boasting* is condemned. It is not merely foolish, it is *evil*.

Any man who thinks for a minute must know this. At least S. James believes that he must, and in consequence concludes: *To him that knoweth to do good, and doeth it not, to him it is sin.* We should have expected him to say: "To him that knoweth that it is evil, and doeth it, to him it is sin." So he might have provided us with a conclusion so obvious as to be unnecessary. As it is he says something that compels us to pause and wonder.

The form that the aphorism takes surprises us. The

Presumption and Plans

disconnected style makes us at first suspect inconsequent thinking. The thought indeed is especially characteristic of the author who insists on *the Royal Law*, on being *doers of the word*, and on *faith without works being dead*. It would be possible to insert this verse several times in the Epistle, and yet it is perhaps particularly appropriate in the place where it occurs.

S. James is dealing with a subject on which his readers could not possibly plead ignorance. They acknowledged a God, and in consequence their dependence upon Him. They must know in consequence that their boasting is evil, because God is denied His meed of praise. Even if they were such as denied the Being of God, they could not escape from recognizing the mutability of fortune. They know this, and so the folly of their boasting is apparent. Again, no reasonable men can argue that to *get gain* is the end of life. But if it be not the end, they must confess that wealth has its responsibilities. They who think so much of wealth cannot be ignorant of the constant opportunities it offers, and the far-reaching possibilities for usefulness it provides. They know this, and cannot deny it. They could do good if they chose: and if they do it not, *to them it is sin*. So S. James brings home to the wealthy how heinous for them are sins of omission. Let them cease from boasting of their profits, and consider how they may be utilized for the good of others and the glory of God.

LECTURE XVI

THE SINS OF THE RICH

"Go to now, ye rich, weep and howl for your miseries that are coming upon you Your riches are corrupted, and your garments are moth-eaten. Your gold and your silver are rusted, and their rust shall be for a testimony against you, and shall eat your flesh as fire. Ye have laid up your treasure in the last days Behold, the hire of your labourers who mowed your fields, which is of you kept back by fraud, crieth out and the cries of them that reaped have entered into the ears of the Lord of Sabaoth Ye have lived delicately on the earth, and taken your pleasure, ye have nourished your hearts in a day of slaughter. Ye have condemned, ye have killed the righteous one, He doth not resist you."—
JAS. v. 1-6

I.—CONNEXION OF THOUGHT.

S. JAMES has denounced the bustling trader for his presumptuous disregard of God. He begins once more with a scornful *Go to,* and in language reminiscent of the Hebrew Prophets denounces as a class the opulent Jews. Their wealth, he tells them, is *corrupt, moth-eaten, and rusted,* and the condition of their wealth is symbolical of themselves. They have made it by fraud; in entire selfishness they have either hoarded or squandered it; and the day of retribution is at hand. *Weep and howl for your miseries that are coming upon you,* he cries. The time has gone by when he might have exhorted them to *weep and howl* for their sins.

II.—THE RICH JEWS

Weep (κλαύσατε) suggests the audible crying of a child that is hurt, while *howling* (ὀλολύζοντες) suggests the semi-liturgical lamentations of Orientals. The rich who have *lived delicately* will cry aloud in their miseries; those who have slain the Just One will mourn in vain before the God of Justice. *The miseries are coming upon them*. The present tense denotes the imminence and the fact that there is no escape. S. James is not uttering a curse, he is writing from the prophetic standpoint. He is announcing the inevitable logic of events. There is no uncertainty about his prediction. It is as convincing as that of Jonah. " Yet forty days, and Nineveh shall be overthrown."[1]

The words are not addressed to *the brethren*, but are rather introduced with the object of making *the brethren* patient under the oppression of the rich. They are written in the Name of Him who says: " Vengeance is Mine, and I will repay."[2] S. James is inspired with the sense of the awful calamities that are coming upon the Jews, and he has no hesitation in ascribing them to God's wrath against sinners. The Jew had ever been inclined to over-estimate the importance of wealth, and to be unscrupulous as to how he acquired it. Amos had denounced " the robbery and violence "[3] of those who dwelt in palaces. Micah had denounced the oppression of the poor by those who coveted houses and fields.[4] Isaiah had cried: " Woe unto them that join house to house, and lay field to field, till there be

---

[1] Jonah iii. 4.
[2] Rom. xii. 19.
[3] Amos iii. 10.
[4] Mic. ii. 2

no place, that they may be placed alone in the midst of the earth."[1]

If S. James, before the second destruction of Jerusalem, calls on men to "weep and howl," Jeremiah, before the previous destruction of the city, had cried: "Gird yourself with sackcloth, lament and howl, for the fierce anger of the Lord is not turned back from you."[2] Nebuchadnezzar stripped the nobles and drove them naked before him to be slaves in Babylon. The camp followers of Titus were to disembowel refugee Jews in the search for gold and precious stones.[3] The warning was for the time, for people then alive; and the prophecy was terribly fulfilled. Those who believe in an unchangeable God will mark His judgments in the days of old, and remember that similar sins may have a similar recompense.

III.—Saving and Squandering Then and Now.

S. James, then, is not concerned with any economic theory, but with the sins of individuals. He does not question the rights of private property as such, but denounces the selfishness of those who possess it. The passage has at first sight this difficulty, that the man who hoards and the man who squanders seem to be confused in the indictment. But the miser and the spendthrift have much in common. The one engrosses more than he can use, and the other wastes what he does not want. Both are selfish, and both use wealth in a way that is unproductive.

It is also well to remember that the East has ever

[1] Isa. v 8. [2] Jer iv. 8. [3] Josephus, *Wars*, bk. v.

been the land of buried treasure. The instinct to hoard where credit is uncertain does not necessarily imply the penurious ways of a miser. The rich fool in the parable, with his well-stored barns, meant "to eat, and drink, and be merry."[1] Dives, who could afford so little in charity, "was clothed in purple and fine linen, and fared sumptuously every day."[2] The man who wastes his substance in senseless luxury is rarely generous and often avaricious. He does not always pay his debts, but he is grasping for the uttermost farthing that is due to him.

S. James first considers the nature of hoarding. He sees that wealth so stored depreciates. He would bring their folly home to the rich when he says: *Your riches are corrupted, your garments are moth-eaten, your gold and silver are rusted*.

Your riches ($\dot{o}\ \pi\lambda o\hat{v}\tau o\varsigma\ \dot{v}\mu\hat{\omega}\nu$) would literally cover all external possessions, but the verb $\sigma\acute{e}\sigma\eta\pi\epsilon$ makes us limit them to stores of perishable goods, such as corn, wine, and oil. Eastern wealth consisted of such things, of rich embroidered garments, and of the precious metals. Gold and silver do not rust ($\kappa\alpha\tau\acute{\iota}\omega\tau\alpha\iota$); they only tarnish. S. James forgot this, and he wanted the word *rust* for the metaphors that follow. Perhaps also he had in mind Our Lord's condemnation of those "who lay up treasure on the earth, where moth and rust ($\sigma\grave{\eta}\varsigma\ \kappa\alpha\grave{\iota}\ \beta\rho\hat{\omega}\sigma\iota\varsigma$) do corrupt ($\dot{\alpha}\phi\alpha\nu\acute{\iota}\zeta\epsilon\iota$), and thieves break through and steal."[3] But if so, by his choice of words he shows that he is not indebted to S. Matthew's Gospel.

The economic conditions of to-day are so different from those of our author that it is somewhat difficult

[1] Luke xii. 19. [2] Luke xvi 19. [3] Matt. vi. 19.

to apply his words directly. A man to-day may have very simple tastes and a very large income, but his accumulations are no longer in a strong box, and his goods are not locked up in barns. His wealth is all invested and far from unproductive. His savings no longer menace the world with want, but are a security for the world's progress. He is, in fact, a trustee for the community, and because his administration is unfettered, he can, if he pleases, afford to be generous and to take risks. Poor men cannot afford to be generous, and public bodies dare not. Poor men ought not to take risks, and boards of management will not. They often waste money from lack of personal interest, and they are too much bound down by red-tape to have any enterprise.

Saving, then, to-day is altogether different from hoarding in the past. In those days men engrossed the necessaries of life, and let others starve in order that they might be idle. To-day the savings of the industrious provide work and wages, that men should not starve. To-day few men hoard, misers are extremely rare, and hardly anyone buries his talent in a napkin. If interest were abolished, and there was no longer a productive employment of savings, the incentive to hoard would again be strong. But socialism in this sense is not imminent. We have learnt the economic lesson that hoarded wealth depreciates, but we have not learnt the moral lesson that the merely selfish employment of wealth is wrong. S. James passes at once from the economic fact to the sin that it presupposes, and to-day he would find the same sin existing, though the conditions of society are so different   He would denounce a man who tried to make a corner in wheat, and thought to grow rich out of the sufferings of the very poor. He would denounce also a man who sold under cost price in order that he might ruin a neighbour and secure a monopoly. He would speak out in all cases where he believed that selfishness and greed were hindering progress, and inflicting hardships on the poor.

IV.—LUXURY, CORRUPTION, AND THE PENALTY.

The mildewed crops, the moth-eaten garments, the rusted metals, all tell their own tale—they have not been used. They also symbolize the men of whom S. James is writing. They are equally idle and useless. They have lost their brightness, their keenness, their zest for life—*their rust is a testimony against them*. They have become dull, and can only relieve their dulness by morbid forms of excitement. In their very pleasures they show themselves corrupt.

So S. James argues, *the poison, or rust* (ὁ ἰός), *shall eat your flesh*. He looks on the rich man, and sees how his strength is enfeebled by luxury and his mind corroded by care. Many diseases can be traced to idleness, and "the deceitfulness of riches"[1] chokes many a life that might otherwise have been fruitful. Many a man has failed because he never learnt to strive. With riches come the parasites who devour them, and the more selfishly a man determines to spend his money, the more certain it is that he will be surrounded by worthless hangers-on who will plunder him.

This was to be brought out very clearly in the days

[1] Matt xiii. 22.

that were approaching. The rich, selfish Jews were to find how true it was. *As fire they had laid up treasure in the last days.*

In the last days (ἐν ἐσχάταις ἡμέραις, without the article) is a general term, and has no reference to *the* Last Day. *The last days* for the rich Jews were very close at hand. "In those days," says the Book of Enoch, "men shall not be saved by gold and silver."[1] On the contrary, says S. James, their gold and silver shall cause their destruction. And so it came to pass, when the rich Jews of Palestine and Syria suffered in the war that was close at hand. They had stored up treasure in order that they at least might be warm and comfortable Others might be chilled by poverty, but they would have a fire. They had it, and were consumed by it. *As fire they had laid up treasure in the last days.* It was their reputed hoards that exposed them as a prey alike to Romans and to Zealots. They were tortured and slain by both sides in the search for plunder.

V.—The Injustice of the Rich and the Lord of Sabaoth.

But it was not simply the folly and danger of hoarding that was in the mind of S. James. He proceeds to consider how they acquired their wealth, and says: *Behold, the hire of your labourers who mowed your fields, which is of you kept back by fraud, crieth out: and the cries of them that reaped have entered into the ears of the God of Sabaoth.*

The Jew at this time was a trader, but he was

[1] Enoch li., *cf* Zeph 1. 18.

descended from agriculturists, and it was still natural for him to invest his savings in land. Lazarus, whom Our Lord raised from the dead, had, we know, a house at Bethany and another in Galilee.[1] Barnabas had property in Cyprus,[2] and Ananias[3] was sufficiently wealthy for him to think that he could withhold part of the price without arousing suspicion. It was the Roman War that divorced the Jews from the land.

Now, if a trader is apt to be grasping, a landlord is apt to be oppressive; so in the Book of Leviticus the labourer is protected, and it is clearly commanded that his wages should be paid at the close of the day.[4] Deuteronomy emphasizes this law: " In his day thou shalt give him his hire, neither shall the sun go down upon it; for he is poor, and setteth his heart upon it: lest he cry against thee unto the Lord, and it be a sin unto thee."[5]

It was this provision that was neglected by the wealthy, who used their wealth as a means of getting credit. The extravagant rich man is reckless as to what he spends, and careless as to when he pays. Anything that he wants he must have at once; but he is careful in parting with ready money, and reduces to beggary those who cannot afford to wait, and who have no credit that others should wait for them. Such a man excuses himself with his good intentions to pay some time; he feels quite exonerated from blame when he pleads that he is good for the money, but S. James carefully stigmatizes his conduct as fraudulent. He does not accuse the rich of repudiating their debts, but

---

[1] Luke x. 38, John xi 1. [2] Acts iv 36. [3] Acts v 1.
[4] Lev xix 13 [5] Deut xxiv. 15.

of keeping back wages. He pictures the miseries of their labourers, whose *cries have entered into the ears of the God of Sabaoth.*

Ages before Jeremiah had cried, "Woe unto him that buildeth his house with unrighteousness, and his chambers by injustice; that uses his neighbour's service without wages, and giveth him not his hire; that saith, I will build me a wide house and spacious chambers, and cutteth him out windows; and it is ceiled with cedar, and painted with vermilion."[1] S. James is contemplating the same sin of wicked extravagance, but he selects an instance of more common occurrence. Only a few are tempted by the building mania, but many a spendthrift retains for his pleasures money that should be disbursed in wages to the poor. So he writes: *Behold, the hire of your labourers who mowed your fields, which is of you kept back by fraud, crieth out* The fields have been mowed; the money is still owing. The rich man, looking into his coffers, should hear the money there crying out against him. The plaint of the starving labourer will not reach him. The man is afraid to speak lest he should lose his place. He goes on hoping against hope, but his cries, that he dare not utter to man, have *entered into the ears of the God of Sabaoth.*

The cry of Sodom and Gomorrah had once been great, but the people "did eat and drink, they bought and sold, they planted and builded": but God had heard, and God came down; "it rained fire and brimstone from Heaven, and destroyed them all."[2] So it was in the days of Moses: "And the Lord said, I have

[1] Jer. xxii. 14 [2] Luke xvii 29

surely seen the affliction of My people that are in Egypt, and have heard their cry by reason of their taskmasters, for I know their sorrows, and I am come down to deliver them."[1] So S. James believed that God's arm was not shortened. He knew that "God would avenge His own elect, which cry day and night unto Him, though He bare long with them." Had not Our Lord promised, "Yea, I say unto you, He will avenge them speedily"?[2]

The God of Sabaoth[3] is only twice appealed to in the New Testament, and here it is with pregnant significance. These rich men have their servants who gather in the harvest and are not paid, but the God of Sabaoth (or Lord of Hosts) has also His servants whom He will send forth to reap. "The reapers are the Angels," said Our Lord; and it was the author of the Apocalypse who tells us what will happen when "the harvest of the earth is ripe."[4] "And the Angel thrust in his sickle into the earth, and gathered the vine of the earth, and cast it into the great winepress of the wrath of God."[5]

VI.—THE OSTENTATION OF THE RICH AND ITS NEMESIS.

Remembering S. James's words, we may well ask ourselves to-day: 'How did I make my money? Should I like my neighbour to know? and Is there a God who weighs to a scruple the balance of my account?' Then come further questions: 'Am I really spending my own money? Have others claims upon it? Do I order things for which I cannot pay, or am I unwilling to pay what is due?' S. James does not even stop there, he

[1] Exod. iii. 7.   [2] Luke xviii 7, 8.   [3] Rom. ix. 29
[4] Rev. xiv. 15.   [5] Rev. xiv. 19

would have us consider further, 'Granted that the money is really my own, is it mine to do what I like with? Is it well spent if spent altogether in self-indulgence? Will such expenditure be for my ultimate good?'

The vulgar rich to-day spend in such a way that neither utility nor art is served, and there are those who mark the evidence provided by their silly ostentation. They would astonish and excite the envy of those who are not equally rich but are equally vulgar. They stir the wrath and indignation of those who have nothing. Is it, in consequence, a wonder that not only the covetous, but good men also, begin to dream of a social revolution which shall "send the rich empty away"?[1] Be that as it may, S. James, facing the plutocracy of his own days, tells them plainly, *Ye have lived delicately, and taken your pleasure; ye have nourished your hearts in a day of slaughter*. The earth has heard of your dissipation, and Heaven the cries of your labourers. Deadened by luxury, you have not perceived that *the day of slaughter has come*.

The Revisers were hardly well advised in altering the old translation, *Ye have lived in pleasure on the earth and been wanton*, for *to live delicately* suggests fastidious refinement, whereas ἐτρυφήσατε rather points to the effeminate and voluptuous life. The other verb, ἐσπαταλήσατε, has a more active sense, and suggests the riot, the waste, and passion of the wanton. Our Lord in vain had uttered His warning: "Take heed to yourselves, lest haply your hearts be overcharged with surfeiting, and drunkenness, and cares of this life, and that day comes upon you suddenly as a snare."[2] None had heeded. The pleasures

[1] Luke i 53. [2] Luke xxi. 34

of the rich had been animal in their nature; they had indulged in the passions of brutes. They had become fat; like the fed beasts they should die. *They had nourished their hearts in the day of slaughter.*

It would perhaps be more natural to interpret these words as pertaining to the moment when S. James was writing. The luxurious nobles were amusing themselves, while the poor were under oppression, against which they rioted and rose in vain. More than one tumult was *a day of slaughter*, and the Romans strove to purchase peace with the severity of the sword. No doubt the rich were heedless, but S. James is writing from the prophetic standpoint. It is the rich themselves whom he thinks of as victims, as of cattle fatted for the slaughter-house. When Jerusalem was besieged many excuses were found for slaying them. The furious leaders, says Josephus, drank to one another in cups that brimmed with the blood of the wealthy. The day of slaughter had come.

VII.—THE SLAYING OF THE JUST ONE.

But S. James is not merely warning the rich that they will be punished by God for their oppression; or that they will be the victims of the hatred and envy which they have so insolently courted. At the back of his mind he ponders a final accusation, *Ye have condemned and slain the Just One.* Let them remember that, and he asks them, *Doth not He resist you?*[1] God may be propitiated, man may be avoided, but the laws of Nature seem to men inexorable. The blood of the slain is upon them. Blood will have blood, let them *weep and howl* as they may.

[1] Westcott and Hort.

Who does S. James intend by *The Just One* (τὸν δίκαιον)? It is obviously some definite person. He evidently assumes that his readers will grasp the force of his allusion, although they live widely scattered in many lands. There is little doubt that he refers to Our Lord, and it is interesting to note that S. Peter, S. Stephen, and S. Paul, spoke of Him at Jerusalem by the same title.[1] It was a title that did not challenge controversy, and was no doubt much used in intercourse with devout Jews who had not accepted Our Lord's claims.

There had been a time when the Sanhedrim had met to discuss the dangers involved in Our Lord's success. They did not argue about His mission, their fears were for their temporal possessions, "lest the Romans should come and take away both our place and our nation."[2] It was then the wealthy Sadducean priest had decided that "it was expedient one man should die for the nation."[3] S. James had probably been in Jerusalem when the Temple was purged for a second time;[4] and Our Lord declared war on the unholy profits and vested interests of the priesthood. He knew also how money had been spent to corrupt Judas, hire false witnesses, and bribe the Roman Guards to silence. Perhaps he guessed that Pilate trembled before the threat of an appeal to Cæsar, because of monetary transactions which must not be made public. So the wealthy had used their power *to condemn and slay*. S. James marks the process. This was no act of wild violence, but a deliberate conspiracy. They had used their wealth

---

[1] Acts iii. 14, vii. 52; xxii. 14
[2] John xi. 48.
[3] John xi. 50
[4] Mark xi. 15 17.

that with all legal forms their enemy might be done to death.

Now the curse they had involved was fallen upon them. They had cried, " His blood be upon us and upon our children."[1] It was in vain that they had beaten the Apostles and taken counsel to slay them, lest they "bring this man's blood upon us."[2] The Divine law was working itself out in the certain consequences of history. The God who had said to Cain, " The voice of thy brother's blood crieth unto Me from the ground,"[3] the God who had decreed, "Whoso sheddeth man's blood by man shall his blood be shed: for in the image of God made He man,"[4] was not silent. They had slain the Just One, who was the express image of the Father's Person,[5] and did they think that they could escape ? Our Lord had foretold how " the blood of all the Prophets, that was shed from the foundation of the world, may be required of this generation; from the blood of Abel to the blood of Zacharias, who perished between the altar and the sanctuary: verily I say unto you, It shall be required of this generation."[6] S. James had probably heard those words spoken. He thought of One greater than all the Prophets, and wrote with conviction, *Ye have condemned and slain the Just One; doth He not resist you?* We have already considered how *God resisteth the proud*, and must not forget our conclusions when considering how the meek and lowly Jesus *resisteth* His insolent and lofty persecutors.

The mystery of blood has stirred the imaginations of

---

[1] Matt. xxvii 25   [2] Acts v 28.   [3] Gen. iv 10
[4] Gen. ix. 6   [5] Heb. 1 3.   [6] Luke xi 50, 51

all races. The instinct, superstitious if you will, that the blood of the slain cries out : " O Lord, how long !"[1] was expressed in pictorial language long before Reason attempted to propound a theory of the moral government of the Universe. The theory remains a matter of faith. Reason has never had sufficient data to prove her thesis, but the language of poet and prophet, due to an instinctive penetration into life, is constantly being verified. S. James had no doubt; blood would have blood; "they who take the sword shall perish by the sword";[2] they who commit murder, however secretly or under whatever legal forms, will be haunted by the blood of the slain, which will resist all attempts to be free from it. Men's sins find them out. They pay the full price, though the recompense comes by devious ways. Resistance to this law is in vain.

It may indeed be asked, Does not the precious Blood of Christ cleanse from every kind of sin, and is it therefore right to speak of Him as resisting the sinner ? The precious blood is indeed available for every sinner that repents, but the sacrifice on Calvary is the eternal witness as to how God resists sin to the very end. When the rich Sadducees conspired to slay Our Lord, they meditated a murder. That He whom they condemned in malice offered Himself as a sacrifice in love only accentuated the nature of their crime. They had not repented, they had not identified themselves with their victim, and S. James is therefore justified in the terms of his final warning : *Ye have condemned, ye have killed the Just One; doth He not resist you?*

Such is the awful climax of his condemnation. He

[1] Rev. vi. 10.   [2] Matt xxvi 52

had started with demonstrating the folly of hoarded wealth and the evil effects of avarice. He had proceeded to show the plaints of the poor against the rich, and the selfishness of the rich in the midst of poverty. He closed with a reference to a crime that seems to sum up the whole sin of the world. His prophecy has been justified by the event—the rich Jews did *weep and howl for the miseries* that came upon them. Cannot we also justify the event? In this world, at any rate, they had merited to *weep and howl*. In saying this, let us also pray that we who have merited condemnation may yet find a place for repentance.

LECTURE XVII

THE PAROUSIA

"*Be patient therefore, brethren, until the coming of the Lord. Behold, the husbandman waiteth for the precious fruit of the earth, being patient over it, until it receive the early and latter rain. Be ye also patient, stablish your hearts for the coming of the Lord is at hand. Murmur not, brethren, one against another, that ye be not judged behold, the Judge standeth before the doors Take, brethren, for an example of suffering and patience, the prophets who spake in the name of the Lord Behold, we call them blessed which endured ye have heard of the patience of Job, and have seen the end of the Lord, how that the Lord is full of pity, and merciful*"—JAS v. 7-11.

I.—THE CONNEXION OF THOUGHT.

S. JAMES is sometimes described as a writer on morals who had no theological interests. His theology is certainly not formulated in this Epistle, but in this passage more clearly than elsewhere his views as to conduct are seen from the standpoint of Doomsday. His moral exhortations throughout are the practical outcome of his religious convictions, and in no case proceed from any ethical theory. So, like a prophet of the Old Testament, having warned the rich of *the miseries coming upon them*, he turns to console his poor *brethren* for the miseries they have been, and are, enduring. The rich may *oppress them, drag them before the judgment seats, and blaspheme the honourable Name that has been called over them*, but *the brethren* must bear and forbear *until the coming of the Lord*. He counsels them not to be downhearted, *for the coming of the Lord is at hand;* not to quarrel or murmur one against another, *for the Judge,* who will set all things right, is even *before the doors.* He returns once more to his opening argument and the last Beatitude of Our Lord. He reminds his brethren, *we call them happy who endured.* He points to the examples of the prophets, and asks them to find, in the story of Job, how "the Lord blessed the latter end of Job more than the beginning."[1]

II.—THE EXPECTATION OF THE "PAROUSIA."

The whole passage, it will be seen, is dominated by the thought of Our Lord's Second Coming—*His Parousia.*[2] In the same connexion the word is found in S. Matthew, S. Paul, S. John, and 2 S. Peter, and it is well to note that it does not mean so much a *coming* as a *visible presence.* Its secular use bears this out. In documents almost contemporary it is used, like the Latin *adventus,* for the state visits of the Emperor.

There are other senses in which the New Testament and the Catholic Church speak of Our Lord's *Coming.* He is coming in the power of His Spirit; He is coming in the progress of the world; in the expansion of His Church, in judgments, like the destruction of Jerusalem, which takes place within the world order. Secretly He comes to the individual heart, or "where two or three are gathered together";[3] publicly He is manifested in the ever-increasing volume of testimony to His power,

[1] Job xlii. 12.
[2] Matt. xxiv. 3, 37, 39, 1 Thess. iii. 13; iv. 15; v. 23, 2 Thess ii. 1, 1 Cor. xv. 23; 1 John ii. 28, 2 Pet 1. 16, iii 4, 12.
[3] Matt. xviii. 20.

and in the growing intensity with which men apprehend the scope of His mission. Economically He comes for adoration and thanksgiving beneath the veils of Bread and Wine, but even then we "show forth the Lord's death till He come"[1] in visible Majesty. The *Parousia* must not be confused with any of these comings; they are only an earnest of what is yet to be. The complete manifestation is to sum up, explain, and justify to all men everywhere, and of every age, the reality, the meaning, and the fruits of the Incarnation. That which is spiritual shall triumph in the material sphere, and the one order shall pass into the other without a break of continuity. The Son of Mary must be acknowledged as God on the earth which witnessed His humiliation.

We may be thankful for the choice of the word παρουσία, for, as it means *a visible presence*, it cannot be explained away in such a context as this. The word is, indeed, used by Josephus[2] for a manifestation of God's presence in an unexpected downpour of rain. The presence (παρουσία) of God was inferred from the rain, and convinced Petronius: but for Josephus, God Himself was by nature invisible. In S. James there is no further object; it is the *Lord* Himself who will be visibly present: S. James was a believer in the Incarnation.

There are writers, indeed, who would label the word "a symbol," and allow each man to interpret it for himself, with the sole proviso that he never assumes his "symbol" may some day be a fact. For Modernists a "symbol" is a counter to which for the purposes of a game you may assign any value that you please, but

[1] 1 Cor. xi. 26.   [2] *Antiquities*, bk. xviii, chap. viii.

which remains a counter without any value in the practical affairs of life.

But for S. James his religion was not a game of speculation: he really expected to see "the Son of Man coming in the clouds of Heaven";[1] and he was concerned in the practical consequences of such a faith when he called on his *brethren* to be *long-suffering*, to *brace themselves up*, and not to *murmur*, for the *coming* of the Lord is at hand.

The word παρουσία is not to be found in the Septuagint, but the Old Testament is full of "The Day of the Lord," of God coming to judgment. Ethnic religions also countenance a similar expectation, for a belief in judgment to come is instinctive in the human heart.

The old Prophets, indeed, insist on the horror of that day. It is a "day of darkness, and not light."[2] It is a day of terror, when men shall creep "into the clefts of the ragged rocks to hide themselves."[3] It is a day especially marked out for the punishment of those who too lightly assume that "the Lord will not do good, neither will He do evil."[4] The old Prophets were, for the most part, urging to repentance a careless, a sinful, and rebellious people.

The Eschatological writers of later Judaism, on the other hand, found in the Lord's Coming a day of restoration, when God will vindicate His own elect; for they were addressing a people spoiled and persecuted, who had no longer any hope of the World Order, who in consequence passionately desired a new Heaven and a new earth.

---

[1] Matt. xxvi 64.
[2] Amos v 18.
[3] Isa. ii 21
[4] Zeph 1. 12.

Both views are of course true, and S. James combines both in his warnings to the rich and in his encouragement of the poor, but it was from Our Lord that S. James had derived his definite faith in the *Parousia*. He looked for the Lord Christ to come and judge His world.

Our Blessed Lord had entered into human life at a definite moment of human progress. He came accepting men as they were, with their hopes and fears, doubts and errors. He came to fulfil the old Law, to sum up the teaching of the old Prophets, to make plain what others had dimly foreseen. He came to endorse all that was good in human achievement and aspiration. He adopted human language, and entered into man's thought, not only as to this world, but as to the world beyond. He rejected in silence much that was crude, fanciful, and untrue. He purified much that had been grossly conceived. He spiritualized and transmuted everything He accepted, and so gave to men an altogether new impulse in living for the future, and a new direction in which their thoughts might run.

Two points alone need emphasis at this stage of our inquiry. First, He taught that the new Kingdom of God was to grow up in and grow out of this world, and so brought this world into logical relation with the other. Here men were to work and wait, to be, like careful servants, preparing against their Lord's return.[1] So His return in glory is not merely to be for judgment and destruction. He is coming to establish a kingdom already existing, to judge the work that has been done, and consummate what men have tried to do: to crown

[1] Matt xxiv 46-51

those who have been loyal to His service, and to complete the subjugation of those who have rebelled.

Secondly, those who, like S. James, had heard and accepted Our Lord's teaching, could never again think of this world except in relation to the other. They could never again even imagine that this world provided an end for their endeavours. Neither were they any more in danger of confusing their sense of values, and preferring earthly prosperity to heavenly joy. The end to which creation moved had become so plain to them that it seemed quite near. They desired it so intensely that they put away from them all thought of "the Lord's delaying His coming."[1] But they never lost their sense of how much remained to do, and their energy was reinforced by the hope that in doing it they were hastening the end.

III.—MEN SHOULD THEREFORE BE PATIENT.

Such was the standpoint of S. James, but such was not necessarily the standpoint of his *brethren*. They were depressed, because oppressed by manifold temptations and trials. Like all oppressed minorities, they tended to gloom, sloth, and irritation—to the gloom that arises from impotent resentment, to the sloth that murmurs "what is the good of trying?" to the irritation one with another which frets any body of weak men. To them comes S. James. He bursts in on them with the glorious certainty which should transform their lives. "Bear up a little longer, for the Lord is coming. There is ever so much to do with the Lord at hand,

[1] Matt. xxiv. 48.

and there is no time for the servants to fume over their little irritations, jealousies, and wrongs when the Master is at the door who will put all things right."

This exhortation starts with the words, *Be patient therefore, brethren, until the coming (παρουσία) of the Lord*. The word *therefore* of course refers back to the judgment on the rich, and reminds the *Brethren* that they are on the side which must ultimately triumph. It is a pity that the Revisers kept to the old translation of μακροθυμήσατε (Be patient), as if μακροθυμία was perfectly synonymous with the ὑπομενή which occurs in verse 11. The first word denotes the *long-suffering* that does not resent an injury, while the second, as suggested in the margin, merely conveys the idea of *endurance*. The point of S. James is therefore in part obscured. The wicked rich men have cruelly afflicted the brethren, but revenge is not permitted to Christians. They must be *long-suffering until the coming of the Lord*. We have already noted that S. James himself does not curse the rich, but as a Prophet warns them of *the miseries coming upon them*, and as a teacher points out the reason of their approach. They, too, S. James would say, are in the hands of the long-suffering God, and His forebearance is another reason for our own.

But the brethren are depressed and gloomy, so he calls on them to think of *the coming of the Lord* and "the brightness of His appearing." It is not for ever they are called on to suffer. The words ἕως τῆς παρουσίας assign a limit. Let them consider the vision of the Psalmist of old time, how "out of Sion hath God appeared in perfect beauty."[1] "God will not

[1] Ps l 2, 3

The Parousia

keep silence" now any more than then. He will come, and "there shall go before Him a consuming fire, and a mighty tempest shall be stirred up round about Him."[1] For whom will He come? Hear His command, "Gather My saints together unto Me: those that have made a covenant with Me with sacrifice."[2] And why does He come? That He may "judge His people," that "He may declare His righteousness," that "He may show the salvation of God."[3]

S. James, however, does not only ask them to contemplate the glory of the *Parousia*. He develops his thought by means of a parable. *Behold, the husbandman waiteth for the precious fruit of the earth, being patient over it, until it receive the early and latter rain.*

The parable was very appropriate, if some of the readers whom S. James had in mind were the labourers who had mown the fields of the rich, and whose wages were kept back by fraud. If the date to which we have assigned this Epistle be correct, it was particularly apt when all men knew how agriculturists had suffered in those long days of drought and famine. It must have carried conviction to readers who remembered how their prayers had been answered by the deluge of rain which ended the long drought, and convinced Petronius that there was a God in Galilee. Anyhow, the reference to *the early and latter rains*[4] is another little bit of evidence to prove that the Epistle was written in Palestine.

But how does the Parable enforce and carry on the point which S. James is striving to make? First, in

---

[1] Ps. l 3. [2] Ps l 5 [3] Ps. l. 6, 23
[4] Deut. xi. 14 , Joel ii. 23 , Hos vi. 3

the husbandman the brethren may find an example of faith and long-suffering: he does his work, and waits on God for the result. He cannot control the weather; and knows that, if he could, still the end that he desires might not be his. During the year he is often anxious; he watches his fields, and wonders; but he also sings with the Psalmist: "They that sow in tears shall reap in joy. He that goeth forth and weepeth, and beareth precious seed, shall doubtless come again with rejoicing, bringing his sheaves with him."[1]

Secondly, the brethren will be reminded of how frequently Our Lord compared His second Coming to a Harvest. It should be a gathering-in of *precious fruit*. Now, the husbandman never forgets the harvest, and views all changes of the weather in respect to it. He does not complain of getting wet, but thinks how the rain will nourish his seed; he is not fierce and bitter in face of the cutting blast, because he remembers how it will dry the ground; he does not droop and despair beneath the pitiless sun, but is radiant with the thought of how his grain is ripening. The gloom and the despondency of the brethren is due to the fact which they have forgotten, that the coming of the Lord is the Harvest of the world, and that *the precious fruits* will well reward their long-suffering. They are longing to escape from pelting rain, stormy winds, and scorching heat, because they think only of their momentary discomfort. They are seeking their own ease and not their Lord's profit.

Thirdly, should they not recognize the slowness of growth? Before the Harvest comes, there must be

[1] Ps. cxxvi 5, 6

both *the early and the latter rains.* Should they not therefore pray to God for showers of blessing? They complain that they can see no progress, but neither can the husbandman. The seed groweth secretly.[1] The husbandman comes and goes, and there is change and growth. The husbandman sits down to watch, and nothing seems to happen. So these gloomy brethren, nursing their wrongs, are sitting, idle and impatient, ready to deny that there is any growth and improvement. Let them be up and doing. The time will pass the quicker, and the harvest will come before they are aware.[2]

Lastly, the Parable suggests the thought of co-operation. Times and seasons are in God's hand, but there is work for the husbandman to do. He is a labourer together with God.[3] So the coming of the Lord will be when He wills, but man may work and prepare for His appearing. The brethren are not only called to be long-suffering towards those who oppress them, but active and vigorous also. So S. James does not merely say, *Be ye also patient,* but *stablish your hearts, for the coming of the Lord is at hand.*

A bright hope disperses gloom, but the tidings that the event hoped for is near stirs men to action. They must get ready, be prepared, be in time for it. The Church had been depressed, and therefore slothful. Each had said, "What can I do?" and had done nothing. Then S. James arouses them with his certainty as to *the Parousia.* "*The Lord is at hand,*" he cries. They must in consequence feel the necessity to have their

---

[1] Mark iv. 26, 27 [2] Acts i 7.
[3] 1 Cor. iii 9

"lamps alight and their loins girded."[1] He would have them pluck up their courage, take heart once more; in his own phrase, *stablish their hearts*. Let them consider how much has to be done ere the Lord comes. There is a world's opposition to be vanquished, there is their own perfection to be attained. With the sense that He is at hand, difficulties are forgotten, and the only fear that remains is the fear of His disapproval.

But another exhortation is also needed. In the light of the *Parousia* everyone should be in a better temper. So S. James writes: *Murmur not, brethren, one against another, that ye be not judged: behold, the Judge standeth before the doors*.

In a community without hope, oppressed by powers that could not be resisted, it was natural that the members should be irritable. Each felt that everything was going wrong, each felt that things would not be quite so bad but for somebody else. Each was suffering, and each felt that his neighbour was insisting with too much iteration on his own trials. Many could, no doubt, face the foe outside with a bold front, but were irritable with the friends within the Church. They were like the enslaved Hebrews striving together, and ready to turn on a peacemaker and say, "Who made thee a prince and a judge over us?"[2] Only they acknowledged that there was a Judge who was coming, and could therefore respond to the tidings, *the Judge standeth before the doors*.

There is also a note of warning in the exhortation. S. James remembers how his Master had said: "*Judge not, and ye shall not be judged.*" The Judge who is

[1] Luke xii. 35   [2] Exod. ii 14

coming will not only "gather the nations, and separate them one from another, as a shepherd divideth his sheep from the goats,"[1] but He will also take account with His servants. He will inquire into their debts towards Himself. He will inquire as to how they have treated their fellow-debtors. There is a terrible warning in the Gospels on the servant who presumes to say in his heart, "My Lord delayeth His coming," and ill-treateth his fellow-servant. The Lord when He comes "will cut him asunder, and appoint him his portion with the hyprocrites."[2]

IV.—AND LEARN OF THE PROPHETS AND JOB.

But S. James knows that there are people who will be deaf to exhortations, and who will not be convinced by his arguments as to the uses of adversity, propounded at the beginning of his Epistle. What they want are examples, and it is to examples he refers them. The Prophets of the Old Testament, he tells them, had suffered as they are suffering now. The Prophets of the Old Testament had endured in hope of the first Advent as they are called on to endure in hope of the second Advent. So he writes: *Take, brethren, for an example of suffering and patience, the prophets who spake in the name of the Lord.* Let them read their histories, and see how "they were tortured, not accepting deliverance . . . . and others had trials of cruel mockings and scourgings. They were stoned, they were sawn asunder, were tempted, were slain with the sword: they wandered about in sheep-skins and goat-skins,

[1] Matt xxv. 32   [2] Matt. xxiv 51.

being destitute, afflicted, tormented."[1] Yet they spake in *the Name of the Lord*, and the Lord accepted their testimony and permitted their sufferings. It was their glory and His. They sealed their testimony with their blood, and His Holy Name was hallowed. They deemed all things worth while, that they might prepare for the Christ that was to come and the Kingdom that was to be. And yet they all died, " not having received the promises, but having seen and greeted them afar off, and having confessed that they were strangers and pilgrims on the earth."[2] Now, says S. James, you have to suffer for the same cause and live for the same hope. Did not Our Lord think of you when He prophesied to the Jews, " Behold, I send you prophets, wise men, and scribes; and some of them you will kill and crucify; and some of them will ye scourge in your synagogues, and persecute them from city to city"?[3]

"It is better to suffer for wrong-doing than not to suffer," was one of the paradoxes attributed to Socrates in the *Gorgias*. S. Peter's proposition is more self-evident, but harder of acceptance. "It is better to suffer for well-doing than for evil-doing."[4] S. James, in some respects, goes beyond both of them when he says, *We call them happy that endured*. He says *we*, though addressing the discontented, for after all he merely states the verdict of mankind. All men shrink from suffering, but all men admire those who have nobly borne unmerited affliction. Even the Jews built the sepulchres of those prophets whom their fathers slew.[5] Men cannot fail to acknowledge that no great thing has

---

[1] Heb. xi 35, 37   [2] Heb xi 13.   [3] Matt. xxiii 34.
[4] 1 Pet iii 17   [5] Luke xi. 47.

ever been done in the world but at the price of suffering; and that the world has been chiefly benefited by those who have despised her rewards. Men dimly recognize that they are not wholly of the earth, earthy, and reverence as heroes and demigods those who have refused to be bound by the earthly standard, those who have rejected the pomp of the fortunate and the ease of the prosperous, to seek for truth, for reality, for God, and found them in the ways of pain, or gone gaily to their deaths as knights of the quest.

Endurance is, after all, the supreme test of manhood; and the best of all evidence for truth is a willingness to suffer for it. It is through endurance also that a man wins his own soul and knows it is his own, and not a plaything or chattel of the world. It is a fact, and no mere rhodomontade, that the martyr has, in countless cases, been a happy man. It is not merely that we call him happy afterwards, when pilgrims frequent his shrine, and Fame trumpets his renown. He was happy at the time—happy in the joy that at least he was not conquered, happy as the athlete who falls a victor at the goal.

All men applaud the heroes, but all men are not heroes, and many of the early Christians were not cast in the heroic mould. They believed sincerely, they did their duty, they hoped for the best, but they wanted some assurance as to their reward. They were like those labourers who came early to be hired for work in the vineyard, but bargained first with the master that they should get not less than a penny a day.[1] S. James has a word for these also: *Ye have heard of the patience*

[1] Matt. xx. 1, 2

of Job, and seen the end of the Lord? There is a proof, in terms that you can understand, that the *Lord is full of pity and merciful.*

Such men were not of the highest type. That is true; but the critic should ask himself the further question, "Am I?" The ordinary Christian living at ease is hardly in a position to criticize adversely those who suffered persecution, even if they were unhappy martyrs and reluctant victims. They had, after all, staked and lost this world for a hope; can we blame them if they wanted assurance that they should receive the stipulated reward either in this world or the next? They were not heroes, let us admit it; but they were Christians who had sacrificed more than we have for Our Lord, and for them the *Lord was full of pity and merciful.*

Modern preachers would not allow them to be "spiritual," for they were not to be satisfied with any fine words. They wanted, in terms that they could understand, to know what they were to gain, and S. James tells them to take heart from the final chapter of Job, where they could see how "the Lord gave Job twice as much as he had before."[1] That was satisfactory. But ought we to say that they were "unspiritual"? I think not. There are many men who have no power of realizing abstractions, and need to have concrete forms for their imaginations to feed on. Seneca had a great grasp of abstract truth, and led a very unspiritual life; while the writer of the Apocalypse, full of the Spirit, nourished his soul with visions of streets of gold and gates of pearl.[2] So the last chapter of Job

---

[1] Job xlii 10   [2] Rev xxi 21.

met the needs of some of his correspondents, and he was justified in appealing to it, for had not Our Lord promised: "Verily I say unto you, There is no man who hath left home, or brethren, or sisters, or father, or mother, or wife, or children, or lands, for My sake and the Gospel's, but he shall receive an hundredfold now in this time, homes, and brethren, and sisters, and mothers, and children, and lands, with persecutions; and in the world to come Eternal life"?[1]

But we can interpret this verse for others than the people we have been considering. Job suffered, and suffered greatly. At first he showed what we should to-day call patience. He said: "The Lord gave, and the Lord hath taken away. Blessed be the Name of the Lord."[2] Afterwards he had still to *endure*, but he was exasperated by his three friends coming as they did to condemn him, and justify God by lying on God's behalf. Then his mind was quickened by his sufferings to question the foundations of thought, to question the Being and Justice of God, to probe the mystery of pain and evil. Stripped of all conventional coverings, he came to grips with the naked Truth, and was foiled in wrestling for the mastery. But it was Truth that Job was seeking. It was a *Lord full of pity and merciful*, who could alone satisfy him, and who could alone command his worship. He wanted such a God, and words that sound like blasphemies are in reality a scornful rejection of any other Divinity. He wanted God, and God revealed Himself. There was in some sense a *Parousia*. Job's questions were not, indeed, answered, but he was convinced that God had heard his cry, and God cared for him.[3] Job

[1] Mark x. 29, 30. [2] Job i. 21 [3] Job xlii. 5, 6.

was satisfied. He was quite content to admit that the problems he had argued were outside his competence. He could leave himself in the Everlasting Arms. Assured of God's character, he wanted no further assurance as to His meaning. For with such a God all things must end in good, and so they did.

Now, here were converts of S. James, enduring many tribulations! They, too, were exasperated by facile assurances that their sufferings must be for their good, and that they needed purification to fit them for the presence of the Lord. S. James tells them to take the story of Job, and learn how the Lord will reveal Himself in due time. They will see the Lord when He comes. In His Presence all their doubts will fade away. The end will yet be good. The end is very near. *Behold, the Judge,* and source of all Justice, *is at the doors.*

V.—THE DIFFICULTIES CONNECTED WITH THE PAROUSIA, THEN AND NOW.

But it may be urged, splendid as was the faith of S. James, he was altogether mistaken. The Lord was not at hand. After nineteen centuries He has not yet come. No doubt the arguments of S. James made life possible for his converts, but why should we to-day dwell on his mistaken predictions? What were the grounds of his hope, and why was it that he was deceived?

First, it must be allowed that S. Paul in his earlier epistles and S. Peter are quite as emphatic in stating their expectations as to the nearness of the Second

Advent.[1] The Apocalypse also ends with the promise, "Surely I come quickly," and the answering prayer, "Even so, come, Lord Jesus."[2] But in his later epistles S. Paul is more concerned with the coming of the Church; S. John's Gospel is dominated by the thought of the coming of the Spirit, and finally 2 S. Peter proclaims what has since been the faith of the Catholic Church as to the *Parousia*.[3] "Beloved, be not ignorant of this one thing, that one day is with the Lord as a thousand years, and a thousand years as one day. The Lord is not slack as concerning His promises, as some men count slackness; but is long-suffering to us-ward, not willing that any should perish, but that all should come to repentance." Then, after stating his full belief in the *Parousia*, he urges men to be "looking for and hasting unto the coming of the day of God,"[4] and calls on them to expect "a new heaven and a new earth, wherein dwelleth righteousness."[5]

But how are we to account for the earlier hopes? Our Blessed Lord had definitely said: "Of that day and hour knoweth no man, no, not the Angels of God which are in Heaven, neither the Son, but the Father"[6]: and after His Resurrection He had told His Disciples: "It is not for you to know times and seasons, which the Father hath put in His own power."[7] The Disciples had remembered His words and recorded them, but they pondered rather on the message of the angels: "This same Jesus which is taken up from you into heaven, shall so come in like manner as ye have seen Him go into heaven."[8]

---

[1] 1 Thess iv 14-17, 2 Thess 1. 7-10, 1 Pet iv. 5, 7, 13, 17.
[2] Rev xxii 20.   [3] 2 Pet iii. 8, 9   [4] 2 Pet. iii 12.
[5] 2 Pet. iii 13.   [6] Mark xiii 32.   [7] Acts 1 7.   [8] Acts i. 11.

It was so natural for them to imagine that the Coming would be at once. They had seen so much of the Salvation of God, and they did so long to see the end. The passion of Christ, His Resurrection, Ascension, and the coming of the Holy Ghost had followed so quickly one upon another, and they found it hard to believe that the final event could be long delayed. In their hope and enthusiasm the Church of Pentecost sold their possessions and had all things in common.[1] The Pilgrims from far lands thought it not worth their while to return home. They wanted all to keep together, that together they might greet the Lord when He came.

There had been certain indications given of what would precede the *Parousia*, and it was natural for those who sought them to find them in their own environment. Our anticipations of the future are always founded on our own experience, and we have been so often disappointed because our experience was incomplete. We may reason quite correctly from the data that we know, but our minds cannot take in the sum of the world's forces; we cannot gauge the potentialities that lie hid in the womb of Time. S. James was arguing from the Jerusalem that he knew. His own land was hastening to a catastrophe, but there was beyond his land the great Empire which he only knew imperfectly, and beyond that again a world but dimly imagined through the mists of fable and myth.

It was on the approaching destruction of Jerusalem that his attention was fixed. The Holy City and its Temple meant so much to the pious Jew. It was the centre of his world and its consecration. He could

---

[1] Acts ii 44, 45.

scarce conceive of life without it. It seemed so appropriate to him that with the destruction of Jerusalem should come the close of the Age. He saw a natural connexion between a judgment within the world order and a judgment outside it. It was with these preconceptions that the Disciples carefully collected all Our Lord's sayings as to either event, and tagged them together according to the scheme of fitness which was in their own minds. This probably accounts for the difficulties we now find in the interpretation of "the little Apocalypse";[1] and it is quite clear that we cannot be certain as to the Order of Our Lord's discourse, for each of the three Synoptists arrange their material differently.

But it is maintained by many that Our Lord Himself confidently looked forward to an almost immediate return. This theory is based on very insufficient evidence. The saying in S. Mark[2] refers to the Coming of the Kingdom and not to the Coming of the Lord. It was exactly fulfilled on the Day of Pentecost. The words, "and He said unto them," are an indication that they originally did not form part of the preceding discourse. The similar saying in "the little Apocalypse" can scarcely be made the basis of an argument for the reason given above. The saying to Caiaphas proves nothing one way or the other, for Caiaphas shall yet see "the Son of Man coming in the clouds of heaven."[3]

Apart from these texts, there are many indications in the Gospels that Our Lord did not intend a speedy return. He compares Himself to one "going a long

[1] Mark xiii [2] Mark ix 1. [3] Matt. xxvi. 64.

journey into a far country "; [1] and to a bridegroom who tarried so long that they all "slumbered and slept"; [2] and to a master bestowing talents on his servants, which may be put out to usury until they increased ten-fold; [3] to a sower planting seed and waiting patiently through the long months for the harvest. [4] So He compares His Kingdom, the Church, which was immediately at hand, to a grain of mustard seed, which should grow until it overshadowed the earth, [5] and to a little leaven which should leaven the whole lump. [6] He told His disciples that in the future there should be false Christs and false prophets, heresies and schisms, ages of faith and ages of apostasy. [7] His careful selection and training of the Twelve was not the work of One who expected an immediate triumph, but of One who was laying the foundations of a great Church. He definitely asserted that before He came His Gospel was to be preached to all nations. [8] He asserted, "all power is given unto Me," [9] but showed that His power was not at once to be directly exercised by Himself, for He put it into commission, sending the Twelve into all the world to discipline all nations. His solemn institution of the sacraments, and His careful provision as to conduct, all point in the same direction. Our Lord was no self-deluded enthusiast who forced the Jews to crucify Him that He might precipitate a revolution of the world order. He was the calm and open-eyed Prophet of Truth who looked far ahead to an assured end.

He did not mislead His disciples; it was their wishes

---

[1] Matt xxv 14 [2] Matt. xxv 5 [3] Matt. xxv. 27.
[4] Matt. xiii. 30. [5] Matt xiii 31 [6] Matt xiii 33
[7] Matt. xxiv 24 [8] Matt. xxiv 14 [9] Matt xxviii. 18, 19

which begat their thoughts The Truths Our Lord insisted on were the suddenness and the unexpected moment of His Coming.[1] He would come as a thief in the night. He wanted men ever to watch and be ready. He wanted them ever to live that they might at any moment appear in His Presence without dismay.

So S. James's teaching was fundamentally sound. Men are only living wisely if they are living in the thought that the *Lord is at hand*, that before to-morrow the trumpet may sound. He pointed quite properly to the Prophets as an example.[2] They saw the promises afar off, and, believing that they were near, lived great lives in the splendour of their vision. No great lives are lived by men who never look beyond a morrow that shall be like to yesterday. The greatness of the Apostolic Church consisted in this, that her members passed each day as if it were the point of transition to eternity. Death came, and yet the Lord delayed.

We know nothing of Time beyond the grave. Even here we recognize that our conceptions of Time are not altogether decided by the mechanism of our clocks. Sometimes we live quicker than at others. What the interval between death and the *Parousia* may be we know not, but it is possible that on that day, when we are all contemporaries, we may congratulate one another on our foresight, and understand how near to each of us the judgment was.

It is, in truth, a great loss to the Christian Church that the *Parousia* no longer maintains a foremost place in her teaching. We still assert that "He shall come

[1] Matt xxiv. 42, 43   [2] Heb xi 13.

again with glory to judge the quick and the dead," but we speak of Doomsday with the same light-hearted indifference which the woman of Samaria showed when she spoke of the coming of the Messiah. She thought to escape an inconvenient argument by flippantly asserting: "When the Messiah is come, He will tell us all things";[1] and to her came the astounding reply: "I that speak unto thee am He." Consciously or unconsciously, most Christians to-day are not waiting or watching. They are infected with the spirit of those who said: "Where is the promise of His coming, for since the fathers fell asleep all things continue as they were from the creation of the world?" We also need to be awakened by a voice like that of S. James, proclaiming *the Judge to be even now before the doors.*

We are sometimes told that the hope of the resurrection really fills the place once held by the hope of the *Parousia*. The modern Christian, we are told, is content to live, to strive, to suffer in the sure and certain hope of a resurrection to eternal life; but a manifestation on the earth of Divine power has but little meaning for him. The doctrine of the Resurrection, it is true, is in some sense for the individual what the doctrine of the *Parousia* is for the race. But to believe only in the one leads to a narrow and selfish view of salvation; we must believe also in the other, not only out of deference to Holy Writ, but because we desire the hallowing of God's name and the glory of His Kingdom. It is not only we who must be saved, but Our Lord also must see of the travail of His soul, and be satisfied with it. It is not only the individual, but

[1] John iv. 25, 26.

the Catholic Church, which is in need of justification. Hence in many ways the Apostolic Church had a wider outlook than our own by emphasizing her belief in the Great Assize, when every eye shall see Our Lord, and every knee shall bow before Him,[1] when justice shall not only be done, but justice shall be manifest to all.

[1] Rev. i. 7 ; Phil. ii. 10.

LECTURE XVIII

OATHS AND TRUTHFULNESS

"But above all things, my brethren, swear not, neither by the heaven, nor by the earth, nor by any other oath but let your yea be yea, and your nay, nay; that ye fall not under judgment."—JAS. v. 12

I.—CONNEXION OF THOUGHT.

S. JAMES has striven to encourage his oppressed *brethren* with the expectation of the *Parousia*. He has told them to be *long-suffering, patient,* and not to *murmur*. He has referred them to the examples of the Prophets, and bade them study the story of Job. Does he now pause to remember that his brethren might learn from the Book of Job other lessons than that *the Lord was pitiful and full of mercy?* The Book of Job is not of the *yea, yea, nay, nay,* order, but shows uncertainty between yea *and* nay, speaking for both with qualifications. It is a book of debate, of hard problems and provisional solutions, of criticism and doubt. Job, indeed, endured unto the end, but it was not with the long-suffering ($\mu\alpha\kappa\rho o\theta\upsilon\mu\acute{\iota}\alpha$) commended of S. James.[1] He cursed the day of his birth, he arraigned the justice of God, he invoked *heaven and earth* to witness in his favour: "O earth, cover not thou my blood, and let my cry have no resting-place. Even

[1] Job III. 1-3.

Oaths and Truthfulness

now, behold, my witness is in heaven, and He that voucheth for me is on high."[1] Job abounded in protestations as to his innocence, not forgetting the characteristic oath, "As God liveth,"[2] while he showed the bitterness of his soul in his answers to his friends.[3] Does the argument, then, run: "Study the Book of Job, that *ye may see the end of the Lord;* but beware of presumptuous railings against God or imprecations on your oppressors, *and, above all things, swear not*'? Does he remember how his Master had taught that he who was "angry with his brother without a cause was in danger of the judgment"?[4] and does he, in consequence, warn his *brethren* against intemperate speech?

Some such thoughts may have flitted through the mind of S. James, but the text reads as if it were an afterthought, written when, for some reason, the question of swearing was uppermost in his mind. It is interesting to note that among the first century papyri discovered at Oxyrhynchus two postscripts begin: *But above all things.*[5] Public speakers to-day often start again, when they ought to finish, with some such words. They recollect a point which they have left out, and for the moment it assumes a supreme importance in their minds. But if this verse be an afterthought, it is certainly not an unrelated postscript. S. James had written, *Murmur not, that ye be not judged;* he now goes on to write: *Swear not, that ye fall not into judgment.* It would have been strange indeed if

---

[1] Job xvi. 18, 19
[2] Job xxvii. 2.
[3] Job xii. 2, xxi. 34, xxvi. 1-3.
[4] Matt. v. 22.
[5] *Vide* Knowling.

S. James, after writing so fully on the perils of speech, had said nothing adequate on the sin of profane swearing.

II.—Limitations of the Text.

When he wrote, *Swear not by heaven, nor by earth, nor by any other oath*, he was without doubt remembering how Our Lord had said, "Swear not at all."[1] We have now to determine as to the scope of the prohibition. Oaths may be solemn acts of attestation or purgation; they may be vows; they may be curses; they may be also merely the careless intensives of the irreverent person who takes God's Name in vain. Did Our Lord and His disciples forbid anything in the nature of an oath, or only the abuse of language, the rashness of those who vowed what they were unwilling to perform, and the misdirected casuistry which restricts the obligation to be truthful?

Provisionally we may answer that in forbidding swearing, Our Lord meant precisely what a modern schoolmaster would mean in issuing a like prohibition; but the subject requires further treatment, which will necessitate a review of Bible teaching.

III.—Solemn Attestations.

In early days when there was no authority to enforce a contract, oaths were of the utmost importance, and were accompanied by ritual acts and other solemnities. For instance, in the Book of Genesis we read of an oath taken with uplifted hand,[2] of one man swearing to

[1] Matt. v. 34.   [2] Gen. xiv. 22.

Oaths and Truthfulness

another by placing his hand beneath the other's thigh,[1] of an oath commemorated by a pile of stones and hallowed by sacrifice,[2] and there is evidence of the curious custom by which the swearer passed between the divided remains of the sacrificial victims.[3] In all these cases the contracting parties acted with the consciousness that God's eye was upon them. They believed either that He was a God of justice, or at least believed that He would vindicate His own honour, by seeing that the oath was kept or the transgressor punished.

An objector to these old customs might urge that men ought always to live in the recollection of God's Presence, and that if they did there would be no need to invoke Him on special occasions. But it is obvious that men do not so live, and it is therefore fitting that the thought should at suitable moments be solemnly recalled. Still to-day in marriage we invoke God's Name, and by our mutual vows make Him a party to our act. We do so not to give the act validity, for consent makes matrimony, but in order to consecrate our lives in the Presence of Him on whom our lives depend. The same idea is found in the Coronation Service. There again oaths are taken, and the nation acknowledges its faith that the world belongs to God.

Now, it is impossible to believe that Our Lord or S. James meant to forbid such religious services, but it is also obvious that the reality and solemnity of such services depend on the exceptional way in which God is summoned to attest the contract.

---

[1] Gen xxiv. 2-3; xlvii. 29.   [2] Gen. xxxi. 52-54
[3] Gen xv. 9, 10, 17.

IV.—WITNESS GIVEN ON OATH.

Secondly, when witnesses cannot be obtained, when the laws of evidence are unknown, or when the State cannot organize the supervision of its people, oaths of purgation fill an important part in criminal jurisprudence. In Exodus xxii. 11, in Leviticus vi. 3, and in Numbers v. 19-22, we find examples of this practice, and from the prayer of Solomon we may infer that such oaths were taken before the altar.[1] But such was the sanctity of oaths, that it was laid down how they might not be demanded of anyone on a trivial occasion. In most cases the form would be, "God do so to me and more also,"[2] if such be not the case. Similarly in our own history we find how important were the purgations, compurgations, and trials by ordeal; and to-day oaths are still tendered and taken by witnesses in our law-courts.

Now, S. James cannot be understood to prohibit such oaths being administered, for Our Lord in His own Person sanctioned the practice, and replied to Caiaphas when put upon His oath by the form: "I adjure thee by the Living God."[3]

Clement of Alexandria indeed teaches that it is an indignity for a Christian to be put upon his oath, as the implication is, that his word could not otherwise be trusted. This is so, but to suffer an indignity is not to commit a sin. Though we feel no need to swear, we need not refuse any more than Our Lord an oath that

---

[1] 1 Kings viii 31.
[2] Ruth i. 17; 1 Sam. iii. 17 2 Sam. iii. 35.
[3] Matt. xxvi. 63.

Oaths and Truthfulness

is legally tendered to us. If men were naturally truthful, such oaths would be unnecessary, but men are often untruthful, and therefore the necessity for oaths "cometh of the Evil One,"[1] "the Father of Lies."[2] Men also are careless and inexact in speech. They tend to exaggeration, and to confuse inference with fact. Therefore, when it is especially necessary that they should think before they speak, it is well that they should be warned how their evidence is being given in the sight of the God of Truth, who marks and will remember what they say.

We can go further, and note that there is sometimes a need of solemn asseverations and the invocation of God's Name, in order to drive home to the heedless minds of men the importance of what is being uttered. So Our Lord appealed to the witness of His Father,[3] and His "Verily, verily" ('Aμὴν 'Aμήν), was an oath, as Origen remarks. S. Paul also did not consider such asseverations to be forbidden. So he writes: "The God and Father of Our Lord Jesus Christ knoweth that I lie not";[4] and with even more energy he says, "I call God for a witness upon my soul,"[5] "For God is my witness,"[6] "For God is my record,"[7] "Before God I lie not."[8] Such confirmation in such mouths carry conviction. "For men swear by the greater, and an oath for confirmation is to them an end of all strife."[9] But while such asseverations may be justified, a common practice of calling upon God to confirm statements which can otherwise be proved, not only impoverishes

---

[1] Matt. v. 37.
[2] John viii. 44.
[3] John v. 37, xi. 41, 42, xii. 49.
[4] 2 Cor. xi. 31.
[5] 2 Cor. i. 23.
[6] Rom i. 9.
[7] Phil. i. 8.
[8] Gal. i. 20
[9] Heb. vi. 16

the power of language, but destroys that reverence for God's Holy Name, which is the beginning of all wisdom.[1]

V — Vows.

Thirdly, in considering oaths, there is the promise and vow taken before God. It may be a solemn dedication of oneself, as in the case of the Nazarite,[2] or a conditional promise to do something if a prayer be answered. Such was the case of Hannah.[3] S. James did not consider such vows to be in themselves wrong, for he counselled S. Paul to fulfil at Jerusalem the ritual obligations of such a vow taken at Cenchrea.[4] There are, then, permissible vows, such as those which the Church demands from candidates for ordination, and permits in the case of those who would dedicate themselves to the religious life.

But besides such vows solemnly taken after thought, prayer, fasting, and trial, there are rash vows taken perhaps in moments of excitement or fear. They are not made with the intent of surrendering ourselves or our goods to God and His service, but for the purpose of attracting His attention and of bribing Him to do our will. In fact the motive is not religious but magical, and therefore not to be commended.[5] In the Old Testament we have the rash vow of Jephthah, which led to the sacrifice of his daughter, and the rash vow of Saul which almost led to the death of Jonathan.[6] Above all, we have that wonderful exposure of super-

---

[1] Job xxviii. 28, Ps. cxi. 10.   [2] Num. vi. 1-10
[3] 1 Sam 1 11, 28   [4] Acts xxi 23, 24, Acts xviii 18
[5] Judg. xi. 30.   [6] 1 Sam. xiv 24, *et seq.*

Oaths and Truthfulness

stition in the Book of Judges, where the story of Micah is told with such grim irony.[1] In the New Testament we read of how Herod Antipas slew S. John the Baptist "for his oath's sake";[2] and of how the Jews "bound themselves under a curse that they would neither eat nor drink until they had killed Paul."[3] We are not told by what casuistry they were saved from the consequences of their oath.

In Leviticus[4] we find that from vows to do evil, and from vows taken in ignorance of all that they imported, there was a way of escape. The man who had taken such a vow had to confess it before the Priest and offer a sacrifice. He might then be absolved: and in the same spirit the Catholic Church has ever maintained that no oath to do evil can be binding, and has claimed the right of absolving men and women from their vows. It is obvious that no man can absolve himself, and should be equally obvious that a man is not freed from a promise because it has become inconvenient to keep it, or freed from a bargain because it will no longer yield the expected profit. In some ways the old respect for the vow shows a superior moral sense to the modern casuistry, which allows a man to break his word, on the score that his expectations have not been realized, or that his intention to benefit himself has been frustrated.

[1] Judg. xvii 1-4
[2] Mark vi. 26
[3] Acts xxiii. 12-21
[4] Lev v. 4-10.

VI.—SWEARING BY THE NAME OF THE LORD.

Fourthly, in the Old Testament we must understand that "to swear by the Name of the Lord" was equivalent to a confession of Faith. "Thou shalt swear by His Name," says Deuteronomy.[1] "Everyone that sweareth by Him shall glory,"[2] says the Psalmist. "He that sweareth in the earth shall swear by the God of Truth,"[3] says Isaiah. "As the Lord liveth" was the oath of orthodoxy for Elijah and Michaiah.[4] Others swore "by the sin of Samaria, As thy God, O Dan, liveth; and, As the way of Beersheba liveth,"[5] or showed themselves completely apostate by calling upon idols. So Jeremiah looks forward to a time when everyone shall swear by God's Name, "As the Lord liveth,"[6] and never by Baal as his contemporaries had been taught to do.

In this sense men swear by that which they believe, and by their oaths express their sense of obligation. So in the Christian Church at Confirmation candidates are made to ratify and confirm in the presence of God their Baptismal promises. So the Church has found tests necessary, and at times also anathemas. But S. James is not thinking of any such solemn protestations, but rather of calling upon God when there is no real recognition of His Presence.

---

[1] Deut. vi. 13.
[2] Ps lxiii. 11.
[3] Isa. lxv. 16
[4] 1 Kings xviii. 15, xxii. 14.
[5] Amos viii 14.
[6] Jer. xii 16

VII.—Hypocrisy, Cursing, Profanity, Equivocation.

There had been a time when the Prophets longed that men would swear by the Lord. The danger of idolatry passed away, and the dangers of profanity and superstition became apparent.

First, there were those who advertised their piety by always having the Name of God upon their lips, while their hearts were far from Him, who by their hypocritical parade of religion made it and God contemptible.[1] We are not, then, surprised to read in Ecclesiasticus: "Accustom not thy mouth to swearing, neither use thyself to the naming of the Holy One."[2] A reaction set in, and the strict Jew passing to the other extreme refused to utter the Name of God even when reading the Scriptures. The Essenes declared all swearing to be sin, and inconsistently initiated their members with the most terrific oaths; and according to the Apocryphal Gospel of Nicodemus the Jews refused to be put upon their oaths by Pilate, alleging that it was against their Law. Thus men are apt to take refuge in rules to escape from principles. Our Lord's command and S. James's exhortation have both been treated with the same narrow literalism.

Secondly, there was the sin of cursing. The Prophets indeed pronounced curses, but it was in the Name of the Lord. Similarly, on Mount Ebal, the people were told to confirm the law and pronounce those accursed whom God proclaimed to be so[3] But these

---

[1] Isa. xxix. 13, Mark vii. 6. [2] Ecclus. xxiii 9.
[3] Deut xxvii. 26

instances are altogether different from the presumption of the man who asks God to damn his fellow. The wickedness is patent, when a man full of hatred and malice would make God a party to his own evil passions, and attempts to bind Him to execute his private vengeance. Yet all primitive people live in constant dread of cursing, though the wise man knows that "the curse causeless does not come."[1] Nay, the Psalmist goes farther, and says of him who "clothed himself with cursing like as with a garment," "His delight was in cursing, and it shall happen unto him: he loved not blessing, therefore it shall be far from him."[2] In Ecclesiasticus comes the word of warning: "Use not thy mouth to intemperate speech, for therein is the word of sin."[3]

Now, *the brethren* of S. James had suffered from great provocation, and were therefore sorely tempted to execration. So he writes, *Above all things, do not swear*. He is mindful of how Our Lord said, "Love your enemies, and pray for them that persecute you, that ye may be sons of your Father which is in heaven."[4]

Thirdly, there is the irreverent person who uses the Name of God without thought or even with a blasphemous intention, who thinks it proves his wit to cheapen what is high and holy, whereas he proves himself a very fool—a man without understanding. Such people hardly come within the purview of S. James's Epistle. They were not among *the brethren* to whom he was writing. He was thinking rather of the man with a temper, the excitable person without self-control, who would fill his mouth with great swelling words,

---

[1] Prov xxvi 2   [2] Ps cix 17   [3] Ecclus. xxiii 13
[4] Matt v 45.

and call *Heaven and earth* to witness the transports of his indignation.

It is very hard for some men not to swear. They can see no harm in strong language, although they recognize it is a sin to use God's Name when in a passion. Casuistry comes to their aid, saying: "There are plenty of expletives which may be used without compromising your religion." So Philo, who was himself opposed to oaths, counselled men if they must swear not to use the Name of God, but to swear by *the earth*, the sun, the moon, the stars, *and heaven*. Similarly it was a proverb among the Jews, " As heaven and earth pass away, so pass away all oaths *by Heaven and earth*." So men swore by their heads, by Heaven, by earth, and by Jerusalem. They satisfied their craving for strong language, and were unconscious that they committed any sin.

Then came Our Lord and proclaimed the whole system a subterfuge. It was not the words used, but the spirit shown, that primarily mattered. It was sinful for a man to lose his self-control, it was sinful for him to indulge his temper, even if he restricted himself to meaningless imprecations. God is not concerned with etymologies, but with the intention of the speaker. He can neither be cheated nor deafened. He marks men's sayings whether He be invoked or not.[1]

So Our Lord taught. God is always and everywhere present. Heaven is His throne, earth is His footstool, Jerusalem is His city. The world belongs to Him, and all things are holy which He has made. We cannot escape His hearing, and our every speech should be

[1] Matt. v. 33, 37.

modulated so that it may enter into His ears without offence. We must, therefore, not merely adjust our oaths, but stifle and control our passion. We must learn in this sense to *swear neither by Heaven nor by earth, nor by any other oath.*

VIII —CASUISTRY.

The Jewish casuist having once decided that swearing of a certain kind was a matter of no importance, was led to discriminate between oaths, and decide which were valid and which not. This was to undermine the whole basis of veracity, and to treat truth as of no obligation unless connected with a special form of words. The Jew acknowledged that he must "perform unto the Lord his oaths,"[1] but he thought himself exempt if the words "unto the Lord"[2] had been omitted. It was on men arguing in this way that Our Lord pronounced sentence. "Woe unto ye blind guides, who say, Whosoever shall swear by the Temple, it is nothing; but whosoever shall swear by the gold of the Temple, he is a debtor. Ye fools and blind: for whether is greater, the gold, or the Temple that hath sanctified the gold? And whosoever shall swear by the altar, it is nothing: but whosoever shall swear by the gift that is upon it, he is a debtor. Ye blind: for whether is greater, the gift, or the altar that sanctifieth the gift? He, therefore, that sweareth by the altar, sweareth by it, and by all things thereon. And he that sweareth by the Temple, sweareth by it, and all things therein. And he that sweareth by Heaven, sweareth by the throne of God, and by Him that sitteth thereon."[2]

[1] Matt v. 33, Deut xxiii. 21-23   [2] Matt xxiii. 16-22

It might, indeed, be urged that it is better for a man to respect something than nothing; and if he recognize no general obligation to speak the truth, it is better that he should tremble at the thought of some specific oath. It is no doubt "better" for society that an utterly unscrupulous man can be controlled by his superstitions, and that the most irreligious of men are often the most superstitious. But it is not "better" for the man himself, neither is it better for society that the propagation of any such superstition should be sanctioned.

IX.—Truthfulness, Sincerity, Trustworthiness.

Our Blessed Lord came to teach that all lying was of the Devil and an abomination unto God.[1] He would have all men always act and speak as if they were conscious that God's eye was upon them. He would in consequence have them understand that an oath added nothing to their obligations. For a Christian *his yea was to be yea, and his nay, nay*. There would never be need of more but for the Evil One. There would never be need of more if men worshipped the God of Truth.

The words *yea, yea, and nay, nay*, had been used before in Aramaic idioms. There is a Midrash which runs: "The good man's yea is yea, and his nay, nay." S. Paul, also, was evidently not thinking of Our Lord's words when, in his fervent protest against the charge of prevarication, he denies that with him there should be "yea, yea, and nay, nay."[2] He is

[1] John viii 44, Prov viii. 7 xii 22.   [2] 2 Cor. i. 17.

merely expressing the truth known to Shakespeare that "Aye and No was no good divinity."[1] We must therefore remember that in this case Our Lord and S. James were giving currency to coin already minted and in circulation. There is no greater proof of Our Lord's originality than the way in which He adopted the language of the streets to enforce new principles of world-wide significance.

The clause in S. James (ἤτω δὲ ὑμῶν τὸ ναὶ ναί, καὶ τὸ οὒ οὔ) is evidently not borrowed from S. Matthew, where neither the rare verbal form nor the articles occur. As Clement of Alexandria, Justin Martyr, and others, insert the articles, it is by some thought to be the original form of the Logion. But this is a matter of little consequence. Three translations of the clause may be offered, and the variation, though slight, is nevertheless real. *Let your yea be a yea, and your nay be a nay*, is an exhortation to truthfulness: men may not prevaricate. *Let yours be the yea, yea, and nay, nay*, is an exhortation to sincerity and consistency: men should know what they mean and stick to it. *Let your yea be yea, and your nay, nay*, is an exhortation to trustworthiness, what a man promises that he should perform. All these translations we may be sure would have the approbation of S. James. He would have men not only tell the truth about events, he would have them also open and sincere in expressing their minds and feelings, and he wanted that in all the business of life their word should be their bond. They needed not to attest their truths by oaths, or protest their sincerity by swearing, or make vows to do this or

[1] *King Lear.*

that. It should be sufficient for each to say to himself, "I have said it, and there is One who weighs and judges every word." When S. James writes, *that ye fall not into judgment*, he would have his brethren remember that he has just warned them *the Judge is before the doors*.

Some have seen in the words, *that ye fall not into judgment*, an additional reason for not swearing. They think S. James was insisting primarily on the perils of perjury. But the text runs: "*Let your yea be yea, and your nay, nay; that ye fall not into judgment*. S. James, therefore, was not by a worldly maxim counselling men to beware of the Law, but was reminding men of Him " who came to bare witness to the Truth,"[1] and was coming again to punish those who deviated from it. The Jew had local courts (αἵ κρίσεις) which took cognizance of perjury, but such courts were not established among the Diaspora, and *the judgment* (τήν κρίσιν) here must be interpreted in relation to *the Judge* (ὅ κρίτης) who is *before the doors*.

The Jew was terribly afraid of being foresworn, but not at all afraid of being untruthful. His view of truth was verbal, but *the Judge* condemned all forms of insincerity and deceit. S. James was writing from Jerusalem, where the awful judgment on Ananias and Sapphira must have been remembered.[2] They had not taken an oath, and they had said what was verbally true; but their intention had been to deceive, they had lied unto the Holy Ghost and been punished accordingly. Arguing from such an example, there is no loophole left for mental reservations. Men do not

[1] John xviii. 37.   [2] Acts v. 1-11.

remain truthful if they prevaricate, nor can they by skilful evasions escape the consequences of lying. They will *fall into judgment* if their yea be less than a yea.

Secondly, the Jew in dealing with heathen was quite willing to protest by forms which he did not consider binding on himself. He who had once spoiled the Egyptians,[1] was willing to cheat any Gentile in business. The Jew trader had not, if we may believe Martial, a high reputation for honesty. *The yea, yea, nay, nay,* was not a motto for commerce.

Truthfulness in trading was very hard to enforce then as now. A man, sincerely religious in other respects, could not understand that the Law of Christ forbade him to take advantage of or overreach his neighbour. He expected no quarter from his neighbour, and argued that it would be unfair to himself if he did not play the game by the accustomed rules. If S. James states generally that any departure from *the yea, yea, nay, nay,* will render a man liable to condemnation, S. Paul more explicitly applies the principle, saying, "That no man go beyond and defraud his brother in any manner, for the Lord is the Avenger of all such."[2]

Thirdly, if commercial morality was low, it was also true that in other relations of life the Jew did not feel obliged to keep faith with Gentiles. Again, S. James would urge that there was no exception to the rule that their *yea must be yea*. They were sons of God in a sense in which the heathen were not. But God, whether invoked or not, is jealous of His own honour, and may be dishonoured in His children. He who is

---

[1] Exod. iii 22 [2] 1 Thess. iv 6, *cf.* 1 Cor. vi 8, 9.

Oaths and Truthfulness

the God of Truth will acknowledge no servants who tell lies. His Name is hallowed when the heathen witness to the truthfulness of His worshippers. When the Gibeonites deceived Joshua, and obtained a treaty by trickery, the people considered themselves bound by their oath, though they kept it only to the letter.[1] But when Nebuchadnezzar made a covenant with Zedekiah and took an oath of him, Ezekiel declared that the bargain must be kept. It was a bad bargain, for the kingdom was only promised security on condition that it should " be base and not lift itself up."[2] Zedekiah rebelled, and the Prophet was commissioned to pronounce sentence. " Thus saith the Lord, As I live, surely Mine oath that he hath despised, and My covenant that he hath broken, even it will I recompense upon his head."[3]

The Bible, then, does not countenance any opinion that it is not necessary to keep faith with heretics or infidels Nations and individuals must keep their word, or beware the judgment.

X.—Summary.

To sum up: this verse of S. James is not to be pressed by narrow literalists into forbidding religious acts by which a man solemnly puts himself into the hands of God, or with due reverence associates God with what he says or promises. Neither does it condemn a man who responds to an oath that is legally tendered to him, though such oaths would be unnecessary if the standard of truth were higher.

[1] Josh. ix. 3-27.   [2] Ezek xvii. 14.   [3] Ezek. xvii 19.

S. James would condemn all cursing and profanity, but he is in this verse chiefly concerned with the casuistry which would undermine the basis of truth by discriminating between the value of oaths. He would teach that truth was of the first importance, that a man's *yea* should be *yea*. He would warn men as Our Lord did, that "for every idle word that man shall speak, he shall give an account thereof in the day of judgment."[1] He probably believed that into the New Jerusalem "there shall in no wise enter anything unclean, or he that maketh an abomination or a lie: but only they which are written in the Lamb's Book of Life."[2]

[1] Matt. xii. 36.   [2] Rev. xxi 27.

LECTURE XIX

IN SICKNESS AND HEALTH

"Is any among you suffering ? let him pray. Is any cheerful ? let him sing praise Is any among you sick ? let him call for the elders of the Church , and let them pray over him, anointing him with oil in the Name of the Lord and the prayer of faith shall save him that is sick, and the Lord shall raise him up , and if he have committed sins, it shall be forgiven him "—JAS v. 13-15.

I.—CONNEXION OF THOUGHT.

S. JAMES has condemned swearing; he now goes on to think of the occasions when *the brethren might* be tempted to swear. First, there are those suffering from persecution. Their natural inclination would lead them to curse their oppressors; but, says S. James, they had much better *pray*. Secondly, there are those who are merry. They seek company and excitement, and in moments of boisterous hilarity are tempted to profane speech and irreverent songs. S. James says: *Is any merry ? let him sing psalms*. Thirdly, there are the sick. In their pain they are ready to make rash vows. They will promise God anything to escape from suffering. S. James, however, knows that they would be better employed in confessing past sins than in promising future excellences. So he tells them to *call for the elders of the Church,* that they may be anointed, prayed for, and forgiven.

II.—Man's Conduct in Affliction.

The Authorized Version is to be preferred in the opening verse, for κακοπαθεῖ does not merely mean *he suffers*, but *he suffers wrong* or *hardship*. This may be seen by the way in which the Revisers have translated the verb in other places.[1] S. James has just condemned swearing, and he turns to those overwhelmed with *manifold trials*, and says: *Is any among you afflicted? let him pray.*

The natural man retaliates when he can, and when he cannot, resorts to cursing. He may be conquered in every other respect, but *his tongue can no man tame*. He glories in the fact that he has not acknowledged defeat, but with execrations has maintained the conflict to the end. S. James, however, was mindful of another example: "Who when He was reviled, reviled not again; who when He suffered, He threatened not; but He committed Himself to Him who judgeth righteously."[2] It was the royal dignity of Our Lord, enduring in silence, that convinced the penitent robber, as to His being the King who must triumph. It was the fact that He committed Himself to One who judgeth righteously that made the Centurion exclaim: "Verily this was the Son of God." So S James calls on his disciples to sanctify their sufferings with prayer. Do they desire deliverance? let them pray to the God who can deliver. Are they conscious that their enemies are sinners? let them pray for them to the God who can redeem men from all evil. There is little we can do for our enemies; there is perhaps

---

[1] 2 Tim. ii. 3, 9, iv 5.   [2] 1 Pet. ii. 23.

nothing which they will receive at our hands: but they cannot prevent our prayers on their behalf. So the aged Samuel when rejected as a judge, said: "God forbid that I should sin against the Lord in ceasing to pray for you." So Our Lord prayed for the soldiers, who crucified Him: "Father, forgive them, for they know not what they do." So S. Stephen cried: "Lord, lay not this sin to their charge." If Our Lord united Himself with us by enduring unmerited sufferings, we are united with Him when we suffer wrongfully, if, like Him, we suffer in patience. In anticipation of His passion, "He prayed yet more earnestly"; and the oppression of the world should drive us to the same sure refuge, so that in communion with God we may find not only solace but also strength, enabling us to be faithful soldiers in a glorious conflict for souls.

III.—Man's Conduct in Prosperity.

Having thought of the persecuted man, S. James turns to the man in prosperity, and says: *Is any merry? let him sing psalms.* Again the Authorized Version is to be preferred. Cheerfulness goes with serenity, but θυμός always denotes the pant of passion, the glow, the ardour of the intoxicated. So εὐθυμεῖ; does not mean *Is any cheerful?* but *Is any elated, merry, or in high spirits?*

Let him sing psalms is also to be preferred to *Let him sing praise*, because the latter is barely English, and because a psalm is after all a song of praise. We need not indeed confine such psalms to those of David, but may accept S. Paul's expansion of our text: "Be not drunk with wine, wherein is riot, but be filled with the Spirit; speaking one to another in psalms and hymns and spiritual songs, singing and making melody with your heart to the Lord."[1]

From merely animal spirits proceed the loud hard laugh, the unseemly jest, the ribald song, and the flippant profanity. Such are not the fruits of cheerfulness, but of reckless self-abandonment. S. James knows the perils of high spirits, admirable in themselves; but he would have men filled with the strongest of all spirits, the Spirit of God. He knows nothing of puritanical gloom, and, like most true ascetics, feels no aversion from innocent gaiety. He would have men sing; and while, no doubt, he thinks first of religious music, we need not restrict his words. A happy child sings as a hurt child cries, spontaneously. It matters little what the words are, for the heart knows what it means; and the heart which is happy in its own estate has only one meaning: "God's in His Heaven: All's right with the world."

Nothing shows more clearly the happy temperament of the early Christian communities, notwithstanding persecutions, trials, and failures, than the fact that they expressed their feelings in song. Psalmody, indeed, had been very highly developed among the Jews, and music was the one art in which they excelled. But it is surprising to find the infant Church singing after the first hearing of S. Peter and S. John before the Sanhedrin;[2] or of S. Paul and Silas singing the praises of God in the prison at Philippi.[3] It was only natural

[1] Eph v. 18, 19, *cf* Col. iii. 16. [2] Acts iv. 24.
[3] Acts xvi 25

that Psalms should be sung when the Church came together as at Corinth,[1] but S. Paul, like S. James in this passage, contemplates songs and melodies on festive occasions.[2] We have already noted a probable quotation from a Christian hymn in the first chapter of this Epistle,[3] and other such quotations may perhaps be found in Ephesians v. 14, 1 Timothy iii. 16, vi. 15, 16, and 2 Timothy ii. 11-13. When S. John came to write his Apocalypse, we find the joy of Heaven naturally expressed in songs, some of them, no doubt, well known in the Church. It was not only in Heaven, but on earth also, that the glories of the Lamb resounded, and a solemn chorus responded with " Amen and Alleluia " to the revelation of God.

The world's idea of merry-making was an orgy, and profanity was the source of its merriment. The Church had in consequence to begin anew and show that festivities need not be associated with riot and undue excitement. So S. James writes, *Is any merry? let him sing psalms.* S. Paul adds that he must sing in his heart: his singing must be spontaneous. The innocent alone can really pour out their hearts in song. Theirs are the songs which no one else can sing, and no one else can learn—the new songs of the Redeemed, who are pure and undefiled.

IV.—Man's Conduct when Sick.

S. James, having dealt with the persecuted and with the prosperous man, turns to consider the condition of the sick. The sick held a very important place in the

---

[1] 1 Cor xiv 26.   [2] Eph. v. 18, 19; Col. iii 16   [3] Jas. i 17.

ministrations of the Early Church, for Our Lord had sent forth the Apostles "to preach the Kingdom of God and to heal the sick."

Sick men are tempted to make rash vows. They may even think that such vows have a religious value, though they often spring from an instinctive love of bargaining, and we may not bargain with God. Besides, the sick man, so bargaining, is at a disadvantage, and is very like the insolvent debtor who will borrow at any interest, and always believes in something turning up which will enable him to pay. It seems to the man in pain so easy to be good in the future; and the more wickedly careless he has been in the past the easier does it seem, for he has not hitherto tried.

S. James, however, fears the result of men promising more than they can perform. He knows that such vows are not the way to bodily or spiritual health. So he counsels the sick brother: *Let him call for the elders of the Church; and let them pray over him, anointing him with oil in the Name of the Lord.*

The first thing the sick man has to understand is that he must ask for help. No man can recover from sickness by the power of his own self-pity. In pain and weakness a man may gain not only sympathy, but support and aid from others. The faith of others will reinforce the sick man's faith; but his faith must exist, and hence the condition, *Let him call for the elders of the Church*. The faith of the Church is of more avail than his own vows, and in asking for its exercise he shows more of the religious spirit than by any private efforts to propitiate God.

In Sickness and Health

It is to be noted that the Elders are to pray (stretching their hands) over him. They are not to rely on any incantation or thaumaturgic power, but only on their union and communion with the Lord of Life. As members of His Body they come confident that "where two or three are gathered together, there is He in the midst of them."[1]

Secondly, they are to anoint the sick man with *oil in* the Name of the Lord, using an outward and visible sign for the communication of God's grace; and S. James is confident that *the prayer of faith shall save him that is sick, and the Lord shall raise him up.* The Faith, it will be noted, is vicarious; but the Gospels tell us how the vicarious faith of the nobleman, the centurion, the Syro-phœnician woman, and the father of the lunatic boy, was effectual. How much more would this be so when all share in the Life of the Lord, and are members of Christ, in His Body, the One Church! It should also be noted that it is *the prayer*, and not *the oil*, which causes the Lord to save. The oil is only the means of conveying to the sick man in a sensible manner the Lord's healing power. And notice the healing power is for the body. *The prayer of faith shall save him that is sick, and the Lord will raise him up.* Salvation in the New Testament has to do both with the soul and the body, and the verb σώζειν is used for both. So Our Lord said to the woman with an issue of blood and also to blind Bartimæus: "Thy faith hath saved thee." He used the same words to the woman who was a sinner.

That bodily healing is here intended, is also clear

[1] Matt. xviii. 20.

from the words ἐγερεῖ αὐτόν (*will raise him up*). This has been obscured by a corruption in the Vulgate text. The Italic version reads *suscitabit*, S Jerome apparently preferred *allevabit*, and the modern text has *alleviabit*, which is no translation of the original Lastly, it is *the Lord who will raise him up*. It is from the Body of Jesus that virtue goes out to heal. He is still alive and still working through His disciples. He is still in conflict with all evil, ghostly and bodily. He still rejoices in all healing as He did when the Seventy returned. Sickness for Him was of the Evil One. It was a result of sin, and it is His will that we should work and pray against it.

This brings us to a third point. The Jews connected sickness very closely with sin. They even went to the length of attributing specific diseases to specific sins. Dropsy was the result of fornication, jaundice of hatred; liver-complaint was a punishment for backbiting, and leprosy for an evil tongue. They also taught that without forgiveness there was no recovery, and so the Rabbis were instructed to seek out sick persons and urge them to confession.

Our Lord corrected the crude thought of His day, when He answered the question, "Did this man sin, or his parents, that he was born blind?"[1] All disease and every defect may be the result of sin, but a sick man may be suffering for the sins of others, and it is only God who can trace the causes and apportion the blame. Similarly Our Lord forbade men to suppose that the slaughtered Galilæans, or those "eighteen upon whom the Tower of Siloam fell, were sinners above all men."[2]

[1] John ix. 2, 3   [2] Luke xii. 2, 4

In Sickness and Health

" God's judgments are unsearchable, and His ways past finding out."[1]

On the other hand, Our Lord was equally clear as to the intimate connexion between mental and physical suffering. He knew what modern science is beginning to appreciate, that body and mind react on one another. A sick man with a troubled conscience is often in more need of absolution than of medicine. He cannot recover until his mind is at rest So Our Lord said, " Thy sins be forgiven thee," before He said, " Arise, and walk."

It was as "the Son of Man" that He forgave sins, and it was His will that the forgiveness of sins should be available for all men everywhere and at all times.[2] He died, we are told, for the remission of sins. He sent His Apostles forth to preach the remission of sins.[3] They were not only to talk about it, for the Lord also said, " Whosoever sins ye forgive, they are forgiven."[4] So S. Peter urged men to " repent and be baptized for the remission of sins."[5] So Ananias called on S. Paul, " Arise, and be baptized, and wash away thy sins."[6]

S. James, however, was writing to the Brethren. They had been baptized, and there is but "one Baptism." There was, however, a way left open by penance and absolution. The sick man is to *call for the elders of the Church*, and *if he hath committed sins, it shall be forgiven him*—so runs the Revised Version. The Authorized reads, *if he have committed sins, they shall be forgiven him*. The Revisers were as unmindful of English Grammar as the older translators were of Greek. The meaning is clear: *Forgiveness shall be his;*

[1] Rom. xi. 33.
[2] Heb. ix. 15, Rom iii 25.
[3] Luke xxiv. 47,
[4] John xx 23
[5] Acts ii. 38.
[6] Acts xxii 16

and we may be sure S. James did not use the impersonal form without a reason. The forgiveness was not a personal act of the Elders, but was bestowed by virtue of their office. They might have the power of the keys, but they exercised it as stewards. It was not they who forgave, but God through them. They were only ministers, and the act was sacramental. What oil was to the body, absolution was to the soul.

Secondly, the Elders could not forgive what they did not know, and therefore previous confession is implied. This is made clear by the way in which S. James goes on to urge mutual confession among Christians. The one thought leads to the other. It may also be noted that *the Elders* are instructed to forgive, whereas mutual confession is advocated for the sake of mutual prayer. This point, however, cannot be pressed, for in the Early Church absolution took a precatory and not an indicative form.

Thirdly, it is well to note the condition, *if he have committed sins*. This sounds strangely from one who has said, *in many points we all stumble*. The natural inference is that S. James intends here the more grievous and deliberate sins, and not the slips and omissions of everyday life. We may also infer from the condition that it was left to a man's own conscience as to whether or no he made his confession. The Elders in most cases would be unable to decide as to whether he was in need of absolution from mortal sins.

Lastly, we must bear in mind that S. James is not promulgating a doctrine of penance. Still less is he explaining it. He is writing to instructed Christians conversant with the practice of the Church. His main object is to show that God and the angels would rather listen to a sick's man confession than to any number of boastful protestations and vows of future good deeds. S. James knows that a man will be the better for unburdening his mind, and that the grace of absolution will at least remove one cause which impedes a restoration to bodily health.

NOTES.

I.—THE ELDERS OF THE CHURCH.

Hitherto we have considered the main drift of the argument, but S. James by his allusions incidentally raises questions as to the discipline and practice of the Church. We must therefore briefly consider: Who were the Elders? Why they anointed with oil? and What is the authority for absolution?

Who were *the Elders of the Church?* Were they merely men of mature age or brethren who were no longer neophytes. This explanation might be possible but for the other references to Elders in the New Testament. There was before the persecution of Herod, and therefore before this letter was written, a body of Elders or Presbyters at Jerusalem, to whom the faithful at Antioch sent their alms by the hands of S. Barnabas and S. Paul.[1] Next we gather that these Presbyters were not merely administrative officers elected by the community, for S. Paul and S. Barnabas ordained ($\chi\epsilon\iota\rho o\tau o\nu\epsilon\hat{\iota}\nu$) them for the Churches which they founded on their first missionary journey.[2] These men were evidently responsible to the Apostolate, and not to the communities which they served. Their importance may be gathered from the fact that in the Council at Jerusalem the Apostles and Presbyters "consider the matter,"[3] though the speeches were made in the ears of the whole Church, and

---

[1] Acts xi. 30.   [2] Acts xiv. 27.   [3] Acts xv. 6.

the decision is of "the Apostles, Elders, and Brethren."[1]
Later we read S. Paul's parting charge to the Presbyters of
Ephesus, where he recognizes them as overseers (ἐπίσκοποι),
pastors, teachers, and rulers, as guardians of the Faith as
well as guardians of the Flock.[2] Both S. Peter[3] and S. John[4]
call themselves Presbyters much as a Bishop to-day often
speaks of his priesthood. And in the Apocalypse the four-
and-twenty Presbyters are sitting about the throne and
worshipping the Lamb.[5] "And in the midst of the throne
stood the Lamb as He had been slain . . . and the four-and-
twenty Presbyters fell down before the Lamb, and having
every one of them harps and golden vials full of odours,
which are the prayers of the saints. And they sang a new
song, saying, . . . Thou wast slain, and hast redeemed us
to God by Thy Blood, out of every kindred, and tongue,
and people, and nation; and hast made us unto our God
kings and priests. and we shall reign on the earth."[6]

Such being the position of Elders or Presbyters in the
New Testament, it is remarkable that, when mentioned, their
existence in the Church is everywhere taken for granted.
We have an account which may be of the founding of the
Diaconate, but not of the Second Order, unless we accept
the traditional view that it dates from Our Lord's commission to the Seventy.[7] That was a second order after the
Apostles, but there is no hint in the Gospels that it was
intended to be permanent. Still, just as we find the Apostolate continued in the election of S. Matthias, in the call of
S. Paul, and in the probable inclusion of S. James and
S. Barnabas, so it is possible that the Presbyterate dates
from the commission to the Seventy, and subsequently
acquired a title which was in accordance with Jewish
nomenclature.

Elder was a title among the Jews, answering to the
Senator or Alderman of other nations. We first meet with
the designation in the camp beneath Sinai, and we read of

---

[1] Acts xv. 22 [2] Acts xx 28-35 [3] 1 Pet v 1
[4] 2 John 1, 3 John 1. [5] Rev. iv. 4 [6] Rev v. 6-10.
[7] S. Luke xi

In Sickness and Health 345

Elders in the Book of Judges, and in other books of the Old Testament [1] In Our Lord's time the local Councils and the synagogues of Palestine had their elders. The title was not necessarily ecclesiastical or restricted to any definite institution or definite functions, so the infant Church could assume it for their ministers without fear of offence and without fear of misunderstanding. It was only the natural title for someone in authority. But it is worth remarking that the title was only current in Palestine. Though so often used in the Septuagint, Jewish inscriptions in the Diaspora often describe a man as ἄρχων and γερουσιάρχης, but never as πρεσβύτερος. It is, in consequence, significant that S. James, writing to the Diaspora, uses the term. It proves that the Christian organization was already independent of the synagogue. There was, however, quite naturally a certain fluctuation as to the use of names. Things come first, names afterwards; and in commending a new thing it is first of all necessary to call it something which will be intelligible to those who are addressed. Writing to Jews, the word Presbyter was available, but when S. Paul passed into Europe he uses words such as the Gentiles would understand. In his first letter he writes tentatively of "those who have the rule over you,"[2] οἱ προιστάμενοι, but he soon accepted the title ἐπίσκοπος, as may be seen from his letter to the Philippians and from the Pastoral Epistles.[3] There is little doubt to-day that in the New Testament Presbyter and Bishop usually refer to the same office; but this by no means proves that Bishops, as we know them, have emerged from the Presbyterate, and are not successors of the Apostolic order. The theory that Bishops began by being chairmen of Presbyterian colleges is recent, and is already passing away. Throughout the New Testament we are always conscious of the subordination of Presbyters to the Apostolate, and there are many indications that the Apostolate in some form was to continue,

[1] Lev iv 15, Num xi 25, Judg. viii 14, etc
[2] 1 Thess. v 12   [3] Phil. 1 1, 1 Tim iii. 1, 2; Tit. 1 7.

and that continuance harmonizes with the witness of the centuries.

It should be clear from what has been said, that it would be a mistake to conclude that the Elders of the Church were limited to the functions of the elders of the synagogue. All the evidence is the other way. The elders of the synagogue were administrative officers largely concerned with legal duties, although, it is true, that they exercised disciplinary powers, and could excommunicate or turn men out of the synagogue. But the Elders of the Church were much more than this, as may be seen from the charge of S. Paul at Miletum, and in the passage quoted from the Apocalypse. So S. James expects his Elders to anoint and absolve, he expects them to act as priests and not merely as churchwardens.

He calls them the *Elders of the Church* (οἱ πρεσβύτεροι τῆς ἐκκλησίας); and in the Septuagint the word ἐκκλησία is used for the whole congregation of Israel, that is, for the Chosen People regarded as a Body in covenant relationship with God. The word in the Septuagint is never used for a local community, for a sect, for the hierarchy, or for a place of meeting. Remembering this usage, and that the mind of S. James was saturated with the Old Testament, it is significant that he speaks of the Synagogue as the place of assembly, and yet calls the ministers *Elders of the Church*. He does so, because they represented each in his place the whole Body. They were not merely the guardians of property, or the elected administrators of local rules. They were stewards of the mysteries of God,[1] and had been commissioned and endued with power from on high.

It may be answered to this, that if Our Lord uses the word ἐκκλησία in the extended sense when He declared that the gates of Hell should not prevail against His Church, He yet said, "tell it unto the Church,"[3] evidently intending a local community. But S. Matthew, who records those sayings, wrote subsequently to S. James, and it would not

---

[1] 1 Cor. iv. 1.   [2] S Matt. xvi. 18   [3] S. Matt xviii. 17

be safe to argue from his Greek rendering of sayings spoken probably in Aramaic. The word Church, it is true, soon attained among the Christians to a varied sense development. This was due to S. Paul's missions. To the Gentiles *synagogue* would be a foreign word, while ἐκκλησία was used very variously in their civil life. So S. Paul retains the word for the whole body of the Baptized, but he also uses it for a local community, for a gathering together of Christians, and when he writes "the Church that is in their house,"[1] he has all but identified it with a building. But again it is our contention that S. James wrote before S. Paul adventured into Europe.

This excursus has been rendered necessary by controversies in modern times, but it is well to remember that S. James never supposed it necessary to tell his correspondents who the Presbyters were, or what they could do. Throughout the Dispersion, wherever there were Christian Jews, this would be understood. He is only urging such Brethren as may be sick to avail themselves of their ministrations—to be anointed and absolved.

II.—UNCTION FOR THE SICK.

It was quite usual to anoint the sick for medicinal reasons. Commentators on this verse cite numerous authorities from Isaiah[2] to Galen in proof of this, but even among the ancients oil was not regarded as a universal remedy, and had S. James been concerned with medicine he would have told his brethren to call for the physicians, and not for the *Elders of the Church*. It was not the mere application of oil that cured, but oil administered *in the Name of the Lord*. In S. Mark vi. 13 we read, that when the Apostles were sent out two by two by Our Lord, "they anointed with oil many that were sick and healed them." In this verse we seem to see a distinction between the miracles of the Disciples and those of Our Lord. He

---

[1] 1 Cor. xii 28; i. 2; xi. 18, xvi. 19 It will be noted that the word Church is used in four senses in one epistle.   [2] Isa. i. 6

healed by word, by touch, or by the saliva from His own mouth; they healed by means of oil, as if to make them conscious that the power which they exercised did not lie in themselves. But at the end of the Gospel they are promised that "they shall lay hands on the sick, and they shall recover."[1] There is no mention of oil here, or in the many miracles recorded in the Acts. We might in consequence argue, that when the Apostles had learnt who Our Lord was, and in whose Name and power they worked, the reason for the use of an outward means had been removed. But then we have this definite precept of S. James evidently referring to a practice well known. We also have the very multifarious evidence as to the use of oil for the sick from his day up to our own. We can only conclude that in the Acts we read chiefly of what was exceptional, and therefore worthy of record, whereas in S. James we have the normal rule of the Church. It is also possible that in some of the miracles, oil was used, although the fact is not recorded.

It has already been noted that the *anointing* and *prayer of faith* were primarily for the restoration of the sick man to bodily health. The Early Church was much concerned with the Body. Their attitude may be summed up in the phrase, "God for the Body, and the Body for God."[2] It was a necessary deduction from their belief in the Incarnation and general resurrection. It was the secret of the new morality which was to purify the world.

But a belief in the Incarnation led to other consequences. If the doctrine did not destroy the distinction between the material and the spiritual, it altogether altered men's views as to the relations which the one had to the other. The earth belonged to God as well as the heavens, what was earthly could be used for spiritual purposes; earthly things could be interpenetrated by spirit and made the vehicles of spiritual power. In fact, men came to look on phenomena not as in themselves unreal, but as types of greater realities

[1] S. Mark xvi. 18 [2] *Cf.* 1 Cor vi. 13.

behind them. For the Early Church the whole of life became symbolic, if by a symbol is understood a real correspondence between the sign and its significance. For the Early Church everything partook of the nature of a sacrament, for the things of earth became the media for the reception of spiritual life. The Early Church found parables everywhere, because they believed that in every thing was somehow revealed the consistent thought of the One God.

Now, oil was naturally associated with healing. It had undoubtedly healing properties, which proceeded from the thought of God. It was therefore the fitting symbol of God's healing power, and sensibly conveyed to the patient what He could do in whose Name it was administered. At the same time we note that repentance and faith were required of the sick man, while *the prayer of faith* was offered by the Presbyters. The rite was moral and not magical. It was an Act of the Church, the Spirit-bearing Body, to exert its privilege of co-operation with God. He who has life in Himself was called upon to reinvigorate the life of one of His members who was in full communion with Him.

But it may be asked, How does the precept of S. James affect the relations of Christians towards surgery and medicine? Are we to assume that the Peculiar People and Christian Scientists are right in refusing medical assistance? We have seen why to the mind of S. James there was no conflict between the material and spiritual, both alike were of God. Familiar as he was with the Book of Ecclesiasticus, he would have been ready with an answer: "Honour a physician with the honour due unto him, for the uses you may have of him: for the Lord hath created him, and from the Most High cometh healing."[1] For S. James to despise the natural means, would be to despise the God from whom *every good gift and perfect boon* proceeds. For S. James to neglect the God-given means of health and expect a miracle, would be a presumptuous tempting of God. He would say

[1] Ecclus. xxxviii. 1, 2

to such: "*Ye ask, and receive not, because ye ask amiss.* You have no more right to believe that God will heal you, while you neglect the natural means which God has placed at your disposal, than you have to believe that your poor neighbour will be *warmed and filled* while you neglect to offer him the assistance in your power. Both beliefs arise from a false spiritualism which repudiates God's control of the world. The son of Sirach knew better. He writes: "My son, in thy sickness be not negligent, but pray unto the Lord, and He will make thee whole. Leave off from sin, and order thine hands aright, and cleanse thy heart from all wickedness." He then orders a sacrifice of a sweet savour, and concludes: "Then give place to the physician, for the Lord hath created him; let him not go from thee, for thou hast need of him."[1]

All material gifts should be received as from God, and all spiritual gifts have either their outward sign or find an outward expression. Through sacramental ordinances this truth is taught with the added lesson that man cannot fathom the mystery of God's working, and that there are powers beyond any which we know. Supposing a sick man prays to God for health, is it not true that God answers the prayer if He sends a doctor who correctly diagnoses and successfully prescribes? Supposing a sick man to be anointed *in the Name of the Lord*, is the anointing less efficacious because God responds to our material symbols by using material means? The skill of the doctor is of God, the laws of hygiene are God's Laws, and the drugs are created by Him, who makes nothing without a purpose. We have no right to dictate or limit the means which God may employ. On the other hand, it would be foolish for the doctor, because God uses him and the means at his disposal, to deny the value of spiritual and sacramental gifts. He knows how limited his knowledge is, and that however many the remedies at his command they do not exhaust the

[1] Ecclus. xxxviii 9-12.

possibilities of God, or, should he prefer the words, the possibilities of Nature. He may be sceptical as to all that savours of the supernatural, but he will readily acknowledge that the mental and moral condition of his patients is often the determining factor in their recovery. He will in consequence find better patients where he finds true penitents with their minds stayed upon God.

Turning to another point, S James tells the sick to call for *the Presbyters of the Church*, but there is good evidence that in the early centuries laymen anointed with oil, that even in some cases men anointed themselves. The oil may have been consecrated by a Bishop or Presbyter. This in some cases is expressly stated, in others it is not only not stated but is not to be inferred. It is true that S James does not expressly limit unction to the Presbyters, but he introduces the rite only in reference to their ministrations, and we can at least conclude, in consequence, that he did not originate the practice, and that it had authority in traditions not derived from him When Christians were few and often isolated, oil was often more available than a Priest, and we may surmise that as the Church does not deny the validity of lay baptism, although she teaches that a Priest is the proper minister of the sacrament, so in early days unction by the laity was permitted when it was impossible to call for the Elders of the Church [1]

Origen, in his second homily on Leviticus, connects this text especially with the Priesthood, but, then, he is writing of Penance rather than Unction. He speaks of the sick man as "not ashamed to show his sin to the Priest, and to seek the remedy," and goes on to quote from the Psalms and the words of "the Apostle James," down to "they shall be remitted him." Similarly S Chrysostom, in his work on the Priesthood, quotes the text in full, but he is thinking first of spiritual aid. He writes: "Not only in chastising, but also in benefiting, God has given to Priests a

[1] 2 *Hom. on Lev.*, § 4.

greater power than that of our natural parents. . . . Our parents can neither avert from us bodily death, nor repulse impending disease; but Priests often heal the soul when it is sick and ready to perish, securing to some a milder punishment and preventing others from falling in any degree; and effecting this, not only by teaching and admonition, but by aiding them through prayer. And they not only have authority to forgive our sins when they regenerate us, but they also have authority to forgive such sins as come afterwards, for he says, 'Is any sick among you? let him call for the Elders of the Church, etc.'"[1]

This passage and others might be remembered by those who quote the passages collected by Bingham, in which S. Chrysostom gives admirable exhortations on the virtue and validity of secret confession to God.

III.—ABSOLUTION.

This brings us to our third subject, Absolution; and the power of absolution is distinctive of Christianity, by it is meant the forgiveness of sins. Moses, indeed, interceded for his people, and Aaron stood with his censer between the dead and the living; but absolution is not the same as intercessory prayer, and Aaron, like David, only strove to avert punishment, which, again, is not the same as forgiving sin. The sin and trespass offerings[2] could only be offered for ceremonial defilement, for unintentional wrongdoing, and for sins of ignorance; there was under the Law no provision for pardoning the wilful offender. Nathan, it may be urged, declared to David, on hearing his confession, "The Lord hath put away thy sin; thou shalt not die;" but the case was exceptional, and the prophet spoke by the direct command of God. Isaiah also, conscious that he was a man of unclean lips, was absolved, but it was by a Seraph, and not by a man, that "his iniquity was taken away and his sin purged."[3] Under the Old Testament there was no real ministry of reconciliation.

[1] *De Sacerdotio*, vi.   [2] Lev. iv, v.   [3] Isa. vi. 5-7.

In Sickness and Health 353

This does not mean that there was no forgiveness. Confession, both to God and man, was urged and practised, as we shall see in the next lecture. Men clung to the thought of possible forgiveness. The Prophets were emphatic on God's willingness to forgive the man who "turned away from his wickedness which he had committed, and did that which was lawful and right";[1] but the sinner was a separated person, and as such he was bound to bear his own burden "No man could redeem his brother or make an agreement unto God for him."[2] Many were assured of forgiveness, but the assurance came from within, and not from without The sinner cried: "Turn Thee, O Lord, and deliver my soul; O save me for Thy Mercy's sake." His prayer was heard, and he was convinced, "The Lord hath heard my petition, and the Lord will receive my prayer."[3]

This being true, it may be asked, what more is wanted? If nothing more was wanted, there was no need of the Cross. When Our Lord, emphatically acting as the Son of Man, forgave the sins of the palsied man, the Jews considered Him a blasphemer, saying, "No man can forgive sins, but God only."[4] This, so expressed, was only a half truth, but it was all of the truth then known to them, for the ministry of reconciliation is inconceivable apart from the Atonement made upon the Cross, and no one would even then dare to exercise it but for the definite teaching of Our Lord.

Before Our Lord's death there was no availing sacrifice that could be pleaded on man's behalf. The Priest of the Old Covenant was restricted by the value of the sacrifices which he offered, and "the blood of bulls and goats could not take away sin."[5] Then came "the Lamb of God," who offered "the one full, perfect, and sufficient sacrifice, oblation, and satisfaction for the sins of the whole world"; and now "the Blood of Jesus . . . cleanseth us from all sin."[6]

[1] Ezek. xviii. 27. [2] Ps. xlix. 7 [3] Ps. vi. 4-9.
[4] Mark ii. 7, *cf.* Job xiv. 4. [5] Heb. x. 4 [6] 1 John i 7

The Life-blood of the Man, Christ Jesus, has been shed. He has passed into the heavens to be our great High Priest, and offers His Sacrifice. His servants here on earth plead that same sacrifice, and render that Blood available for individual needs.

Men before Our Lord's advent might be sure that there was a good God who might forgive, but there was still need of the historic Sacrifice on Calvary to win and to convince the world. So in the old days, and even now, the truly penitent may rest in a subjective assurance of God's pardon; but there is likewise a need of a ministry of reconciliation, that God's pardon may be effective for many harassed souls. Men hope, men pray, they are the victims of their temperaments, they are deluded by their emotions, they are tempted to despair. They need help, and Our Lord has provided help. They are not to live by themselves or trust in themselves, or bear their own burdens. They are to be members of His Body, to trust in one another, so that each to the other, according to his vocation, becomes a minister of grace.

We no longer ask men to speculate on the possibilities of God forgiving sin, or to accept our deductions on the subject: we point them instead to the Cross of Calvary. We no longer condemn men to wrestle like Jacob in the darkness and alone for a blessing,[1] but ask them to accept from Our Lord's accredited servants the absolution which He intends for them.

But did He intend this particular grace? First, He promised S. Peter: " I will give unto thee the keys of the kingdom of heaven . and whatsoever thou shalt bind on earth shall be bound in heaven: and whatsoever thou shalt loose on earth shall be loosed in heaven."[2] The promise was for the future, but it was no merely personal endowment, for the context has to do with the foundation of the Church. The promise was made first to the chief of the Apostles, as

---

[1] Gen. xxxii. 24   [2] Matt. xvi. 19.

In Sickness and Health 355

the representative of all who were to be united in one body. Shortly afterwards, when Our Lord was dealing with the man who should be regarded as a heathen and a publican, He promised all the Apostles: "Verily I say unto you, Whatsoever ye shall bind on earth shall be bound in heaven: and whatsoever ye shall loose on earth shall be loosed in heaven."[1] Here it might be argued from the context, though I think wrongfully, that the power was purely disciplinary: that it accounts for S. Peter's treatment of Ananias and Sapphira,[2] and his condemnation of Simon Magus;[3] for S. Paul's punishment of Elymas[4] and reproof of the soothsaying girl,[5] and for the excommunication of the incestuous man at Corinth;[6] for S. John's threats against Diotrephes,[7] and for some of the warnings to the Seven Churches.[8] But when we go on to the commission in the Upper Chamber on the evening of Easter Day, there is no ambiguity. Our Lord said: "Whose soever sins ye forgive, they are forgiven; and whose soever sins ye retain, they are retained."[9] These words cannot be restricted to disciplinary powers affecting a man's status or outward condition. To forgive sins has an effect upon character, and alters a man's relationship with God. Some rigorists in the Early Church, and the Novatians afterwards, restricted this power to the granting or withholding of Baptism; but no one to-day would go on to maintain the awful but logical consequence, which the Novatians did not shrink from, that there is no forgiveness for post-baptismal sin.

Granting that Our Lord spoke the words, it may still be asked, to whom were they addressed?[10] From S. Luke it is clear, though S. John does not mention it, that others beside the Apostles were present upon the occasion. Those who believe the commission was to the Apostles alone, may answer that S. Luke was principally concerned in

---

[1] Matt. xviii. 18   [2] Acts v. 3, 4, 9.   [3] Acts viii 20-23
[4] Acts xiii 10-12.   [5] Acts xvi 18   [6] 1 Cor v 4
[7] 3 John 10.   [8] Rev ii. and iii.   [9] John xx 23.
[10] Luke xxiv. 33.

stating the evidence for the Resurrection, and therefore recorded all those who were present; but S. John, who was principally concerned in stating the nature of the commission, only mentions those to whom it applied. On the other hand, it may well be argued that the power was given to the whole Body there assembled, to the whole Church as it then was. This seems the best explanation, for as the Society was meant to be permanent, so the power was meant to be permanent, and the Society does not die, as the Apostles have done.

Assuming, then, that Our Lord bestowed the power on the Church as a Church, it is obvious that the Church must exercise that power through some or all of her members, but only as she determines to grant faculties for that purpose. Just as the power of life and death possessed by the State does not justify any citizen slaying his fellow, so the power of forgiving sins possessed by the Church does not empower any Churchman to absolve. We learn from S. James that in clinical cases *the Presbyter of the Church* forgave the sick. We also find that in the Early Church the Bishop ordinarily reserved to himself the power of absolution.

As Penance became more general, the power was entrusted generally to the priesthood, and S. Cyprian permitted deacons to exercise it in exceptional cases. The validity of absolution by deacons was upheld by Alcuin (*circa* 800 A.D.), and was recognized in a council at York in 1194, and in another at London as late as 1200. The Church, then, does not regard the power as inherent in the priesthood, but as inherent in herself. It is now restricted to Bishops and Priests, but that is because they alone have jurisdiction for the purpose. However, in such cases, such as a man stricken on the battle-field, lay absolution has been recognized as valid.

If the Church has varied her rules as to the minister of absolution, she has also exercised her power at different times in different ways. She has only absolved in the

In Sickness and Health

public congregation and at special festivals, and she has made absolution a secret of the confessional. She has absolved before, or only after penance has been performed. She has, and has not, demanded protracted discipline and probation. She has restricted absolution to offences of the gravest magnitude, and she has urged the faithful to receive it for the most venial offences. She has made it a condition of communion, or she has left each man free to decide whether he needs it. She has appointed special confessors, or allowed everyone to choose his own priest. At times we may believe she has been wiser than at others. We may also believe that, as a Living Church, she has been wise in reference to the conditions of succeeding times. She has never doubted her powers, and we need not doubt but that in the ages to come she will use them as occasion shall require.

Disputes have not only arisen as to the minister, form, and method of absolution, but the fact itself has been explained by theologians in a variety of ways. Theories, however, do not alter facts, and God's pardon is not dependent on man's skill in explaining it. The following thoughts are offered tentatively, and the reader must remember that, while they are concerned first of all with sacramental absolution, there is no idea in the author's mind of forgiveness being limited to that ordinance.

God is ever ready to forgive the penitent, but nothing man can do by contrition or confession can merit that forgiveness. It remains the free gift of God. Every sinner, who is penitent, knows this. He cannot claim forgiveness, for he cannot even forgive himself. He remembers, however, that he is a member of Christ; he asks for Jesus Christ's sake; he pleads His merits, having none of his own to plead. Now, if we remember that the merits of Christ are the Treasury of the Church, we have a clue to understanding how the ministers and stewards of Christ's Church may exercise that "charity" which "covers a multitude of sins." To put the same truth in another way,

He is our Head, and His life, with all its healing and invigorating powers, flows through the whole Body. In that Body all the members have functions which should contribute to the life of the whole, and the function of some is to absolve in the power of the Precious Blood.

This is sometimes denied, owing to a confusion of thought. Men confuse a willingness to forgive with an act of forgiveness. Now, God is forgiving: He never ceases to love the sinner, for God is love; but inasmuch as enmity implies the separation of two parties, so forgiveness implies the union of two parties, and man has to be reconciled with God. The ministry of reconciliation is therefore more concerned with man's attitude towards God than with God's attitude towards man.

To argue from analogy, a mother loves her passionate little son who stamps in a corner, refuses to be good, and repels all her advances. She cannot forgive him, much as she wants to do so. When the child is sorry, it would not comfort him if he were sent to bed with a treatise on forgiveness. He wants to see his mother, to sob out his penitence, to be taken in her arms and covered with her kisses. The mother was always forgiving, the moment she knew of the child's penitence her forgiveness went out to him; but his actual absolution took place when he felt her touch and heard her words of love.

It may be replied that in this forgiveness there is no intermediary; but was not the mother herself really an intermediary? As certainly as the Priest she was acting for God. The child's naughtiness was a sin against God; it may have been a sin which did not affect the mother. Yet what mother doubts her power to forgive, and what child questions the validity of his mother's absolution?

It has sometimes been contended that the Old Testament provides a type of absolution in the declaration of the Priests that a leper was cleansed. This may be true, but is inadequate, for the Priests merely declared a man clean who had been cleansed, altogether apart from their

In Sickness and Health

ministrations. Now, in absolution, God's pardon is not merely declared, it is also conveyed to the penitent. When the prodigal "came to himself" he was at once forgivable. He came home, confessing his sin, to find a father who had never ceased to love him, who had always longed to forgive. But when the father ran to meet him, fell upon his neck and kissed him, the pardon was conveyed; and who will say that the act was without significance both to father and son? So God is ever forgiving, the sinner who repents is at once forgivable, and absolution is one means, the outward means, by which the forgiveness is conveyed.

The fact that absolution is not merely declaratory is brought out also in the commission of Our Lord. The word "Whose soever" certainly implies discretion. The fact that sins may be "forgiven" or "retained" implies power. We must, in consequence, conclude that a Priest is not merely a herald, but in some sense a judge.

To understand why a judge is necessary, we must again remember that the obstacles in the way of forgiveness are on man's side, not God's. There are many who believe in a general way that God forgives, who find it hard to believe that He can forgive them. They need encouragement, they need also the authoritative voice from outside if they are not to despair. Secondly, many have consciences that are not very enlightened, they misunderstand and imagine sins, or are scrupulous self-tormentors. Some, on the other hand, commit heinous sins and offend against the most elementary laws of morality without much compunction. They have become so accustomed to them that they call them natural; or they argue that, as they are condoned by their neighbours, they cannot be very bad. Such people need instruction. Thirdly, there are sinners who loathe their sins and long to be rid of them, but have no love of God and no real desire for forgiveness, and the mutual obligations which forgiveness entails They would accept any punishment that did not entail self-surrender. They want to save themselves, and will not submit to be saved by the Precious Blood. They need to be convinced of sin. Lastly, there are those who require to be brought to penitence, for they are only moved by fear. Their sins are a terror to them, but they only wish to escape the penalties, and they confuse remission of sin with remission of punishment. But in the Church absolution comes first and penance afterwards, and a man does not cease to be a penitent because he has been absolved. He ought to go away full of joy and gratitude, marvelling at the miracle by which he and God are at one again; but just in so far as he is a true penitent, so he will be the more sorry for his sin when he has experienced in absolution the amazing love of Him whom he offended.

But this discretion of the Priest to examine the penitent and give or withhold absolution gives rise to difficulties. It is asked: 'Supposing absolution is denied to a really penitent man, is he forgiven or no?' The answer seems to be: 'When God is forgiving, and the sinner forgivable, the denial of absolution causes the sinner to forfeit the joy of conscious reconciliation. It is a real deprivation and a wrong to him here and now, but it cannot affect his eternal relations with God.' On the other hand, it is asked, 'Supposing the Priest is deceived and grants absolution to one who is not penitent, is such a man forgiven or no?' Again comes the answer that God is forgiving, but in this case the man has no use for the forgiveness granted him. In despising God's gift he adds to his sin, and so the Priest feels the responsibility which he may incur.

The dangers are great, and the difficulties men feel on the subject are real, but they have their analogies in all life. Children are entrusted to parents that they may be brought up in the fear and nurture of the Lord. Whether they are or are not brought to God depends largely on how far those parents recognize their responsibility. Our lives and properties and well-being depends on rulers and judges. We are taught that "the powers that be are ordained of God";[1]

[1] Rom. xiii. 1.

but we know that they have often been corrupt, unjust, and tyrannical, and are always fallible. God's own most Holy Faith is entrusted to men, who are not always wise or well instructed, who, being human, are prone to error. A man is shocked to think of the possibility of a true penitent being denied absolution; but how many millions of the human race to-day, through the negligence of the Church, have never had the chance of hearing the Gospel of salvation! God has entrusted the task to men, and waits with patience for them to obey Him. We can only conclude that it is God's purpose that we should receive His grace at the hands of our fellows. Not only the Church, but the whole world, is conceived in accordance with a mediatorial plan. and of that plan Christ crucified is the fullest interpretation man on this earth can receive.

Believing, then, in the solidarity of the race and the mutual interdependence of its members, we believe that as sin separates men, so the forgiven man is not only united with Our Lord, but restored to the full fellowship of the Church. The consequences of his sin which remain are no longer a burden on himself alone As they are part of the burden borne upon the Cross, so the Church, identifying herself with that Holy Sacrifice, responds to S. Paul's command: "Bear ye one another's burdens, and so fulfil the Law of Christ."[1]

Lastly, as all obstruction to the inflow and circulation of grace has been removed, the forgiven sinner finds a Saviour, and the Saviour finds a son in whom, and with whom, and for whom, He can work. The forgiven man is "in Christ," and Christ is in him.

[1] Gal. vi. 2.

LECTURE XX

A MEDIATORIAL CHURCH

"*Confess therefore your sins one to another, and pray one for another, that ye may be healed The supplication of a righteous man availeth much in its working. Elijah was a man of like passions with us, and he prayed fervently that it might not rain, and it rained not on the earth for three years and six months And he prayed again, and the heaven gave rain, and the earth brought forth her fruit. My brethren, if any among you do err from the truth, and one convert him, let him know, that he which converteth a sinner from the error of his way shall save a soul from death, and shall cover a multitude of sins.*"—JAS. v 16 20.

I.—THE MEDIATORIAL KINGDOM.

IT was natural for S. James to proceed from the particular to the general. *Respect for persons* in a synagogue leads him to expound *the Royal Law;* emulation among teachers causes him to dilate on the perils of speech; and the administrations of Presbyters to the sick brings to his mind the mediatorial activity of the whole Church. If the sick man should confess to the Presbyters and be forgiven, all the brethren should confess and pray for one another. This leads him still further to insist on the immeasurable value of intercessory prayer, and he establishes his contention by an example which shows that the very elements can be affected by fervent supplication.

But a man's duty to his fellows does not end with praying for him. He is to regard himself as his

A Mediatorial Church

brother's keeper, both in the *way of truth* and in the way of conduct. The Truth for S. James is not a private possession, neither is it for him a matter of opinion. Men are not to be left alone to believe what they please and act as they see fit. To *the Word of Truth* he has traced the origin of the Christian life, the *way of Truth* he sees stretching before him to a definite goal; both alike are summed up for him in that *Faith of Our Lord Jesus Christ*, which he would have the brethren keep. Our Blessed Lord had said, "I am the Way, the Truth, and the Life";[1] and to Him the erring brother is to be brought back converted and convinced. The Gospel for S. James is a common inheritance; and the salvation of sinners is the work, not of the Presbyters only, but of all the brethren.

Men sometimes say, "No one shall come between my soul and God"; but such a sentiment would have had no meaning for S. James and the other New Testament writers. For them each was to minister to the others, each was to pray for the others, each was to convince the others. No one was to think merely of himself or the cultivation of his own soul. Each was to think of others first, each was to be in some sense a mediator between God and his fellow. On no other terms could men be "in Christ" and save their own souls.

The Church of the New Testament was sacerdotal to its core. Not merely the officers with special functions, but the whole body consisted of Priests.[2] One was the Celebrant—that was a matter of order—but all offered with him and said Amen at his Eucharist.[3] The Presbyters were called on to anoint

---

[1] John xiv. 6. [2] 1 Pet. ii 9 Rev 1 6; v. 10 [3] 1 Cor. xiv. 16.

and absolve the sick, but all the brethren were to make the sins of others the subject of their prayers; and each was to confess his sins that others might have the opportunity of praying for him.

Christianity, then, was not a matter of " God and the soul, the soul and God." It was not a sentimental philosophy or a subjective religion. Christianity was concerned with God and the Church, the Church and God, while to the Church as to God every individual soul was important.

This mediatorial conception arose quite naturally out of the relationship of Our Lord with His disciples effected by the Holy Spirit. As there is only one God, so in a sense there can be but one Mediator;[1] for no one can perfectly represent men to God but a Man, so no one can perfectly represent God to men who is not Himself God. This perfect mediatorship was made possible by the Incarnation. But through the power of the Spirit men are members of Christ and enter into His life, that they may share His work and become mediators in Him and with Him. So "supplications, prayers, intercessions, and eucharists," could " be made for all men,"[2] Christians or not. So men, like S. Paul, were ordained as preachers and apostles that, through their mediatorial endeavours, others might be joined to Our Lord.

II.—THE PLACE OF CONFESSION IN IT.

Remembering this, we are enabled to understand the command of S. James, *Confess your sins one to another.* If the Presbyters of the Church were to offer *the prayer*

[1] 1 Tim. ii. 5.   [2] 1 Tim. ii. 1

A Mediatorial Church

of faith that a brother's body might be *saved*, all the brethren were bound to pray that one who was spiritually sick might be *healed*. If the man with a sick body was to call for the Presbyters to minister to him, the man with the sick soul was also to make his ailments known. If a man's bodily health concerned the whole Church, much more did his spiritual health, for "when one member suffers, all the members suffer with it."[1]

It is worth noting that the word for *confess*, ἐξομολογεῖσθε, is nowhere used in the New Testament for secret confession to God. The verb was not used in this sense until the time of S. Chrysostom. Neither is it a general confession that is commanded. S. James, like S. John, speaks of the confession of *sins*,[2] not of sin. He does not say, "confess your sinfulness" or "confess you are a sinner," but *confess your sins*—the specific acts which you have committed.

The *Textus Receptus*, indeed, reads παραπτώματα, which the Authorized Version correctly translates as faults, but all the best manuscripts are in favour of ἁμαρτίας, sins. The alteration apparently was due to careless quotations, which in time reacted on the text. It was, indeed, much easier to justify the confession of faults than the confession of sins. By faults a neighbour is wronged, by both faults and sins God is alienated. There is a moral duty, easily understood, to own up to and offer an apology for faults, while the duty of confessing sins to a neighbour, who has not obviously suffered by them, is by no means so clear. A man could say, " I will confess my faults to my neighbour,

[1] 1 Cor. xii. 26.   [2] 1 John i. 9.

and, if forgiving, he will be able to pray, 'Forgive us our trespasses, as we forgive them that trespass against us';" but in saying this he would altogether miss the point of S. James, when he says, *Confess your sins one to another, and pray one for another, that ye may be healed.* S. James was certain that everyone was bound to pray for the neighbour who had wronged him, whether he confessed or not. The whole point of the confession in this case is that one tells the other what he would not otherwise know, and therefore gives him fresh matter for disinterested prayer. To confess our faults is a moral obligation, but the command to confess our sins is based on a spiritual relationship—we are all one in Christ Jesus.

To-day a recommendation to confession would be prefaced with argument and explanation. S. James mentions it quite incidentally, for he was a Jew writing to Jews, well grounded in the Scriptures and well acquainted with their national practices. To them teaching like that of S. James was very familiar. Sins had ever been confessed orally. So the people wept before the Lord at Bochim,[1] so the Levites confessed their sins during the Passover in the reign of Hezekiah,[2] so those who had married strange wives confessed in the days of Ezra.[3] They could quote also the words of admonition addressed by Joshua to Achan: "My son, give, I pray thee, glory to the Lord God of Israel, and make confession unto Him, and tell me what thou hast done: hide it not from me."[4]

The practice also was familiar. It was not only

---

[1] Judg. ii. 5   [2] 2 Chron. xxx. 22.   [3] Ezra x 10 *et seq.*
[4] Josh. vii. 19.

enjoined by the Rabbis, but it was connected with the sacrifices offered in the Temple. All Jewish authorities concur that oral confession was made over the Sin and Trespass Offerings. The High Priest even was not exempt. A Jewish commentator says: "The Law commands that the Sin offering of the High Priest be burnt publicly in the place of the ashes, that no man might be ashamed to confess his sin; for lo, the High Priest sinned and confessed his sin, and brought his Sin Offering."[1]

"Be not ashamed to confess thy sins,"[2] said the son of Sirach, who knew "there is a shame that bringeth sin; and there is a shame which is glory and grace."[3] "Whoso covereth his sins," says the Book of Proverbs, "shall not prosper: but whoso confesseth and forsaketh them shall have mercy."[4] Men could hide their sins from men, but not from God. They should wish to do neither, but say, with the Psalmist, "I will acknowledge my sin unto Thee: and my unrighteousness have I not hid."[5]

This same spirit of openness we see in Our Lord's command to the lepers: "Go show yourselves to the Priests."[6] We find it again in the way Our Lord insisted on the woman who had been healed of an issue of blood, telling what she had done.[7] We see it in the openly expressed penitence of Mary Magdalene,[8] and in the Lord's approval of Zaccheus.[9] We find the teaching summed up in the confession of the prodigal to his father: "I have sinned against heaven and before thee."[10]

[1] Quoted by Lightfoot, *Temple Service*, chap. viii., § 2
[2] Ecclus iv. 26
[3] Ecclus. iv. 21.
[4] Prov xxviii 13
[5] Ps. xxxii. 5.
[6] Luke xvii. 14.
[7] Mark v. 33.
[8] Luke vii 37 *ff*.
[9] Luke xix. 9.
[10] Luke xv. 18.

These are all individual instances, but in the case of S. John the Baptist, we have crowds who were baptized in Jordan, "confessing their sins";[1] while at Ephesus we read, "Many also of them that had believed came, confessing (ἐξομολογούμενοι) and declaring their deeds."[2] In both these cases the movement appears to have been spontaneous and unexpected. Hearts convicted by the Holy Spirit of sin, of righteousness, and judgment found a natural outlet for their penitence. So quite recently in the soberly conducted Presbyterian Mission at Mukden, Chinese converts were constrained by the same Spirit to rise one after another and confess their sins. "Never," says a witness, "have I experienced anything more heart-shaking, more nerve-racking, than the spectacle of those souls stripped naked before their fellows. It seemed to violate the privacy of the being, to outrage every instinct of the individual. And yet those most racked and torn by their emotions, once they had made a clean breast of their sin, seemed to find peace, and their faces shone with an ecstasy that their streaming eyes could not belie." This was in China, where a man is chiefly preoccupied with "saving his face." We do not wonder that word went the round of the villages: "Avoid these Christians. Their God is a Spirit of confessing." S. John the Divine would have agreed to the accusation, for he says: "If we confess (ὁμολογῶμεν, openly own to) our sins, He is faithful and just to forgive us our sins, and to cleanse us from all unrighteousness."[3]

When speaking of the Presbyters and the sick, we noted the sacramental character of their ministrations,

[1] Mark i. 5, *cf* Luke iii 10-14   [2] Acts xix 18.   [3] 1 John i. 9.

A Mediatorial Church

and dealt at length with the subject of absolution. In the verse that we are now considering, the command to confession of sins is given in the widest possible terms, and while the Church is free, under the guidance of the Holy Spirit, to settle her rules of discipline, she cannot interpret this text as teaching the necessity of sacramental confession. It no doubt admits of confession to a priest, but it also admits of confession to a next-door neighbour; it does not say whether the confession should be made in church or in the open field. It may be made on a public occasion, or closeted with a friend alone. The command is equally fulfilled when a little child confesses his naughtiness to his mother in the nursery, or when a hoary-headed criminal pours out his sins in the hearing of a priest. It may be pleaded in justification of the mutual confidences of friends, the mutual confessions of monks, or the mutual testifyings of members at a Wesleyan Class Meeting. It covers what goes on in an Enquiry Room after a Revivalist Meeting, or the tales that are told from the Penitent Form during a Salvation Army Campaign.

Though the command is of so general a nature, the purpose of S. James in urging confession in this place is much more restricted. He desires that each may pray for the other, and that each may be healed by the other's prayers. In fact, he is, for the moment, only regarding confession as a means to an end.

There was a scoffing proverb in Palestine—"Physician, heal thyself"; but a physician generally admits his incompetence when his own sickness is concerned. If he prescribes for himself, he is like the lawyer who acts for himself and has a fool for his client. Now, what is true of physicians and lawyers is equally true of the saints. The wisest and most devout of men is often tortured by silly scruples, when his own sins are in question. He prays, and rightly prays, to his Father in secret; he humbles himself, and "waters his couch with his tears."[1] Doubtless he is also forgiven, but his mind is not at rest, until through human sympathy and human intercourse his wound is healed. As S. Paul says, "None of us liveth to himself."[2] We are all dependent on the ministrations of others.

Besides, however keen our insight into spiritual realities, we only see in part. We look through a glass darkly,[3] and sin obscures our vision just in those directions where sin intervenes. It is the pure in heart who see God,[4] and therefore consciousness of impurity must render us sightless. We are like blind men needing to be taken by the hand, until, through the prayers of another, the scales fall from our eyes.[5]

But blindness is not S. James's metaphor; for him each sin is like a wound that needs to be healed. It is noteworthy that he speaks of the *saving* of the body and of the *healing* of the soul. We should have expected him to have transposed his verbs. But just as the salvation of the body was one of the new thoughts arising out of the Incarnation, so the *healing* of the soul was a new thought dependent upon the Atonement. He did not think of a passing over of sins as of things best forgotten, or of a mere salvation from such penalties as the sins entailed. The Saviour had not come to

---

[1] Ps. vi. 6   [2] Rom xiv 7.   [3] 1 Cor xiii 12.
[4] Matt. v. 8.   [5] Acts ix. 8-18,

accept a man as a sinner. He had come that the integrity of the soul might be restored. He had come that the soul so restored might be joined to His Church; and the whole Church was to be concerned in the winning of that soul for Him. The Church was enlarged when that soul was won.

III.—THE VALUE OF INTERCESSION.

The next sentence of S. James, *the supplication of a righteous man availeth much in its working*, may be interpreted as justifying the command just given. The argument then would run: "Confess your sins to your neighbour, that he may pray for you; and you should know that the prayer of a righteous man will aid in the healing of your soul."

This may be true, but it is obvious that the words of S. James have a wider reference; and this becomes clear when he illustrates the availing power of prayer by the work of Elijah, which had nothing to do with the confessing of sins. We note the sequence of his thought from the preceding verse, but we must not limit the application of his words. S. James knows no limitations to the scope and power of prayer.

The word for *supplication* (δέησις) always implies a known need for which petition is made. S. James, then, does not mean vague or general prayer, or the commendation of a soul to God, but definite petitions for others that they may have what they need. He has spoken of the man in affliction, and commanded, *Let him pray* (προσεύχεσθω); but he did not restrict him to *supplication*, for the man's prayer might be all the better, if in it he accepted God's discipline and surrendered himself to God's Will. He told the Presbyters to offer the *prayer* (εὐχή) *of faith*, but prayer in that case had primarily a sacramental sense: it implied in some sense a consecration of the sick man. But he is here thinking of definite petitions, and uses the word δέησις accordingly.

There has been a suggestion that by a *righteous man* is meant one who is dead, for on this earth "there is none that doeth good, no, not one."[1] That the departed saints should pray for us would have been no foreign idea to the mind of S. James; neither would he have been so impious as to suppose that their prayers would be unavailing. Probably, like the author of the Epistle to the Hebrews, he thought of his struggling brethren "as compassed about with a cloud of witnesses";[2] he thought of them like athletes in the arena who might owe their salvation to the suffrages of the spectators. So in the Book of Enoch we read: "The righteous in their dwellings with the angels interceded for the children of men, and righteousness flowed before them as water, and mercy like dew upon the earth."[3]

But while we believe that the souls of the righteous are in the hands of God,[4] and that those united with Our Lord must share in His work of intercession, we cannot limit S. James's assurance to their supplication. There is not the least authority for limiting the word δίκαιος to the dead. It was a title conferred by the Jews on S. James himself. Neither does such an interpretation agree with the context. S. James has just spoken of mutual confession among brethren as an occasion for

[1] Ps xiv. 3, Rom iii 12. [2] Heb. xii. 1.
[3] Enoch xxxix. 4 *et seq*. [4] Wisd. iii. 1.

prayer by the brethren and not by the departed saints. He goes on to illustrate his statement by the example of Elijah, and carefully reminds us that his prayers were availing while on earth, and while he was *a man of like passions with ourselves*. S. James is not merely telling men of the benefits that they may receive from *the supplication* of the righteous; he is, as we shall see in the concluding verses, even more anxious that all should intercede.

Why, then, it may be asked, does S. James introduce a new term into his argument? and would it not run better had he written " supplications to God avail much " ?

The answer to this question is to be found in the concluding word of the sentence, ἐνεργουμένη. No one, I suppose, is contented with the translation of the Revisers. *In its working* does not make sense. Neither can we return to the Authorized Version, for as availing prayer must be *effectual* the result is tautological. Besides, from the position of ἐνεργουμένη in the sentence, it is clear that it must not be treated as an adjective qualifying *supplication*, but as a participle explaining in some way how or why *the supplication of the righteous man avails*. The question then arises, is this participle middle or passive? If it were possible to treat it as passive, we should remember the use of ἐνεργούμενοι for people possessed, and translate *the supplication of a righteous man avails much, being inspired*. This would agree with S. Paul's teaching: " The Spirit itself beareth witness with our spirit. . . .[1] Likewise the Spirit also helpeth our infirmities: for we know not what we

[1] Rom. viii 16.

should pray for as we ought: but the Spirit itself maketh intercession for us with groanings which cannot be uttered. And He that searcheth the hearts knoweth what is the mind of the Spirit, because He maketh intercession for the saints according to the Will of God."[1]

But the most weighty authorities will not allow of ἐνεργουμένη being treated as a passive participle. We are therefore led to translate the verse as follows: *The supplication of a righteous man availeth much, being fervent*—*i.e.*, full of energy. Such a translation accounts for the introduction of a *righteous man* into the argument, and shows that he is only to be preferred because of his greater capacity in praying. S. James does not wish to discourage anyone from intercession, he wants only to intensify their fervour. The way to righteousness is the way of intercession, and when we have learnt to plead for others we are accepted ourselves.

IV.—THE VALIDITY OF PRAYER.

This translation also agrees with the illustration which follows. Elijah, we are told, "prayed fervently." Literally the clause (προσευχῇ προσήυξατο) means *prayed with prayer*: the author wishing us to understand that his praying was prayer indeed. What an example! Picture the Prophet on Mount Carmel praying with his face between his knees, while his servant returns again and again to say no change can be discerned in the weather. In the end the prayer of the righteous man was availing ![2] As the greatly daring Tertullian says: "Sola est oratio quæ Deum vincit."

[1] Rom. viii. 26, 27.   [2] 1 Kings xviii. 42-46.

A Mediatorial Church

To a man of the simple and practical mind of S. James, it is just as sensible to ask a saint to pray for you, as it is to ask a lawyer to plead for you, or a carpenter to make you a box. We are not isolated individuals, but belong to a society where each has his own functions and his own gifts—functions and gifts which are entrusted to each for the good of all. The saint has a great, though often unrecognized, part to play in the social economy. Again, we believe with Tertullian that "the world standeth firm through the prayers of the saints."

But the question immediately arises, 'for what may we pray?' S. James would no doubt have answered, for everything and anything that is not forbidden by God. At any rate he selects an illustration as to the power of prayer, which shows that it is availing in the realm of Nature, and not only of effect in the sphere of grace. *Elijah was a man of like passions with us, and he prayed fervently that it might not rain; and it rained not on the earth for three years and six months. And he prayed again, and the heaven gave rain, and the earth brought forth her fruit.*

Legend had been busy with the life of Elijah, and it is noteworthy that S. James does not apparently depend upon the story as told in the Book of Kings. There is nothing there to suggest that the drought was occasioned by Elijah's prayers, unless it be the words "the Lord before whom I stand,"[1] and the words of Ahab about his "troubling Israel";[2] but in the Book of Ecclesiasticus we are told, "he brought a sore famine upon them . . . he shut up the heavens."[3] Neither

[1] 1 Kings xvii. 1.   [2] 1 Kings xviii. 17   [3] Ecclus xlviii. 2, 3.

from the Book of Kings should we gather that there was no rain for three years and six months, for Elijah was commanded to appear before Ahab "in the third year,"[1] although it is true that this may mean the third year of his sojourn at Sarepta. S. Luke,[2] however, agrees with S. James as to the time; and there is no doubt that they represent the current tradition of their age.

Some have wondered why the instance of Elijah's raising the son of the woman of Sarepta[3] was not preferred. For them it is a much greater example of the power of intercessory prayer. But for S. James, quite rightly, the prayers that affected the lives of the whole people were much more important than those which expressed and resulted in an act of private benevolence. The instance he selects was also more appropriate to his time, if he were, as I believe, writing in a time of drought. Let men pray for rain, for what had been might be again. All would remember the recent instance recorded by Josephus, when rain had fallen in Galilee as an answer to prayer. Besides, the instance illustrates both the binding and loosing powers promised by Our Lord to His disciples Such powers had been exercised, says S. James, by one of *like passions with us*, a man capable of mighty fervour, but also subject to doubt and depression, a man who did not *count it all joy when he fell into manifold trials*. S James was not unmindful of Elijah on Mount Horeb[4] when he refers to his conduct on Mount Carmel. Yet, he urges, his prayers were availing, and he implies that the

---

[1] 1 Kings xviii. 1.
[2] Luke iv. 25
[3] 1 Kings xvii. 20, 21.
[4] 1 Kings xix 14.

unchangeable God will answer such prayers now as then.

Such an argument, it may be said, was quite natural in the first century, but it does not appeal to the modern man. We no longer think much of the unchangeable God, but we think more of the unchangeable laws of the universe. Is it any longer conceivable that God will interfere with those unchangeable laws, because *a man of like passions with us* requests him to do so?

So speaks the modern man, and goes forth to control and adapt the laws of Nature in a variety of ways to suit his own convenience, without pausing for a moment to ask whether or no he is interfering with them. He exercises his will, and is proud of his knowledge. He can to some extent control steam and electricity, but he cannot control the weather, and with arrogant dogmatism declares that God cannot do so either. He asks a telegraph clerk to send a message, but he will not ask God to send rain. He believes in the knowledge and power of the telegraph clerk, but he does not believe in a God "who can hear and understand." S. James, on the other hand, believed in a personal God of boundless wisdom, knowledge, and power. He therefore believed that if a man could in many ways control the forces of Nature, much more could God do so. As he asked his fellow-men to help him with their knowledge and their skill, so he could see no reason why he should not supplicate the God who knoweth all things and holds all things in the hollow of His hands.

V.—THE WEAKNESS AND STRENGTH OF THE CHURCH.

But while arguing on the validity of prayer, we must remember that for S. James his argument needed no justification. He is not teaching men why they should pray, he is exhorting men as to how they should intercede: and while his words admit of intercession for material needs, he is primarily interested in progress towards spiritual perfection. After all, though Elijah's prayers were for drought and rain, his object in praying for them was that the people of Israel might be converted *from the error of their ways* and brought back to the Living God. They had gone astray in the worship of Baal, the supposed God of Fertility, and they were to learn that they were mistaken through the famine that ensued. When they shouted on Carmel "the Lord He is God,"[1] they had learnt their lesson, and the rain proved that their confidence was not misplaced. Many have yet to learn that not in Nature, but in the power above Nature they should trust; that if they "seek first the kingdom of God and His Righteousness,"[2] they may leave to God the sending of rain and sunshine and fruitful seasons.

Elijah converted the people, and S. James, remembering this, writes: *My brethren, if any of you do err from the Truth, and one convert him, ye know that he who converteth a sinner from the error of his ways shall save a soul from death, and shall cover a multitude of sins.*

He is no doubt still thinking of the power of

[1] 1 Kings xviii. 39.   [2] Matt vi. 33

A Mediatorial Church 379

intercession, but his words cannot be limited to that. His thought widens out; and our intercessions would not be very real unless we were prepared to seize on such opportunities as God vouchsafes of doing the work for which we pray.

In the first clause it will be noted that S. James contemplates one who *errs from the Truth*, and in the next of one returning *from the error of his ways;* and it is sometimes in consequence maintained that *the Truth* for S. James were the rules of right conduct, and had nothing to do with a creed or with dogmas. This is to overlook his earlier references to *the Word of Truth, the implanted Word*, and *the Faith of Our Lord Jesus Christ;* it is also altogether to misconceive his attitude towards *Faith and Works*. Conduct for S. James was the test of sincerity as regards the Faith, but he had never even thought of anyone walking in the narrow way of the Christian life while careless about its direction and its goal. The men to whom he was writing had sacrificed everything for the Faith of Christ; had they been content with morality they could have remained within the pale of Judaism. For them it was only by loyalty to *the Truth*, that they hoped to *save their souls from death*.

What was this Truth? It was bound up with the Life of a Person, believed to be the Son of God. All His words were true, and all His commands must be obeyed. The brethren lived to serve Him, and were conscious that they must not disgrace their Master. To be like Him was their inspiration, and to hold communion with Him was their joy. Jesus was in a very real sense their Gospel; and that Gospel was summed up afterwards in the single text, "God so loved the world, that He gave His only begotten Son, that whosoever believeth in Him should not perish, but have everlasting life."[1] That this was true the brethren were witnesses: it was for them the only possible explanation of the life they had known. Their creed was a short recital of the facts which had convinced them. This is abundantly clear from S. Peter's sermon on the day of Pentecost and his subsequent address in Solomon's Porch. It is clear also from the two speeches made before the Sanhedrin, and from the address given in the house of Cornelius.[2]

Some, however, found the strain of loyalty too great, and fell away. "The care of this world and the deceitfulness of riches"[3] seduced them from their allegiance. They could not bear the world's scorn, they grumbled at their hard lot, they were impatient at Our Lord's delay in manifesting His triumph. Some left their first love,[4] some tried to compromise, some hesitated, and were perplexed. If Christ had come, how was it that none of their leaders or the learned had believed on Him? There was the glorious Temple, its ordered services, and vast crowds of worshippers challenging comparison with the worship of the little flock. It was so hard for the brethren to reconcile their traditional customs and God-given Law with the New Teaching which abounded in hard sayings. Then the Cross was to them a stumbling-block,[5] the conversion of men like Cornelius provoked them to jealousy,[6]

---

[1] John iii 16
[2] Acts ii 14-36, iii. 12-26, iv 8-11; v 30-33, x 34-43.
[3] Matt xiii. 22   [4] Rev. ii. 4.
[5] 1 Cor. 1 23.   [6] Acts xi. 1-3

the doings at Antioch caused them disquiet.[1] The old barriers of race and exclusiveness which had protected them so long were being thrown down. Old things were passing away, all things were becoming new.[2] There were all the doubts and difficulties incident to a period of transition; there were the cruel family estrangements, the breaking with old ties, the parting with hallowed traditions. The new Creed was simple, but to apply it was difficult. The foundations were secure, but the cost of building on them seemed ruinous. The way was plain, but steep and narrow. Men believed and then hesitated, started on the way and turned aside, rushed to meet danger and opposition and fell. So S. Jude called to the Church: " On some have mercy who are in doubt; and some save, snatching them out of the fire, and on some have mercy with fear."[3]

For S. James, then, to desert the Truth was to lose the way and imperil the life of the soul. It was the Master who had shown *the way*, it was the Master who was *the Truth*, it was to the Master that *the life* of the erring brother was precious. He had shed His Blood for that life, and His servants could not be true to their calling unless, like the Good Shepherd, they sought for him who was lost.[4]

[1] Acts xi. 22.
[2] 2 Cor v. 17.
[3] Jude 22, 23
[4] Luke xv. 5; John x 11.

VI.—The Ministry of Each to Other.

The command to intercede and work for the conversion of sinners is quite clear. The brethren are to care for one another, minister to one another, and rescue one another. It is, however, by no means so clear as to whether S. James encourages them in this by a promise that in so doing they will save their own souls and cover a multitude of their own sins, or whether he is setting before them the greatness of such achievements—for to convert a brother means to save the brother's soul from death and to atone for his sins.

The latter view is generally supposed to be more in accordance with the Christian spirit, while the former is more in line with contemporary thought. Which view represents S. James's meaning it is impossible to say, for both explanations are admissible, and both are also true.

Assertions that "Almsgiving covers sins" may be found in Tobit and Ecclesiasticus,[1] while in the Book of Daniel we read: "They that be wise shall shine as the brightness of the firmament, and they that turn many to righteousness as the stars for ever and ever."[2] The Jews had a proverbial saying: "Whoso maketh many righteous, sin prevails not over him."

As Our Lord taught that in His Judgment of the Nations He would accept those who had visited the sick and prisoners, who had comforted the afflicted, fed the poor and clothed the naked,[3] so it seems clear that He will say to His servants, "Well done," should they

[1] Tobit iv. 10; Ecclus iii. 14. [2] Dan xii 3. [3] Matt. xxv. 34-36.

A Mediatorial Church

have *converted the sinner from the error of his ways.* At least S. Paul imagined as much when he wrote to S. Timothy: "Take heed to thyself and to the doctrine; continue in them: for in doing this thou shalt both save thyself and them that hear thee."[1] So in the Epistle to the Hebrews we read: "God is not unrighteous to forget your work and labour of love, which ye have shewed toward His Name, in that ye have ministered to the saints and do minister."[2]

It will be noted that the use of future tenses—*will save and will cover*—accords best with reference to the brother who converts. The conversion has taken place, and he who brought it to pass may expect his reward. In some sense this is an appeal to self-interest, but so are all God's promises. It is not an appeal to selfishness, for it follows that a man is not to be absorbed in his own perfection but in the saving of others. There is a religion and a morality which ends in egotism and produces prigs. Our Lord, however, taught that, "Whosoever would save his soul shall lose it, and whosoever shall lose his soul for My sake and the Gospel's, shall save it."[3] There is no reason for Pharisaic self-satisfaction in the man who strives to save his brother, though conscious of *the multitude of his own sins.* He can only come, like Mary Magdalene, as a penitent to Our Lord, and may be accepted on the same terms. Our Lord said, "Her sins, which are many, are forgiven; for she loved much";[4] and so we may interpret S. James as saying, "The brother who

[1] 1 Tim. iv 16.
[2] Heb. vi. 10
[3] Mark viii. 35.
[4] Luke vii 47.

has shown his love by converting others shall be forgiven the multitude of his own sins."

On the other hand, the language suggests a reference to the Book of Proverbs, where we read, "Love covereth all transgressions,"[1] though this seems to mean that the man who loves refuses to see faults. Were S. Peter and S. James thinking of this verse? The former writes: "Have fervent charity among yourselves: for charity covers (καλύπτει, R.V.) a multitude of sins."[2] These words must be explained in connexion with "the end of all things" referred to in the previous verse, and so S. Peter, like S. James, by his use of future tenses, is looking forward to a Divine judgment, and not counselling human forbearance. If, then, we are to interpret *the saving of a soul and the covering of sins* as referring to the man converted, we must argue in some such way as follows: The love of Christ covers and atones for sins, and so the love of those who are His has in some sense an atoning power. There is indeed but one Sacrifice for sin, but that one Sacrifice is continually being offered, and all true Christians identify themselves with it, while they participate in its fruits. To interpret S. James on these lines brings out most clearly the mediatorial character of the Church, and is in accord with what has been said of Absolution in the last lecture. The converted man, then, is in a state of salvation, and if he continues therein may hope to be finally saved.

I have preferred the reading γινώσκετε[3] to γινωσκέτω, because it is obvious that *the brethren* are not being

[1] Prov x. 12.   [2] 1 Pet. iv. 8
[3] R.V , margin , Westcott and Hort

A Mediatorial Church

commissioned to announce something to others, but are being urged to do something themselves. I have also preferred to translate γινώσκετε as indicative, because I do not believe that S. James was issuing a rhetorical proclamation, but was recalling familiar words. The ambiguity of this concluding sentence is probably due to the fact that it is a quotation. It may be a saying of Our Lord's, for in the Didascalia we read: "As the Lord saith, love covereth a multitude of sins." Regarding it as a quotation, the form of the sentence is accounted for, and regarding it as a quotation of Our Lord's saying, the termination of the letter becomes intelligible. The author reaches a natural climax, and *the bond-slave of Jesus Christ* ends with an appeal to the authority of His Master.

VII.—CONCLUSION TO THE WHOLE EPISTLE.

There is no real reason for believing that the end of the Epistle is lost. Working slowly, as we have done, from sentence to sentence, the sequence of thought has often seemed haphazard, but looking back over the whole Epistle we find that it is complete. S. James was writing to men oppressed by outward persecutions and tormented by inward temptation. He tells them how they should meet both; but he would have them think not so much of the injustices from which they were suffering, he would have them think rather of their sins and shortcomings which called for correction. Briefly, he sets before them how they should hear the Word, how they should speak, and what they should do. Then he goes on to deal with sins of commission and omission, and expounds *the Royal Law*. Next he deals with the sins of speech, and shows the need of Heavenly Wisdom. Thirdly, he deals with sins of pride and presumption, and extols humility.

The brethren were suffering many wrongs, but they were also very sinful; let them think of the *Parousia*, and remember that, when the Lord comes, not only will all wrongs be righted, but all sins will be judged. In the sure and certain expectation of His Advent their lives should be given to prayer and praise, to the ministry of the sick, and the conversion of the sinner; for the Church does not merely exist as a refuge from trial and difficulty, it is an army ever advancing to the conquest of the world.

FROM B. H. BLACKWELL'S LIST.

THE YATTENDON HYMNAL. Edited by ROBERT BRIDGES and H. E. WOOLDRIDGE. Music, Words, and Appendix, containing expository notes on the Hymns. A few remaining copies. Demy 4to., boards, raised to 30s. net (original price £1).

"The Yattendon Hymnal is a monument of fine taste both in music and in verse, and it is only to be regretted that its merits are so little known and appreciated."—*The Church Times*

THE WORD BOOK OF THE YATTENDON HYMNAL. Ed ROBERT BRIDGES, *Poet Laureate*. Fcap. 8vo, sewed, 2s. 6d net. 16mo., sewed, *for use in Churches*, 6d. net.

"... First among living hymn writers ... it may be confidently predicted that Dr Bridges will be remembered in future ages by his hymns, even should his other verse come to be almost forgotten."—Dr Dearmer in *The Daily Mail*

THE SWEET MIRACLE. Translated from the Portuguese of EÇA DE QUEIROZ. By EDGAR PRESTAGE. Fourth Edition. Royal 16mo, art boards, 1s net.

"It is perfect—a minute jewel, but flawless and of the first water and cut by a master hand."—*The Academy*

GEORGE HERBERT'S "COUNTRY PARSON." Edited, with Introduction, by H. C. BEECHING, *Dean of Norwich* Post 8vo., antique boards, 3s. 6d. net; wrapping parchment, 5s. 6d. net.

"Breathes there a lover of books . who . . will not welcome this attractive little volume? The get-up and printing are so good that we regard it as a model reprint."—*The Literary World*

A SHORT HISTORY AND EXPOSITION OF THE APOSTLES' CREED AND OF THE FIRST EIGHT OF THE THIRTY-NINE ARTICLES OF RELIGION. By E J. BODINGTON, M.A. (*Ven Archdeacon of Wilts*). With a Preface by the LORD BISHOP OF SALISBURY. Large fcap. 8vo., cloth, 3s. 6d.

"A Manual that the Clergy may without hesitation put into the hands of pupil-teachers, readers, lay preachers, and others for whom Pearson and the more complete works on the Creed are not quite suitable We recommend the Clergy to keep a copy at hand for lending to enquirers The book deserves every word said in its favour by the Bishop of Salisbury."—*The Church Times*

THE PRIMACY OF ENGLAND. With facsimile of the signatures to the "Accord" of 1072. By S F. HULTON. Crown 8vo., cloth, 6d. net.

"An admirable account of the long strife for precedence between the Archbishops of England."—*The Manchester Guardian*.
"For general impartiality and accurate and interesting treatment of its subject-matter the book is beyond praise."—*The Law Journal*.

LYRA EVANGELISTICA. Missionary Verses in Mashonaland. By ARTHUR SHEARLY CRIPPS. Third Edition. Fcap. 8vo., cloth, 2s. 6d. net.

"A NEW POET."

"In Mr Arthur Cripps we have a poet of a wild land who will not consent for one moment to forget the classic tradition. He is best, perhaps, in his short pieces, cut like a jewel, for which the true model is the epigrams of the Greek Anthology."
—*The Spectator.*

BY THE SAME AUTHOR

PILGRIMAGE OF GRACE. Verses on a Mission. Fcap. 8vo., cloth, 2s. 6d. net.

"The work of a real poet . . . Here are vivid landscapes of Mashonaland, little etchings of native life, and the unconquerable yearning, despite the joy of his mission work, which makes the writer long for the green of an English spring, the beauty and companionship of Oxford."—*The Church Times*

THE GOLDEN WISDOM OF THE APOCRYPHA. With Explanatory Preface and an Appendix containing some of the Proverbial Wisdom of the Talmud. By W. KNIGHT (Emeritus Professor of Philosophy in the University of St. Andrews). Crown 8vo., paper boards, parchment back, 2s. net.

"The selection is severly limited. . . We do not complain. Prof Knight's object is to 'attract to these books something of the attention which is their due, and it was judicious to insert nothing but what was of unquestionable value,' literary and spiritual. There is certainly nothing that is not worthy of its place."—*The Spectator.*

A SUBSIDY COLLECTED IN THE DIOCESE OF LINCOLN IN 1526. Edited by Rev. H SALTER. Complete volume: 8vo., art linen, 12s. 6d. net. In separate parts, sewed: I. Lincolnshire, 4s. net, II. Leicestershire, Rutland, and Northants, 3s. 6d net; III. Herts, Hunts, and Beds, 2s. net; IV Bucks and Oxon, 3s net.

"Mr Salter has done an excellent service for ecclesiologists and historians . . it gives details of the clerical subsidy or taxations of the great diocese of Lincoln, supplying the names of the incumbents and curates of almost every parish, together with various particulars as to their incomes and church expenditure, and also throws new light on the administration of Cardinal Wolsey."—*The Athenæum.*

AN ANALYSIS OF THE CHURCH OF ST. MARY, CHOLSEY, IN THE COUNTY OF BERKSHIRE. (University College, Reading, Studies in Local History.) Twenty-three plates. By Professor F. J. COLE, D.Sc., Oxon. Demy 8vo., paper boards, 5s. net.

"His method is admirably scientific, and his beautiful photographs and sections make his arguments intelligible even without a visit to the spot"—*The Oxford Magazine*

"The book is one that antiquarians and architects will delight in."—*The Catholic Times.*

B. H. BLACKWELL, BROAD STREET, OXFORD.

www.ingramcontent.com/pod-product-compliance
Lightning Source LLC
Chambersburg PA
CBHW050611300426
44112CB00012B/1452